ROADSIDE HOLLYWOOD

Happy Travels.

Love Al & Mike

Christmas 1993

ROADSIDE HOLLYWOOD

The Movie Lover's State-by-State Guide to Film Locations, Celebrity Hangouts, Celluloid Tourist Attractions, and More

JACK BARTH

CB
CONTEMPORARY BOOKS
CHICAGO

Library of Congress Cataloging-in-Publication Data

Barth, Jack.
Roadside Hollywood : the movie lover's state-by-state guide to film locations, celebrity hangouts, celluloid tourist attractions, and more / Jack Barth.
p. cm.
Includes index.
ISBN 0-8092-4326-1 (pbk.) : $9.95 FPT
1. Motion picture locations—United States—Guide-books.
2. United States—Description and travel—1981. I. Title.
PN1995.67.U6B37 1990
791.43'02573—dc20 90-19658
CIP

Line drawings by Doug Kirby

Published by Contemporary Books, Inc.
180 North Michigan Avenue, Chicago, Illinois 60601
Manufactured in the United States of America
International Standard Book Number: 0-8092-4326-1

Contents

Acknowledgments

Most film commissions—except New York State and Washington, D.C., which were hopeless—proved terrific sources of local information. I'm grateful also to many chambers of commerce and historical societies. The following, however, *really* went out of their way to supply detailed information and photos. They are my friends:

Michael Blowen (Boston)
Jim DeBrosse (Cincinnati)
Violet Fallone (Fonda, New York)
Von Glasgow (New Orleans)
Dancy L. Jones (Tennessee Film Commission)
Ann McFerrin (Kansas City)
Oklahoma Film Office
Andrew Peterson (Minneapolis)
Philadelphia Film Office
Joe Trabert (Baltimore)
Tom Trusky (Idaho)

Research: Julie Kuehndorf
Additional research: John Spingola

Editor: Linda Gray
Copyeditor: Gerilee Hundt
Special thanks:
Deborah Brody
Michael Carlisle
Susan King Kirby
Matthew Bialer
Cara White
Howard Karren

Publicity: Clein + White

Original drawings: Doug Kirby

Introduction and User's Guide

Roadside Hollywood is a travel guide for movie lovers—even armchair movie lovers. With this book, you have two options: one passive, the other active, both fun, fun, fun.

PASSIVE: You can discover the real America—at your leisure and in the comfort of your living room. Just pick a part of the country you wish to visit, turn to the proper page, and find out which movies best convey the flavor of that region.

ACTIVE: You can head out on the highway and visit the sites connected with your favorite movies and stars.

Roadside Hollywood, a TV set, and a VCR are your ticket to unlimited fun and frolic across the greatest nation ever committed to celluloid. But if you insist on seeing it live and in person, that's OK, too. The heart of *Roadside Hollywood* is a section called What's There. This tells you where to find tangible evidence of your favorite stars and films: childhood homes, museums, graves, celebrity-run establishments, notorious love nests, festivals, possessions of the stars, death sites, and much, much more!

The other two sections under each state are "Made in . . ." and "Gifts to Hollywood." Made in . . . lists chronologically the major films produced in the state. This is your video travel guide. Films were chosen for quality, for "sense of place," for visitable locations, and for whether there's something cool to say about them. With a few exceptions, television shows, including made-for-TV movies, were avoided.

The first town listed after a title is the primary location. Other towns named were secondary locations. Second-unit locations—that is, places where a cameraperson was sent for local color, but where no stars ever set foot—are generally not included. Also, a distinction is made between films set in a location and films shot on location.

Often, a place will not look enough like the director's vision of that place—or shooting there is just plain unfeasible—so the film is set in that location but actually shot somewhere else.

Gifts to Hollywood are the film people who were born or raised in each state. Birth dates are not listed; there are disparities among sources, and I didn't want to waste my time tracking down more misinformation.

Our turf is the continental 48 states minus the Los Angeles and New York City areas. These two movie meccas have been excluded because:

1. It's not surprising to encounter stuff there. This book will help you find things in *unexpected* places.

2. There are already two good books, Richard Alleman's *Movie Lover's Guides*, that cover New York and Hollywood.

The information in *Roadside Hollywood* was provided by state and city film commissions and chambers of commerce, by cooperative local film critics and historians, and by driving around like crazy for several years. Nonetheless, it's always a good idea to call ahead—fame can be fleeting.

OK, now, it's time to hit the road. Grab your steering wheel, or your remote control, and head out for Roadside Hollywood. Or bust!

ROADSIDE HOLLYWOOD

SCHOOL BUS
KIRBY

Chapter 1

CALIFORNIA (minus LA)

CALIFORNIA

MADE IN CALIFORNIA

Let's start in the belly of the beast. Actually, *Roadside Hollywood* is going to bypass the belly—Los Angeles—and give you, I don't know, the entrails or something. And it's not exactly a "beast" we're talking about, either . . .

I know, let's start again.

Even excluding L.A., California has seen far more filmmaking than any other state. That's because 1) It's big and 2) It's close to L.A. But what's striking about the Golden State is that it has so many identifiable, dramatically different subsections. The Mojave is nothing like the Sierras are nothing like the redwoods country is nothing like the agricultured valleys. And nowhere else is like San Francisco.

So unlike the way most of the other states are organized, the Made in California section is ordered not by release date or theme but by region. After all, even though they're two cities in the same state, it's meaningless to compare the development of filmmaking in San Francisco to that in San Diego—but Kansas is Kansas is Kansas.

HIGH SIERRA

Lake Tahoe: This popular resort was a location for *A Place in the Sun* (1951): Montgomery Clift dunks whiny Shelley Winters in favor of Elizabeth Taylor (*tough choice!*). Harrah's Lake Tahoe Resort Casino, in Stateline, Nevada, is the hotel where Don Ameche and Joe Mantegna camp out in *Things Change* (1988). They also visit megagangster Robert Prosky at the Ehrman Mansion, in Sugar Pine Point State Park on Highway 89.

Lone Pine: *High Sierra* (1941) was shot along the slopes of Mount Whitney and at Arrowhead Springs. *Star Trek V* (1989) was shot at Owens Dry Lake and at Yosemite National Park. The Alabama Hills, a group of weird rock formations, is a popular movie backdrop. To check it out, go west on Whitney Portal Road to Movie Flat Road.

Mammoth Lakes: Mammoth Mountain Ski Area doubled as the Himalayas for *Indiana Jones and the Temple of Doom* (1984) and *The Golden Child* (1986), and appeared in *Born on the Fourth of July* (1989).

NORTHERN COAST

***Johnny Belinda* (Fort Bragg, Mendocino, 1948):** This story of a deaf-mute was set in Prince Edward Island, Canada, but the filmmakers were able to obtain the same chilly, misty verdure in northern California.

***The Birds* (Bodega Bay, San Francisco, 1963):** Hitchcock's wild horror fantasy was set and shot in this tiny fishing village north of San Francisco.

***Serial* (Marin, San Francisco, 1980):** This is based on Cyra McFadden's funny observations about upscale, fern bar–clogged Marin County, the first community in America to adopt a "lifestyle."

CENTRAL COAST

This rainy region of crashing waves and blustery beauty is portrayed in movies as a locus of offbeat, arty types—a pretty fair depiction. The area is known these days as Clint Eastwood's stomping grounds.

***East of Eden* (Salinas, Mendocino, 1955):** James Dean's starring debut, the film is a John Steinbeck adaptation shot in the old man's backyard.

***Play Misty for Me* (Monterey, 1971):** The original *Fatal Attraction*: Clint is pursued by a deranged groupie.

***Heaven Can Wait* (Woodside, 1978):** The Filoli Mansion, Warren Beatty's home in the movie, is also seen in the opening of "Dynasty." It was built by William Bourn, Jr., with the profits from his Empire Mine in Grass Valley. You can visit—see What's There.

***The China Syndrome* (Ventana, 1979):** Perhaps the timeliest film ever, the release of this film—about a near meltdown at a nuclear power plant—coincided with the disaster at Three Mile Island.

***Cannery Row* (Monterey, 1982):** Another Steinbeck adaptation shot in Steinbeck country. Debra Winger wrested the female lead from Raquel Welch, who blasted the producers for demolishing her "reputation."

***The Lost Boys* (Santa Cruz, 1987):** The Santa Cruz Boardwalk, one of the country's few remaining vintage amusement piers, was an inspired location for this teen-vampire flick.

SMALL-TOWN CALIFORNIA

***The Adventures of Robin Hood* (1938):** This film, in which Errol Flynn buckled lots of swash, was shot in Chico's Bidwell Park. Years later, on "The Beverly Hillbillies," Jethro tried to re-create the excitement in L.A.'s Griffith Park.

***All the King's Men* (Stockton, 1949):** Residents were used as extras; some even had speaking roles. Its said that Broderick Crawford's character, a demagogue based on Louisiana's Huey Long, became almost *real* to locals.

***American Graffiti* (Petaluma, San Rafael, 1973):** The great cruising movie, set in 1962 in George Lucas's hometown of Modesto, which by 1973 had become too developed for filming.

***Gates of Heaven* (Petaluma, 1978):** This documentary by Errol Morris (*The Thin Blue Line*) about a pet cemetery isn't as funny as it's reputed to be. It's set at the Bubbling Well Pet Memorial Park, 2462 Atlas Peak Road.

***Peggy Sue Got Married* (Petaluma, 1986):** Francis Coppola, who produced *American Graffiti*, returns to Petaluma for this gentle *Back to the Future*–style dramedy starring Kathleen Turner and Coppola's nephew, the criminally miscast Nicolas Cage.

MOJAVE DESERT

The Mojave has served both as itself and as a stand-in for arid foreign lands—or, as in *Star Wars*, for an arid foreign planet. Its appeal is in both its great natural beauty and its proximity to the fancy nocturnal hangouts of Hollywood.

Films shot in the desert include *Chinatown* (1974),

which was all about the desert's major omission—water; the opening scenes for *Close Encounters of the Third Kind* (1977), scenes that were expanded in the film's "special edition"; *Lawrence of Arabia* (1962), which found northern Africa at the Imperial Sand Dunes; *The Professionals* (1966), in which Death Valley stood in for Mexico; *Spartacus* (1960), which also filmed in Death Valley; and *Them!* (1954), which featured giant ants scurrying around Palmdale.

SAN DIEGO

Until the last few decades, San Diego was basically a navy town. It has since become a faceless SoCal Boomville—the city now has no image whatsoever. Try to remember *one* memorable San Diego location from any of the following: *The Big Mouth* (1967); *Tora! Tora! Tora!* (1970); *Airport '77*; *Attack of the Killer Tomatoes* (1980), with a cast that includes the town's most famous resident, the San Diego Chicken; *Heartbreak Ridge* (1986); *Top Gun* (1986); or *Spaceballs* (1987).

The one notable location in the San Diego area is the magnificent Hotel del Coronado on Coronado Island, which was a Florida resort in *Some Like It Hot* (1959) and was also a major set in *The Stunt Man* (1980). It still looks pretty much the same, and you can stay there. 1500 Orange Avenue. Reservations: 619/435-6611.

SAN FRANCISCO

Now *this* is a movie town. The memorable location shoots are countless. But one film *not* shot here was *San Francisco* (1936), about the 1906 earthquake: only background footage was lensed here.

The San Francisco area is home to filmmakers Francis Coppola, George Lucas, and Philip Kaufman. Coppola's masterful *The Conversation* (1974) is one of the few films to use the town without making it look like a postcard. Kaufman shot his 1978 remake of *Invasion of the Body Snatchers* here.

Location shooting in the sound era began in S.F. at

the beginning, with *The Jazz Singer* (1927), and is still going strong in the Dirty Harry era and beyond. A company called Showbus offers tours of movie locations; the number is 415/775-7469. You'll find a movie tour of San Francisco in What's There, but other S.F. films to remember are:

***The Maltese Falcon* (1941):** John Huston and Humphrey Bogart demonstrate what a *great* film noir town San Francisco can be.

***Lady from Shanghai* (1948):** Orson Welles shot the stunning climax for his valentine to Rita Hayworth at the San Francisco Fun House Hall of Mirrors. He also filmed in Sausalito, a cutesy art colony in the East Bay.

***The Birdman of Alcatraz* (1962):** The island prison is now a tourist attraction; you can see the Birdman's actual cell.

***Harold and Maude* (1972):** This cult favorite was written by Colin Higgins, who directed another S.F. film, *Foul Play* (1978). Production ranged all over the Bay Area, including Redwood City, Palo Alto, Oyster Point, Oakland, Daly City, and Cabot.

***Play It Again, Sam* (1972):** Director Herb Ross makes nice use of S.F. locations, but if this film had been directed by Woody Allen and made a few years later, it would surely have been set in New York.

***What's Up, Doc?* (1972):** Peter Bogdanovich's screwball-comedy homage uses the hills of San Francisco to great slapstick effect in the chase scenes.

***Chan Is Missing* (1982):** Shot for $20,000 in S.F.'s Chinatown, the film was compared by the *New York Times* to the work of cinema genius Luis Buñuel.

CALIFORNIA'S GIFTS TO HOLLYWOOD

★ ★ ★ ★ ★ ★ ★ ★ ★ ★ ★ ★ ★ ★ ★ ★

Mel Blanc (San Francisco): The cartoon world's man of a thousand voices, including Bugs Bunny, Daffy Duck, and Porky Pig.

Cher (b. Cherilyn Sarkisian, El Centro): Living proof

of . . . something, something very American. A few years back, a study showed that some American high school kids thought Chernobyl was Cher's full name. Films include: *Silkwood, Mask, Moonstruck, Mermaids.*

Robert Duvall (San Diego): The American Olivier, a man who is *always* well-reviewed, regardless of the film. Films include: *The Godfather, Network, The Great Santini, Apocalypse Now, Tender Mercies.*

Clint Eastwood (San Francisco): America's great action hero had to go to Italy in the 1960s to make such spaghetti westerns as *The Good, the Bad and the Ugly* and *A Fistful of Dollars* before hitting it big stateside with the Dirty Harry series. Eastwood can direct, too: his work includes *Play Misty for Me* and *Bird.*

Gene Hackman (San Bernardino): Like Duvall, an actor's actor who hit pay dirt in the early 1970s with an action film, in his case with *The French Connection.* Other films include: *The Conversation, Hoosiers, Mississippi Burning.*

Tom Hanks (Concord): Hanks's star continues to rise steadily, despite his lacking any skill beyond likability. Films include: *Bachelor Party, Big, Turner and Hooch.*

George Lucas (Modesto): Lucas abandoned the drudgery of directing right after *Star Wars.* His special-effects company, Industrial Light and Magic, based in San Rafael, is at the forefront of filmmaking technology. He produced the Indiana Jones series and had earlier directed *American Graffiti,* based on his 1962 graduation from Thomas Downey High School. See What's There.

Russ Meyer (Oakland): The most stylish exploitation director ever, by a long shot. Meyer's epics feature big bazooms, blockhead men, rapid cutting, and women who know what they want.

Gregory Peck (La Jolla): A Hollywood elder statesman with a commanding voice, Peck continues to be sought after as he approaches 80. Films include: *Spellbound, Duel in the Sun, Moby Dick, To Kill a Mockingbird, The Omen, Old Gringo.*

Sam Peckinpah (Fresno): The master of poetic violence, a stylist in the use of slow motion and offbeat editing. Films directed include: *The Wild Bunch, Straw Dogs, The Osterman Weekend.*

Molly Ringwald (Roseville): The pubescent queen of such John Hughes movies as *Sixteen Candles* and *The Breakfast Club,* she's having a tough time finding good roles as she ages.

Natalie Wood (San Francisco): Cute child star who, like Elizabeth Taylor, only got better-looking as she aged. Her death while boating with Christopher Walken and her husband, Robert Wagner, is a mystery. Films include: *Miracle on 34th Street, Rebel Without a Cause, West Side Story, Bob & Carol & Ted & Alice.*

WHAT'S THERE

Alhambra: This is the site of the nation's first multiplex. A single theater was opened in 1923; a second was added in 1939 when the owner annexed an adjacent grocery store. Fittingly, the primitive "twin" theater was demolished in 1987 and replaced by an octoplex.

Carmel: The Hog's Breath, on San Carlos, between 5th Street and 6th Street, is Clint's saloon. Ever since Clint was elected mayor (he is no longer), this town has been choked with tourists.

Cholame: The James Dean Crash Site Memorial, a modern, angular, chromium cenotaph, looks like the entrance sign to an industrial park, and indicates that a great cultural leader was felled in the vicinity. The memorial was installed in 1983 by a Japanese businessman, Seita Onishi, who also commissioned a 120-ton, $200,000 wall sculpture for the site.

Little James Dean medallions are embedded in the wooden frame around the monument; avid souvenir seekers have pried some of them loose. The cenotaph is maintained by the adjacent Aggie's restaurant (805/238-5652), which sells James Dean sunglass visors, postcards,

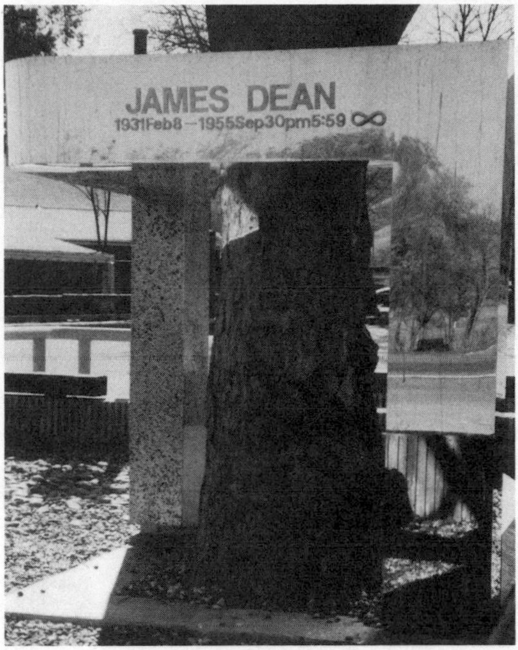

The James Dean death site marker.

and T-shirts. Hanging near the register is an enlarged copy of the speeding ticket Dean received at 3:30 P.M. that fateful day—he was never able to pay it. The lady at the Post Office (805/238-1390), right behind the cenotaph, displays a scrapbook chronicling the fame of this tiny dot on the map.

Soon after Dean's fatal 1955 car crash, the Greater Los Angeles Safety Council displayed his mangled Porsche Spider as an advertisement for safe driving; it was gradually dismantled for souvenirs, and—like the bulk of Dean's artifacts—hasn't resurfaced since.

Each year, on the anniversary of his death, September 30, a group of admirers retraces Dean's route from L.A. and stays at the Paso Robles Inn. The cenotaph is really about ½ mile closer to Cholame than the actual crash site. It's near the intersection of Highways 41 and 46.

The James Dean Death Road is adorned with gory billboards proclaiming the stretch Blood Alley.

Hanford: The Fox Theater dates back to 1929; it's one of few original Fox theaters that have been restored. 326 North Irwin.

Hillsborough: Bing Crosby was one of the richest men in show biz; his estate is at 1200 Jackling Drive.

Kenwood: The gift shop of the Smothers Brothers Winery sells corkscrews with their pictures on them, along with a variety of "Mom liked you best"-themed merchandise. It also features a yo-yo exhibit. Highway 12 and Warm Springs Road. 707/833-1010.

Modesto: Since the mid-1970s, tens of thousands of cruisers have been bringing traffic on McHenry Avenue to a standstill on American Graffiti Night, the Saturday night after local high school graduation—usually the second week in June. The town recently had to ban cruising on all other nights; even so, the annual festival is unofficial, unsanctioned, and downright unwelcomed. Cops shut it down after 10:00 P.M., but until then it's a whirl of custom cars, vendors, an oldies concert, and wall-to-wall traffic. In George Lucas's Modesto youth, and in the movie, the cruise strip was 10th Street, but now 10th isn't even a through street. Of course, since 1962 Modesto's population has grown from 30,000 to 160,000.

Ojai: This pleasant burg was the Shangri-La location for *Lost Horizon* (1937). There's a marked bench at the site of filming on East Ojai Avenue.

Palm Desert: The Bob Hope Cultural Center is at 73-000 Fred Waring Drive, thus combining a tribute to a comedian and to a bandleader in one handy address. For information call 619/340-ARTS.

Palm Springs: The Gene Autry Hotel has recently been renovated. 4200 East Palm Canyon Drive. Reservations: 619/328-1171. This is an area that sure knows the value of celebrity names.

Rancho Mirage: The Streets of the Stars neighborhood has streets named after Jack Benny, Burns & Allen, Claudette Colbert, Bing Crosby, Greer Garson, Bob Hope, Danny Kaye, Frank Sinatra, Barbara Stanwyck, and Gerald Ford. It's 10 miles southeast of Palm Springs, in and around the Blue Skies Village Mobile Home Park, just north of Country Club Drive on the east side of Highway 111, west of the Morningside Country Club. Need more directions?

Also in Rancho Mirage is The Betty Ford Clinic. Calling all autograph hounds! Past sightings include Liz Taylor, Chevy Chase, and many, many more! 39000 Bob Hope Drive, Eisenhower Medical Center.

A HISTORICAL TOUR OF SAN FRANCISCO AND THE MOVIES

1921: The career of Roscoe "Fatty" Arbuckle, the Jazz Age John Candy, ends in scandal after a wild party at the Hotel St. Francis, at which a starlet named Virginia Rappe died. You can sleep right where it happened: Rooms 1219, 1220, and 1221. Westin St. Francis, 335 Powell Street. Reservations: 415/397-7000.

1923: Saints Peter and Paul Church is filmed while under construction in Cecil B. DeMille's *The Ten Commandments.* Almost 50 years later, a sniper aims at a priest here in *Dirty Harry.* 666 Filbert Street.

1924: Erich von Stroheim's *Greed,* a landmark adaptation of Frank Norris's dental saga *McTeague,* is filmed in San Francisco and edited down to only 8 or 10 hours. The dental parlor location was at Laguna and Hayes streets—Stroheim had the company sleep at the site for the duration of filming.

1937: The Golden Gate Bridge opens and instantly becomes the cinematic shorthand for establishing an S.F. setting. It also becomes a photogenic battlefield for many a cinematic climax. In 1947, Humphrey Bogart fights Clifton Young at the foot of the bridge in *Dark Passage.* Whoops—Young falls onto the rocks belo-o-o-o-w. The bridge is wrecked by an atomic octopus in *It Came from Beneath the Sea* (1955). Christopher Reeve scoops a school bus from the teetering span after an earthquake in *Superman* (1978). Dirty Harry finds a victim at a lovers' lane overlooking the bridge in *Sudden Impact* (1983). Roger Moore and Christopher Walken duke it out atop one of the bridge's towers in *A View to a Kill* (1985). The bridge is lashed by a storm and a Klingon ship flies under it in *Star Trek IV* (1986).

1947: Bogie's art-deco hideout snugaway with Lauren Bacall from *Dark Passage* is at 1360 Montgomery Street.

1952: Joan Crawford lives at 2800 Scott Street with Jack Palance, who wants to kill her, in *Sudden Fear.*

1958: Kim Novak dives into the bay at scenic Fort Point, beneath the Golden Gate, in *Vertigo* (1958). She lives at the Brocklebank Apartments, 1000 Mason Street, across from the Fairmont Hotel. [The building is later seen in *The Woman in Red* (1984): Gene Wilder teeters on a ninth-story window ledge.] Later, a brunette Novak lives at the Empire, now the art-deco York Hotel, 940 Sutter Street. You can stay there; it's pretty ritzy. Reservations: 415/885-6800.

1968: The Fairmont Hotel lobby is seen in *Petulia,* starring a young and foxy Julie Christie. Many a major movie moment has come down in this grand hotel. Orson Welles ran into William Randolph Hearst in an elevator here; Hearst had tried to have Welles's *Citizen Kane* destroyed, then refused to review it or any other films from its distributor, RKO Pictures, in his many newspapers. In the 1980s, the Fairmont became the model for the TV show "Hotel." California at Mason, atop Nob Hill. Reservations: 415/772-5000.

1968: Steve McQueen researches his role in *Bullitt* by cruising with San Francisco police. The film's unforgettable car chase lasts 11 minutes, with the only music being the sound of squealing tires and bouncing suspensions. McQueen insists on doing his own driving for the picture. Frank Bullitt's home is at 1153-57 Taylor Street. He shops across the street, at the V-J Grocery, 1199 Clay Street.

1972: The steps in Alta Plaza Park, used for a wild chase in *What's Up, Doc?*, are wrecked by the filmmakers. Clay near Steiner Street.

1974: The Hyatt Regency is used for exterior and lobby scenes in *The Towering Inferno.* 5 Embarcadero Center. Reservations: 415/788-1234.

1983: San Francisco filmmaking reaches its apex at Burger Island during the filming of *Sudden Impact.* Clint Eastwood challenges a punk with the immortal words, "Go ahead—make my day." 701 Third Street.

San Jose: The Winchester Mystery House is located here. A 1981 John Wayne commemorative rifle is displayed in the Winchester Museum, a sidebar to the tour of this bizarre edifice. Names of the Duke's westerns are inscribed on the stock of the rifle to inspire marksmen.

San Simeon: The Hearst Castle, off Highway 1, was the inspiration for Xanadu in *Citizen Kane.* One building served as Olivier's Roman villa in *Spartacus.* The best part of the tour is finding out that tour guides get to party at the castle in off hours. Tickets must be reserved in advance: 805/927-4622.

Santa Barbara: Ronald Colman's grave is at the Santa Barbara Cemetery, East Cabrillo Boulevard. He's in the Ridge section, lot 663.

Olivier and Vivien Leigh were married, the JFKs honeymooned, and John Huston polished the script of *The*

African Queen at the San Ysidro Ranch. It's in the foothills of the Santa Ynez Mountains, near town.

Stanford: Shirley Temple's Doll Collection (she lives in nearby Woodside), including some of herself and Bill "Bojangles" Robinson, is on display for free in the lobby of the Children's Hospital at Stanford, 520 Sand Hill Road.

Temecula: El Rancho de Jaklin is Jack Klugman's horse ranch. Jaklin is the Klugman horse that placed third in the 1980 Kentucky Derby. De Portola Road, off Highway 79, near town.

Victorville: The Roy Rogers–Dale Evans Museum displays memorabilia from the careers of this singin' western duo, including a Last Supper beach towel in the Our American Religious Heritage room, a family table

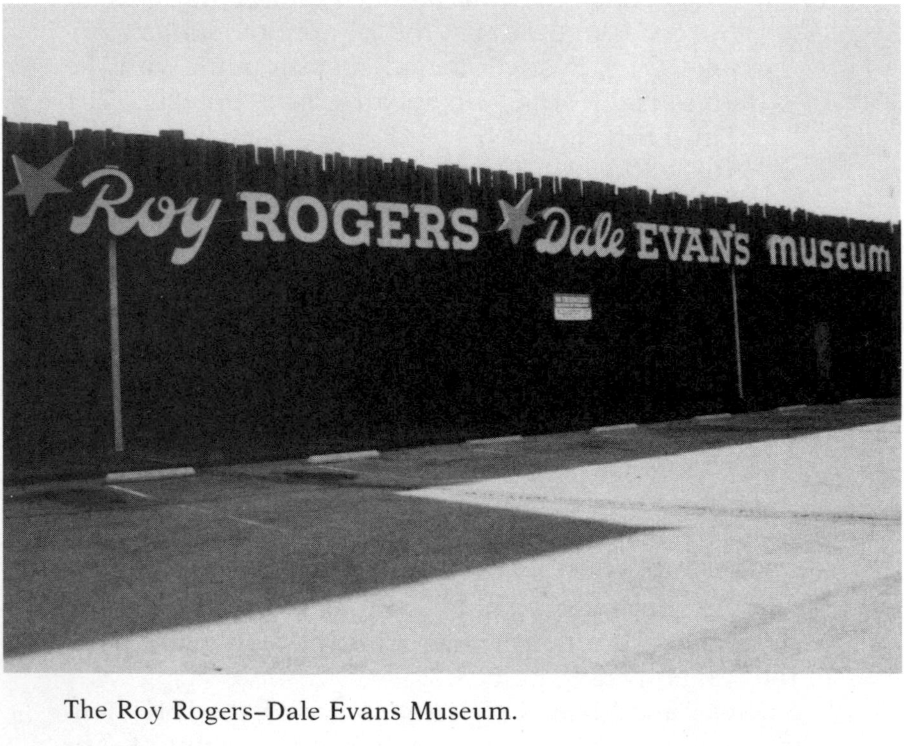

The Roy Rogers–Dale Evans Museum.

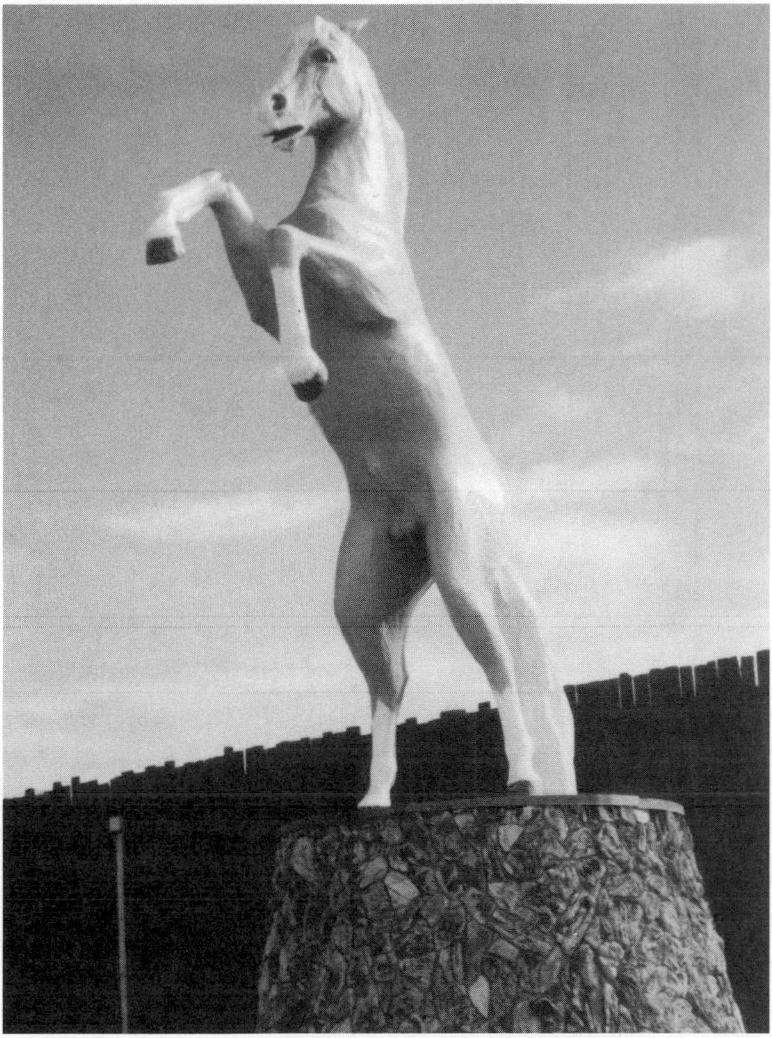

And heeere's Trigger! (Roy Rogers–Dale Evans Museum)

made by George Montgomery, and Roy's horse, Trigger, stuffed and mounted. Palmdale Road exit off I-15.

Woodside: The Filoli Mansion, seen in *Heaven Can Wait* and "Dynasty," can be toured almost year-round. Canada Road. Reservations: 415/364-2880.

ΔΤΧ
ANIMAL HOUSE
KIRBY

Chapter 2

The GREAT NORTHWEST

Idaho •
Oregon •
Washington •

IDAHO

MADE IN IDAHO

RUGGED, HAIRY-CHESTED PIONEERS

***Northwest Passage* (McCall, 1939):** King Vidor's Technicolor extravaganza stars Spencer Tracy and Robert Young. By all accounts, the shoot was as grueling as the actual experiences of Rogers's Rangers. Slews of locals were employed, including 250 regional Indians. The film's setting was actually supposed to be New York State and eastern Canada.

***The Unconquered* (Ashton, 1946):** Cecil B. DeMille, Gary Cooper, and Paulette Goddard—big adventure! White-water scenes were shot on the Falls and Snake rivers.

***Breakheart Pass* (Lewiston, 1975):** Charles Bronson plays a lawman aboard a train looking for baddies. The Lewiston area subs for Nevada.

***Bronco Billy* (Boise, Meridian, 1980):** Clint threw his fans for a loop when he played a screwy Wild West Show loser.

***Heaven's Gate* (Wallace, 1980):** This small mining town was dressed as the main street of Casper, Wyoming. The buzz at the location concerned the hazards—to both humans and animals—of working for director Michael Cimino, and his cavalier attitude of "anything for the movie."

***Pale Rider* (Sawtooth National Recreation Area, 1985):** Clint's overlong homage to *Shane* delivers great western vistas, courtesy of the U.S. Department of the Interior.

SNOW BUNNIES

***I Met Him in Paris* (Sun Valley, 1937):** Sun Valley stands in for the Swiss Alps as Claudette Colbert flirts with Melvyn Douglas and Robert Young. The resort had opened just prior to filming.

***Sun Valley Serenade* (Sun Valley, 1941):** Ski footage for this Sonja Henie vehicle was shot here, but none of the principals actually made the trek. The film seems to play constantly at a local theater. Many other films of the forties and fifties did second-unit work here as well.

***Ski Party* (Sun Valley, Sawtooth National Forest, 1965):** Frankie Avalon, Deborah Walley, and Dwayne Hickman in a beach movie on snow.

SILENT WITH GOOD STORIES

***Told in the Hills* (Lewiston, 1919):** Unusually sympathetic to Indians, this six-reeler actually employed hundreds of Nez Percé; it was the first time they'd been allowed to gather since losing the Nez Percé War in 1877. A few years ago, Boise State film professor Tom Trusky wangled a few reels of this lost film from the only place on earth that had preserved a copy—the Soviet film archives.

***Back to God's Country* (Priest Lake, 1922):** Nell Shipman, a writer, director, and actress, came here with a menagerie in the 1920s, searching for authentic locales for her dramas. In this one, her first, she performs a brief nude scene! (She was good-looking, too.) Other titles include *The Grubstake, The Light on Lookout,* and *Trail of the Northwind.* Shipman's career never got very far after her studio collapsed.

ALSO . . .

***Bus Stop* (Ketchum, Sun Valley, 1956):** Marilyn Monroe wears some amazing outfits, and acts, too. See What's There: Ketchum.

IDAHO'S GIFTS TO HOLLYWOOD

★ ★ ★ ★ ★ ★ ★ ★ ★ ★ ★ ★ ★ ★ ★ ★

Wilford Brimley (Nampa): This crusty old character actor lived most of his life here; he left only about 10 years ago.

Walt Disney (Lewiston): Diz worked briefly here and married a local girl. KLEW-TV in Lewiston is still owned by the Retlaw Corporation. (That's Walter spelled backwards.)

Jack Hoxie (Riggins): A popular silent cowboy, Hoxie faded shortly after the advent of sound. Tom Trusky recently uncovered evidence that Hoxie was born Jack Stone, murdered his brother Earl, changed his name, and became a big cowboy star, with nobody ever suspecting his past.

David Lynch (Boise): The director of *Eraserhead, Blue Velvet,* "Twin Peaks," et al., famous for his consumption of coffee and sugar, was born in Missoula, Montana, but grew up here.

Lana Turner (b. Julia Jean Mildred Frances, Wallace): Turner claims she's from Wallace, but she's actually from Burke, a rowdy little mining town nearby, a real Sin City. Her father was a rough character, a gambler. A former baby-sitter employed by Turner says that when she returned to Wallace for a War Bond drive, instead of receiving a warm, effusive welcome she was instantly besieged by her father's creditors. She turned around and left in a huff, and that was it for her and Idaho.

Craig Wasson (Boise): Wasson was a brief phenom in the early 1980s, starring in a flurry of films such as *Body Double, Ghost Story,* and *Four Friends,* but his flavor went out of favor. He attended Borah High.

WHAT'S THERE

Hayden Lake: This neo-Nazi stronghold was the summer home of Bing Crosby, who was also known as . . . Der Bingle. The house is on English Point Road (US 2).

Ketchum: The North Fork Store, a location from *Bus Stop,* has a photo display of the movie. It's 10 miles north of town on Highway 75, on the west side of the road.

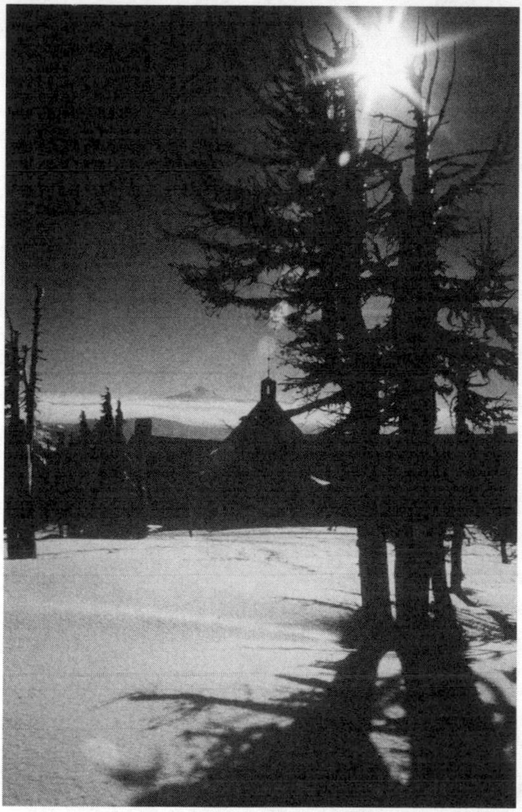

The Timberline Lodge, location for *The Shining*. Because all work and no play . . . . *(Courtesy of Tony Price)*

MADE IN OREGON

In the 1920s, the Portland-Beaverton area was a hot location for pristine-wilderness adventures, particularly those of J. J. Fleming and Premium Pictures. Big names like King Vidor, William Wellman, and Raoul Walsh later found their way up here. In recent times, Oregon, like Washington, has become a refuge for filmmakers seeking nice, clean suburban settings without too much congestion or pollution.

FRONTIERLAND

***Paint Your Wagon* (Baker, 1969):** Oregon subs for gold-rush–era California with one of the strangest casts ever assembled for a musical comedy: Clint Eastwood, Lee Marvin, Jean Seberg.

***Rooster Cogburn* (Bend, 1975):** This *True Grit* sequel brought the Duke to Big Trail country with Katharine Hepburn, in an *African Queen*–ish story.

TREES, TREES, TREES

***The General* (Cottage Grove, 1927):** One of Buster Keaton's best, it required lots of space to run the vintage locomotive. Buster found it here in the Oregon woods, which subbed for the Civil War–era South.

***Abe Lincoln in Illinois* (Eugene, 1939):** Raymond Massey became typecast as a Lincolnesque mug after this, but Henry Fonda in John Ford's *Young Mr. Lincoln* is less pompous, more Lincolny. Woodsy Oregon provided plentiful rails for Lincoln to split.

***Sometimes a Great Notion* (Central Coast, 1971):** Based on Oregonian Ken Kesey's novel, this is filmdom's finest look at the beauty and brutality of the logging life in Oregon, with Paul Newman directing himself and Henry Fonda.

***Search for Sasquatch (Legend of Bigfoot)* (Bend, 1975):** They didn't find him.

***Stand By Me* (Eugene, Cottage Grove, Brownsville, 1986):** Neo–Brat Packers go tromping in the woods; Rob Reiner directs. Based on Stephen King's short story "The Body."

A NICE CLEAN PLACE POPULATED BY WHITE PEOPLE

***Drive, He Said* (Eugene, 1970):** Jack Nicholson returned to the Northwest after his *Five Easy Pieces* triumph to direct his pals, including screenwriter Robert Towne and director Henry Jaglom, in an arty character movie. Filming included a naked man running through the University of Oregon quad.

***Animal House* (Eugene, Cottage Grove, 1977):** After 50 other schools turned down requests to be used as locations, the University of Oregon agreed to be represented as Faber College, home of the infamous Delta House. University officials say the cast and crew were pussycats in real life.

***The Black Stallion* (Gearhart, Nehalem, 1979):** Ultralush photography meets ultralush Oregon landscapes in Mickey Rooney's umpteenth comeback.

***Personal Best* (Eugene, 1982):** The University of Oregon, one of the nation's top track-and-field schools, is the setting for this lesbian relationship between two track stars.

***Short Circuit* (Astoria, Portland, Columbia Gorge, North Bonneville, Washington, 1986):** Ally Sheedy lives the prototypical posthippie Oregonian life until she meets smiley guy Steve Guttenberg and a "funny" robot.

ALSO . . .

***One Flew Over the Cuckoo's Nest* (Salem, 1975):** Shot at Oregon State Hospital, the film won Oscars for everybody involved, got Michael Douglas's moviemaking career in gear, and brought recognition to Czech émigré director Milos Forman.

***1941* (Cannon Beach, 1979):** Rare Spielberg flop about a Japanese wartime invasion of Hollywood. It supposedly had one shot costing $1 million per take—and Spielberg went for *three takes*! Farther down the Oregon coast is a town that actually *was* buzzed by a Japanese bomber during the war: Brookings. (The pilot of the plane, Nobuo Fujita, later became a beloved honorary citizen of the town and was feted at the 1962 Azalea Festival. It seems that in trying to erase Brookings from the map, he inadvertently placed it *on* the map.)

***Breaking In* (Portland, 1989):** The outstanding Scottish director Bill Forsyth, who wanted to shoot his *Housekeeping* in the northwest United States but was forced to

Canada by economics, finally gets to roll 'em on U.S. terra firma.

***Drugstore Cowboy* (Portland, 1989):** Druggies on the run in the Great Northwest: *Bonnie and Clyde* meets *Wired.*

OREGON'S GIFTS TO HOLLYWOOD

★ ★ ★ ★ ★ ★ ★ ★ ★ ★ ★ ★ ★ ★ ★ ★

Howard Hesseman (Salem): A former member of the comedy group The Committee, he starred as a dippy hippie in *Billy Jack* and made millions in sitcoms.

River Phoenix (Madras): Hippie offspring who throbs young hearts with his affected but effective acting.

WHAT'S THERE

Timberline: Mount Hood National Forest's Timberline Lodge was the unforgettable location for Stanley; Kubrick's *The Shining.* The majestic lodge was used for exteriors only; the interiors were filmed in a studio. Reservations: 800/547-1406

Vale: The Bates Motel was built in 1952; after *Psycho* came out in 1960 the motel's towels, keys, matchbooks, and other items began disappearing at an alarming rate. According to owner Steve Bates, people still stop to take photos under the motel's sign.

Neither Tony Perkins nor Janet Leigh has stayed here, but Burl Ives and Tennessee Ernie Ford have. Rates at this writing are approximately \$22–\$26 per night. The towels no longer bear the motel's name. Common question asked of Mr. Bates: "Your name isn't Norman, is it?" Highway 20 (1101 A Street West), west side of town. Reservations: 503/473-3234.

MADE IN WASHINGTON

SEATTLE

***It Happened at the World's Fair* (1963):** Elvis bops at the 1962 World's Fair, one of the last great world's fairs on U.S. soil.

***Cinderella Liberty* (1973):** James Caan is a Navy dude involved with sailor's delite Marsha Mason, a likable actress in her pre–Neil Simon days.

***The Parallax View* (1974):** The assassination in this paranoid Alan Pakula–Warren Beatty adventure takes place on the observation deck of the world's fair Space Needle.

***Streetwise* (1984):** Effective, touching documentary about Seattle street kids.

***The Stepfather* (1987):** This wonderfully creepy film uses the quiet beauty of the area as a counterpoint to Dad's gruesome butchery.

***The Fabulous Baker Boys* (1989)** No San Juan Islands cruises in this cool, downbeat film; it's the urban Seattle that tourists barely notice.

***Say Anything* (1989):** Seattle came of age as an Anywhere USA in 1989 with this film and *The Fabulous Baker Boys,* neither of which makes a big deal about the area's natural beauty.

PUGET SOUND

***Five Easy Pieces* (Seattle, San Juan Islands, also Eugene and Portland, Oregon, 1970):** Jack Nicholson's stuffy family lives in peaceful isolation in the rainy, verdant San Juan Islands. Directed by Bob Rafelson, who also directed . . .

***Black Widow* (Seattle, 1986):** Theresa Russell seduces nerdy Nicol Williamson at his bucolic island retreat.

WAR GAMES

***To Hell and Back* (Fort Lewis, 1955):** Audie Murphy re-creates his wartime heroism on the Yakima Firing Range.

***An Officer and a Gentleman* (Port Townsend, Seattle, Tacoma, 1982):** Historic Port Townsend was the setting for this naval-air romance between Richard Gere and Debra Winger.

***WarGames* (Newhalem, Mount Vernon, Steilacoom, Seattle, 1983):** Hacker extraordinaire Matthew Broderick nearly starts a war.

SASQUATCH COUNTRY

***Call of the Wild* (Mount Baker, 1935):** Clark Gable tromps through Yukon country near Mount Baker. This popular locale for generic barren wilderness was also used for hunting scenes in *The Deer Hunter.*

***St. Helens* (1981):** Art Carney plays crusty Harry Truman, who refused to vacate during the 1980 volcanic eruption and got buried under millions of tons of mud. Oops, I gave away the ending.

***Harry and the Hendersons* (Snohomish County, Kittitas County, Seattle, 1987):** John Lithgow and his family take bigfoot home with them. Amazingly, this never became a sitcom.

AND . . .

***The Runner Stumbles* (Roslyn, 1979):** Dick Van Dyke plays a priest accused of murdering a nun. The rear of the Brick Tavern, the oldest bar in the state, became the courtroom. Two wooden jail cells were added to a steel one already in the basement for the jail scenes.

***Heart Like a Wheel* (Olympia, 1983):** Bonnie Bedelia is great as Shirley Muldowney, one of the first prominent female race-car drivers.

***I Love You to Death* (Tacoma, 1990):** Lawrence Kasdan's marital infidelity comedy, starring Kevin Kline and Tracey Ullman.

WASHINGTON'S GIFTS TO HOLLYWOOD

★ ★ ★ ★ ★ ★ ★ ★ ★ ★ ★ ★ ★ ★ ★ ★

Dyan Cannon (b. Samille Diane Friesen, Tacoma): Giggly, busty blond good at screeching. Bore Cary Grant's only child. Films include: *Bob & Carol & Ted & Alice, The Anderson Tapes, Heaven Can Wait.*

Bing Crosby (Tacoma): Mr. Cool. A mellow crooner who always looked and sounded as relaxed as a man in a bathtub. He and Bob Hope were the sultans of Hollywood in the forties and fifties. See What's There: Tacoma; Spokane; Hayden Lake, Idaho.

Frances Farmer (Seattle): Good-looking, talented actress who was too sensitive for her own good, so Mom had her lobotomized. Scenes from her screen bio, *Frances,* were shot in Seattle. See What's There: Steilacoom.

Chuck Jones (Spokane): Bugs Bunny's daddy, he also helped create Porky Pig, Daffy Duck, and many other great Warner Bros. characters.

Kevin McCarthy (Seattle): Silver-haired smoothy remembered for *Invasion of the Body Snatchers* (1956, though he had a role in the 1978 remake as well). His sister was known as Mary "The Group" McCarthy.

WHAT'S THERE

Snoqualmie and North Bend: These two tiny towns are the setting for Northwest native David Lynch's "Twin Peaks" TV show. In the center of Snoqualmie is the Big Log, a 39-ton log seen in the opening credits. One mile north of town is the Salish Lodge, exterior for *Peaks*'s Great Northern Hotel; bookings tripled after the show's premiere. 37807 Southeast Snoqualmie Falls Road. Reservations: 800/826-6124.

In North Bend is the Mar T Cafe, *Peaks*'s Double R Diner. Unfortunately, as of this writing the Mar T has failed to exploit the possibilities of promoting a "damn fine" cup of coffee. But at least you can get pie here. 137 West North Bend Way.

Spokane: On display in the Bing Crosby Room at Gonzaga College, Bing's alma mater, are his Oscar for *Going My Way*; gold records; a 1957 trophy from *Fisherman* magazine proclaiming him "Fishing Father of the Year"; the graduation program from Gonzaga High School, at which Bing spoke on "The Purpose of Education"; and a 1944 award certificate from the India Film Journalists Association, saying he had "Perfect emotional acting with action expressed from the jaws, in acting serious roles. A perfect film-face for negative and positive emotions." Amen. There's also a statue on campus. 502 East Boone Avenue.

Also in Spokane may be found the Crosby Alumni House, his boyhood home. Here are Bing's more casual artifacts: his pipe, dressing gown, and Gonzaga blanket. 508 East Sharp Street.

Steilacoom: Here, at the Western State Mental Hospital, Frances Farmer spent her most hellish years in confinement. Steilacoom Boulevard.

Tacoma: The Bing Crosby Historical Society and Gallery of Washington State Entertainment was founded in 1977. Here are his slacks and other belongings, as well as a clan of true Crosby lovers. The group publishes a fan-club newsletter, *The Crooner*, and hosts an annual May tribute. The society is based in the historic Pantages Center, at Ninth and Broadway. Info: 206/627-2947.

Bing's birthplace, 1112 North J Street, has a historical marker placed by the Sons of the American Revolution. It's about the fifth step up from the street.

A stone marker heralds the Bing Crosby Rose Bed in Point Defiance Park.

Bob's Java Jive, a coffeepot-shaped bistro, was seen in *I Love You to Death*. It's at 2102 South Tacoma Way, and well worth a stop.

The Pantages Building, at the corner of Ninth and Commerce in downtown Tacoma, is the home of the Bing Crosby Historical Society. *(Courtesy of The Bing Crosby Historical Society)*

KIRBY

Chapter 3

The WILD WEST

- Arizona
- Colorado
- Nevada
- New Mexico
- Texas
- Utah
- Wyoming

MADE IN ARIZONA

Studio facilities in Arizona include the soundstage at the Old Tucson tourist attraction, near Tucson, and Carefree Studios, near Phoenix. "The New Dick Van Dyke

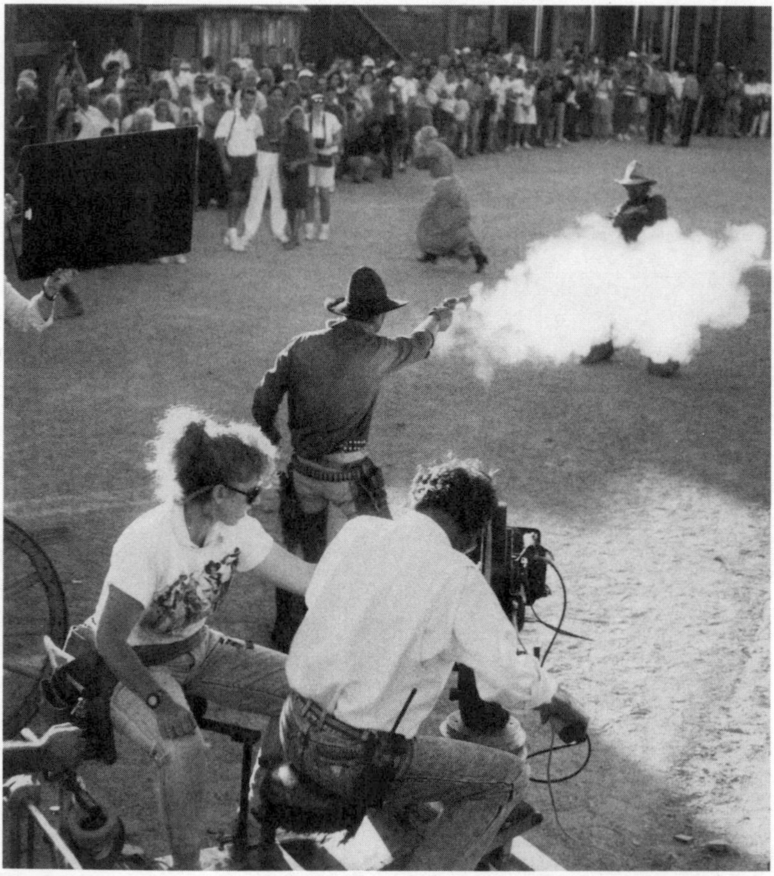

"Reality gives way to imagination" in Old Tucson, the "Hollywood in the Desert." *(Courtesy of Old Tucson Studios)*

Show" and *Raising Arizona* were shot at Carefree. Orson Welles began shooting his much-anticipated *Other Side of the Wind* here, starring fellow directors John Huston, Dennis Hopper, and Henry Jaglom. But the revolt in Iran caused his backers to withdraw support. Huston attempted to finish the film after Welles died. Perhaps someday it will surface, like ashes rising from Phoenix.

A $250 million movie studio is under construction near Laveen, southwest of Phoenix, and is expected to open in 1992. The studio will also be geared for tourists à la the Disney and Universal tours.

DESERT SANDS

***The Sheik* (Yuma, 1921):** This definitive Rudolph Valentino film required endless desert sands.

***Beau Geste* (Yuma, 1926, 1939, 1966):** All three versions of the story, considered classic enough to be commemorated in U.S. postage, did some Arizona shooting to simulate the sands of Arabia.

***Gunga Din* (Yuma, 1939):** Another postage-stamp classic (the others were *Gone with the Wind* and *The Wizard of Oz*). This time, Arizona mimes India.

***Flight of the Phoenix* (Yuma, Buttercup Valley, 1966):** As in *Beau Gest,* the setting is Arabia. James Stewart, a real WWII pilot, plays a pilot in the film. A stunt pilot crashed and died during shooting.

***Planet of the Apes* (Page, 1968):** The setting is a barren, ape-run future; why, it's Page, Arizona!

***Return of the Jedi* (Yuma, 1983):** The setting is a distant planet in a galaxy far, far away. Arizona it is.

***Spaceballs* (Yuma, 1987):** This *Star Wars* parody spent four days of filming at sand dunes near town.

GUNSLINGERS

***Stagecoach* (Kayenta, Mesa, 1939):** John Ford's great western, which revived the genre; the Duke's breakthrough role. Orson Welles screened this film before making *Citizen Kane.*

***Red River* (Elgin, Whetstone Mountains, San Pedro River, 1948):** Director Howard Hawks had five dams built to bring the San Pedro to flood stage.

***Violent Saturday* (Bisbee, 1955):** A vivid, violent look at a small-town bank robbery, based on a Jim Thompson novelette.

***Gunfight at the O.K. Corral* (Old Tucson, Elgin, Phoenix, 1957):** The setting is the O.K. Corral in Tombstone. *My Darling Clementine* (1946) covers the same subject.

PHOENIX: LIKE ONE BIG 'BURB

***Real Life* (Phoenix, 1979):** Albert Brooks's character, Albert Brooks, has to choose between a family in Phoenix and one in Green Bay, Wisconsin, to be the subject of his parody of PBS's "Family." He chooses Phoenix. "*You* spend the winter in Wisconsin," he chortles.

***Raising Arizona* (Phoenix, Scottsdale, Carefree, 1987):** Outstanding use of locations, as well as outstanding everything else.

***Bill and Ted's Excellent Adventure* (Phoenix, Scottsdale, Mesa, 1989):** The New Southwest is here in all its suburban glory.

AND...

***Saboteur* (Boulder Dam, 1942):** Robert Cummings, on the run in a Hitchcockian case of mistaken identity, hits this landmark, then heads for the Statue of Liberty.

***War of the Worlds* (Florence, 1953):** The dark side of *Starman*—a Martian invasion.

***Oklahoma!* (San Rafael Valley, 1955):** This classic musical was filmed at the Green Cattle Company Ranch.

***The Nutty Professor* (Tempe, 1963):** Jerry Lewis's undisputed masterwork—"Gimme an Alaskan polar bear heater"—was filmed at Arizona State University. Other films shot there include the lame-o 1976 remake of *A Star Is Born* and Robert Zemeckis's coolest film, *Used Cars* (1980).

***Easy Rider* (Valentine, 1969):** At the Collins Ranch, now the Hunt Ranch, Peter Fonda fixes a flat in the background while a cowboy symbolically shoes a horse in the foreground. The ranch is located along the country's best remaining section of fabled Route 66, on the south side of the road, just west of the Indian agency.

***Alice Doesn't Live Here Anymore* (Tucson, 1975):** Ellen Burstyn goes to work in a Tucson diner when her husband dies. Directed by Martin Scorsese, this melancholy film somehow spawned the idiot sitcom "Alice." Seen in the film is the groovy Big Horn Restaurant, in Amado, for which the front entrance is a 25-foot steer skull. It's still there, off I-19, across the street from the Cow Palace.

***Starman* (Winslow, 1984):** The impressive Meteor Crater, a major tourist attraction, is the site of alien docking for Jeff Bridges. It is located 20 miles west of town on I-40.

***Million Dollar Mystery* (Page, Lake Powell, Lake Havasu, Bisbee, 1987):** Lots of Arizona is seen in a cross-country hunt for $$. The film's promotional hook was that some lucky moviegoer would win $1 million—unfortunately, it failed to take in that much at the box office. Nonetheless, a woman in Bakersfield was awarded the cash.

***Midnight Run* (Globe, Flagstaff, Williams, Sedona, 1988):** Lots of outdoor Arizona locations. The famous jump, however, was filmed in the warmer waters of New Zealand.

ARIZONA'S GIFTS TO HOLLYWOOD

★ ★ ★ ★ ★ ★ ★ ★ ★ ★ ★ ★ ★ ★ ★

Rex Allen (Willcox): The singing cowboy star of the fifties is well remembered in his hometown. See What's There: Willcox.

Ted Danson: The *Three Men and a Baby* and "Cheers" star was born in San Diego and raised in Flagstaff.

Andy Devine (b. Jeremiah Schwartz, Flagstaff): One of the great western sidekicks, he was famous for his crotchety fretfulness and raspy voice, which was caused by a childhood accident in which he jabbed a curtain rod through the roof of his mouth. He hosted a bizarre kid's TV show in the fifties, "Andy's Gang." ("Froggie, plunk your magic twanger!") See What's There: Kingman.

WHAT'S THERE

Amado: Many a star has haunted the Cow Palace Restaurant, a desert canteen that dates back to the 1930s. Photos on the walls include Joan Blondell, Douglas Fairbanks, Jr., Al Jolson, John Wayne, Mae West, and Loretta Young. Mounted buffalo, moose, and elk adorn the spaces between the stars, and the eatery features live entertainment and singalongs. Off I-19.

"Rub elbows with the famous motion picture horses," invite the folks at the Hitchin Post Stables, which features "motion picture livestock" from films galore.

Flagstaff: Ride "famous movie horses" at the Hitchin Post Stables, including horses from *The Gambler II* and *Wanda Nevada.* (Peter Fonda rode a mule in *Wanda.*) 448 Lake Mary Road, 4½ miles southwest of town. Info: 602/774-1719.

Florence: A cenotaph of a sad, riderless Tony, Tom Mix's horse, marks the spot where America's Champion Cowboy died when his Cord crashed into a gully and a suitcase flew forward and smashed his skull. Tony has been stolen twice, in 1980 and again in 1989, but was most recently replaced through the efforts of a devoted nonagenarian. At Tom Mix Wash, 15 miles south of town on Highway 80/89.

Kingman: The Mohave Museum of History and Arts has a permanent exhibit of Andy Devine memorabilia—clothes, pictures, movie posters, his Golden Boot award—along with oil paintings of all the presidents and first ladies. 400 West Beale Street.

The Beale Hotel, which Devine's parents owned and where he grew up, is "under renovation." It's at 325 East Andy Devine Avenue. For the past dozen Octobers, the town has hosted Andy Devine Days, which include a rodeo and a parade (in which Andy's widow struts).

Oatman: Clark Gable and Carole Lombard spent their wedding night in Room 15 of the historic Oatman

From the Oatman, Arizona, brochure.

Hotel; they were married in Kingman on March 29, 1939. The hotel is said to be haunted: toilets flush themselves, the jukebox starts up on its own, lights flicker, footsteps are heard.

The spook-ridden hotel is now an attraction. An old movie projector, posters, and other memorabilia can be found in the Theater Room. The room has been restored to its 1939 look—tours cost 50¢. There are big photos of stars on the wall, but the door is blocked off with chicken wire.

No rooms are rented out anymore. Oatman has a few hundred residents; it formerly had 12,000 or so. Off Old Route 66.

Scottsdale: Rawhide, a cheesy Wild West theme park, has the wagon train from *How the West Was Won* but no other authentic memorabilia. Rawhide is geared to happy hour, not tourism—the place is only open after 5:00 P.M. 23023 North Scottsdale Road.

Tombstone: Tombstone is not a movie attraction per se, but it is every western fan's dream of the old West. The town is preserved not so much for historical accuracy as for fun. At the O.K. Corral, wax figures re-create the poses that were re-created in *Gunfight at the O.K. Corral* and *My Darling Clementine*. If you stay at the Hacienda Huachuca Motel, you'll be, according to the brochure, "staying where John Wayne stayed." Reservations: 602/457-2201.

Tucson: Old Tucson, a movie set converted to a tourist attraction, is the second largest pay attraction in the state. (Number one is the Grand Canyon.) On the premises are authentic props from *The Alamo*, Lolita's Fruit Stand and Dean Martin's hideout from *Rio Bravo*, locations from *Three Amigos*, and much, much more.

On a tour of the working soundstage, visitors can admire a tribute behind glass to John Wayne—a big Oscar with a little *True Grit* eye patch. The soundstage tour includes a special-effects-heavy look at the location's history. Recent additions include a stunt fall off a 21-foot tower and a ride through a mine shaft.

The Tres Amigos Cantina in Old Tucson *(Courtesy of Julie Kuehndorf)*

Harry Cohn, the boss of Columbia Pictures, commissioned the construction of Old Tucson in 1939 for a $2.5 million epic, *Arizona* (starring Jean Arthur and William Holden). The ruins of this set are on display here. It went pretty fallow for 20 years till Robert Shelton built it up again. At one time, the wardrobe department here had the world's largest collection of western costumes. A Boardwalk of Fame has names of stars who worked here branded into a wood-plank sidewalk.

Old Tucson is located at 201 South Kinney Road. Info: 602/883-6457.

Willcox: The Rex Allen Museum has videos of his movies, the stagecoach he drove in "The Frontier Doctor" TV show, costumes, scenes from his early childhood, and a mural of him on his horse, Koko. Next door is the Rex Allen Theater, "under renovation," which will show his movies when completed. The museum opened in October 1989 and is open daily 10–5. It's on North Railroad Avenue.

The Palace Bar, 118 North Railroad Avenue, has a bronze statue in the bar of Allen riding Koko. The town plans a large statue in the park on Railroad Avenue someday. There is also a Rex Allen Drive. The house where he grew up has burned down.

Allen now lives in Sonoita, Arizona, on a ranch. He comes into Willcox every few weeks and stops at the museum, so you just might get lucky.

Tom Mix death monument, in Florence. *(Courtesy of Julie Kuehndorf)*

MADE IN COLORADO

ROCKY MOUNTAIN HIGHLIGHTS

Around the World in 80 Days **(Durango, 1956):** The well-preserved, upscale art enclave of Durango was one of 140 locations for this ambitious production.

Butch Cassidy and the Sundance Kid **(Durango, Silverton, 1969):** The film that temporarily revived the western.

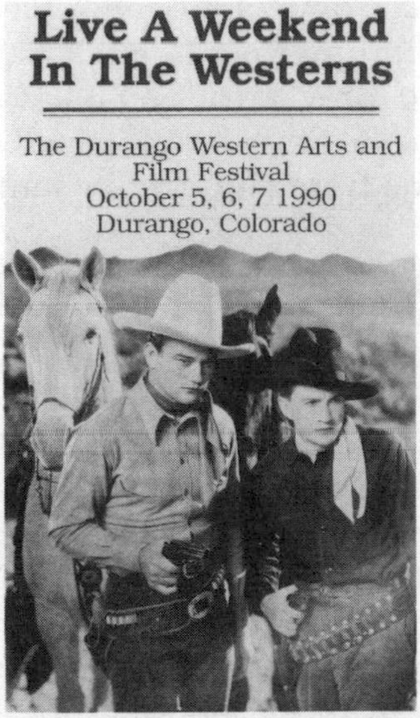
Live A Weekend
In The Westerns
The Durango Western Arts and
Film Festival
October 5, 6, 7 1990
Durango, Colorado

The Durango Western Arts and Film Festival brochure.

Downhill Racer **(1969):** Robert Redford got paid to go skiing in the Rockies for Michael Ritchie's profile of an egocentric skier. Bill Johnson of the 1980 Olympics must have based his life on this film.

True Grit **(1969):** The film that launched a thousand eye-patch tributes to the Duke and won him an Oscar.

Badlands **(1973):** Based on the career of multiple murderer Charles Starkweather. Although the film was set in the Dakotas, the fantastically gorgeous landscapes of this cult favorite, starring Martin Sheen and Sissy Spacek, were shot in Colorado.

***Sleeper* (Genesee, 1973):** The film's futuristic house is located on Route 74 between Denver and Evergreen.

***Continental Divide* (Custer, Pueblo County, also Cedar Falls and Crystal Mountain, Washington, 1981):** John Belushi's a chain-smokin' Chi-town newshound. Blair Brown's an outdoorsy ornithologist. Between them, there's a *Continental Divide!* Get it?

***National Lampoon's Christmas Vacation* (Breckenridge, 1989):** An early melt imperiled the start of production and required the trucking of snow from other areas—until a 77-inch snowfall hit a few days later. Locations included the Summit County High School gym, the local Wal-Mart, and Breckenridge Golf Course (which was Jolly Jerry's Saw 'n' Save Xmas Tree Ranch). Scenes of the Griswold home were shot in Burbank, California.

COLORADO'S GIFTS TO HOLLYWOOD

★ ★ ★ ★ ★ ★ ★ ★ ★ ★ ★ ★ ★ ★ ★ ★

Lon Chaney (Colorado Springs): The silents' Man of a Thousand Faces had a gift for portraying such scary types as the Phantom of the Opera and the Hunchback of Notre Dame. His son, Lon Junior, carried on the tradition.

Douglas Fairbanks (Denver): Like Chaney, Fairbanks was a prolific silent-screen star whose son made it in the talkies. He married America's Sweetheart, Mary Pickford; they lived in the legendary Pickfair mansion, and the two of them founded United Artists with Charlie Chaplin and D. W. Griffith.

Joseph Walker (Denver): A major cinematographer who shot many classics, including *It Happened One Night, Lost Horizon, The Awful Truth, His Girl Friday, It's a Wonderful Life,* and *Born Yesterday.*

Arriba: Tarado Mansion, open for tours, was designed as a replica of *Gone with the Wind*'s Tara. Inside is a privately owned collection that includes the tea coat of the Unsinkable Molly Brown and General Custer's wife's harp. It is located ¼ mile south of 1-70 exit 383.

Aspen: There is great stargazing in this movie-colony hangout. Don't worry about bothering them—if they were *really* looking for privacy, they wouldn't be here.

The Hotel Jerome opened in 1889, built by Macy's magnate Jerome Wheeler. Gary Cooper used to girl-watch out front. Lana Turner, Lex Barker, Hedy Lamarr, and John Wayne have also hung out here. 330 East Main Street.

Cañon City: Buckskin Joe, a 160-acre western theme park, has been the location for movies with John Wayne, Tom Selleck, and James Arness. Films shot here include *Cat Ballou, The Dutchess and the Dirtwater Fox* (Buckskin Joe was Dirtwater), *The White Buffalo* (Charles Bronson), *The Sacketts* (about 75 percent was shot here),

"Stay an hour, stay a day—you'll love Buckskin Joe, Old West's Largest Theme Park".

The Cowboys (this is where the Duke came to get the kids), *Barquero* (Warren Oates), and *How the West Was Won.*

The location was opened in 1958 as a tourist attraction and movie set. Before 1958, Tom Mix did a lot of filming in the Cañon City area. Parts of *Stagecoach* and *Wells Fargo* were also shot nearby.

Buckskin Joe consists of an array of structures transplanted from various parts of the region after a master plan was drawn up by Malcolm Brown, a former MGM art director. One of these buildings is a saloon from Prospect Heights where Mix was arrested for disturbing the peace in 1904. (He was working as a cowboy in this area when he started making movies.) Also here is a transplanted bunkhouse where Mix bunked during his cowboy days.

Buckskin Joe is located eight miles west of town; take the Royal Gorge exit off Highway 50.

Durango: The Durango Western Arts and Film Festival, held in October, includes performances by cowboys and Ute Indians and trips on the famous Durango and Silverton Narrow Gauge Railroad. Former western star Harry Carey, Jr., has retired here and appears at the film festival, which each year features classic westerns. Other stars such as Ben Johnson, Tommy Lee Jones, and Dennis Weaver have shown up for the events.

Information: 800/525-8855.

Estes Park: The Baldpate Inn was the basis for the comedy-mystery novel *Seven Keys to Baldpate,* which has been adapted for the screen five times. On display within is the largest collection of keys in the world, including keys to Hitler's desk, Mozart's wine cellar, Fort Knox, and Westminster Abbey. It's seven miles south of the park on Highway 7. Open Memorial Day through Labor Day, 303/586-6151.

Monte Vista: At Best Western's Movie Manor motel, you can enjoy drive-in movies while lying in bed! A big picture window looks out over the screen of the adjacent

Enjoy drive-in movies while lying in bed at Best Western's Movie Manor Motel.

theater. The soundtrack is piped into the room; you control the on–off switch and volume. One disconcerting side effect is that you might start nodding off, only to hear, "The snack bar is closing in five minutes" loudly interrupting the film.

Next door to the motel is the Academy Award Dining Room, which has posters, movie decor, and such menu items as the Italian Stallion (Italian sausage) and the Big Duke Burger. Stars' names are written (not signed) in the cement sidewalk in front of the restaurant. Rest rooms are labeled Actor and Actress.

In 1926, the parents of owner George Kelloff opened a movie theater in Aguilar, in the southeast part of the state; they were pioneers in this part of the country in presenting talkies. The younger Kelloff opened a normal drive-in in 1952 in Brownsville, Texas. He founded another drive-in here in Monte Vista in 1955; nine years later, he opened his "motel with a view." Kelloff says he plans to buy the highest lot in the cemetery across the street so he can continue to keep an eye on things. 2830 West US 160. Reservations: 303/852-5921.

Telluride: Every September, one of the most prestigious film festivals in the world takes over this picturesque town. Information can be obtained from the Chamber Resort Association: 303/728-3041. Or write: Box 653, Telluride, Colorado 81435.

NEVADA

MADE IN NEVADA

Nevada had always been popular with filmmakers looking for nondescript wide-open spaces, and since the emergence of Las Vegas—and, to a lesser extent, Reno—as a pleasure center, the state has enjoyed a continual stream of Hollywood production.

In 1946, Allied Pictures announced it would set up a studio at the Basic Magnesium plant in Henderson, southeast of Vegas. It was to be a haven for independents who were getting the cold shoulder from Hollywood. The dream never materialized, and the altruistic Allied execs ran up an unpaid bill of $2,933.76 at the El Rancho Hotel.

LAS VEGAS

Las Vegas is a funny place. All-out orgiastic decadence is its theme, but it still maintains a small-town hypocrisy that mandates an appearance of morality. Hookers abound, but whorehouses, sanctioned in the state, are illegal in Clark County. Bare-breasted chorus lines are de rigueur, but total nudity onstage is strictly forbidden.

So it's not too surprising that when the producers of *Fever Pitch* (1985), starring the great Ryan O'Neal as a man with a gambling disease, approached the local film commission for assistance, they were forced to sign an agreement that *nothing in the film would be anti-Vegas*: "Yes, we know that the lead character's life goes down the toilet because of his gambling addiction—just sign the paper."

Still, Vegas is Vegas, one of the country's unmitigated fun zones. *Oceans 11* (1960), the first Rat Pack movie, is about a simultaneous robbery of five casinos. During filming, the all-Vegas-headliner cast would join together for legendary performances at the Sands. *Diamonds Are Forever* (1971) has a great time with the setting: this James Bond romp includes a fantastic chase that trashes 20 cars. The International Hotel, now the Las Vegas Hilton, was evil mastermind Jimmy Dean's Whyte House.

The MGM Grand is ridiculously prominent in MGM/UA's *Rocky IV* (1985) and not as much so in *Lookin' to Get Out* (1980). In *Oxford Blues* (1984), Rob Lowe plays a carhop at the Dunes who cons his way into Oxford. *The Electric Horseman* (1979) has Robert Redford as a broken-down cowboy who kidnaps a degraded Vegas show horse. In *Corvette Summer* (1978), Mark Hamill searches Vegas for a stolen sports car. And in *The Gauntlet* (1977), cynical Vegas gamblers place long odds on whether Clint Eastwood can escort a witness to trial, as both bad guys and corrupt "good guys" are trying to kill him.

Jonathan Demme's *Melvin and Howard* (1980), about

how Melvin Dummar, a normal guy, allegedly rescued Howard Hughes in the desert and became Hughes's heir, filmed scenes in a Clark County District courtroom. Hughes, who practically owned Vegas in the fifties and sixties, tried his hand at a Vegas film, producing *The Las Vegas Story* in 1952. Ironically, the film's great flaw is its unconvincing setting. The man who owned Vegas in the 1970s, Elvis, shot *Viva Las Vegas* (1964), and the documentary *Elvis: That's the Way It Is* (1970) here.

One memorable oddity that captures the wacky Vegas zeitgeist is *Las Vegas Hillbillies* (1966), which stars the unlikely duo of Jayne Mansfield and Mamie Van Doren along with country-music middleweight Ferlin Husky. But the one to be topped is Albert Brooks's *Lost in America* (1985). In a classic scene, Brooks tries to convince bemused casino boss Garry Marshall to give back the nest egg that his wife, Julie Haggerty, has lost in one reckless night. He and Haggerty have their nest-egg quarrel at Hoover Dam, the art-deco masterwork in Boulder City. [By the way, the Man of Steel foils a plot to rupture Hoover Dam in *Superman* (1978).]

One serious constraint on filmmakers is that it's illegal to film inside an actual casino. Two very Vegas films, *Desert Bloom* (1986) and Francis Coppola's *One from the Heart* (1982), were shot entirely off campus. *Bloom,* which parallels the early days of Vegas with the booming of the atomic age, was shot on a Tucson soundstage. *Heart* was shot entirely at Coppola's short-lived Zoetrope Studio, in Hollywood.

RENO AND TAHOE

Reno's famous BIGGEST LITTLE CITY IN THE WORLD arch is seen in Robert Altman's *California Split* (1974), *Jinxed!* (1982), *Pink Cadillac* (1989), and many other films. *Jinxed!,* with Bette Midler and Ken Wahl, also included scenes shot at Bally's Cabaret and Harrah's. *California Split* was lensed at the Mapes Skyroom.

Much of *Pink Cadillac,* which disastrously paired Clint with Bernadette Peters, was shot in the area: at

Harold's Club; at the Eldorado, where the Caddy went crashing into a casino; at John Ascuaga's Nugget Casino in Sparks; in Hazen; and in the state capital, Carson City, turning the Fuji Park Fairgrounds into rodeo grounds. Clint had better luck—although he dies in the picture—with *Honkytonk Man* (1982), which was filmed at the Pony Express Hotel in Carson City and at the Dayton Hotel in Dayton, Nevada.

. . . *All the Marbles* (1981), a Robert Aldrich comedy about female wrestlers, was filmed in Bally's Cabaret. Perhaps the best evocation of Reno is *Desert Hearts* (1985), a stylish lesbian love story set in the fifties, when Reno was chiefly a divorce mill; it was shot at the Riverside Hotel, Mapes Casino and Skyroom, and the downtown railroad depot.

In *The Godfather II* (1974), the Corleones make their move in Nevada. The lakeside Corleone compound was Henry J. Kaiser's former estate at Lake Tahoe. *Things Change* (1988), an amiable mob spree set in Tahoe, was filmed at Harrah's Tahoe and the Cal Neva Lodge.

A little farther out, three classics were shot in the desert. John Ford's epic *The Iron Horse* (1924) was filmed near Wadsworth. *Bad Day at Black Rock* (1955), a Technicolor Cinemascope nailbiter with Spencer Tracy stuck in Nowheresville, was filmed at Black Rock, Washoe, and Pershing. And *The Misfits* (1961), the curtain call for Marilyn Monroe and Clark Gable, was shot near Black Rock as well as in Quail Canyon, at Odeon Hall in Dayton, and at the Mapes Casino in Reno.

NONDESCRIPT DESERT: "WHAT A NUCLEAR DUMP"

Valley of Fire State Park is harsh, scenic land that's close enough to Vegas to be very attractive to filmmakers. *One Million B.C.* (1940), *The Professionals* (1966), and Sam Peckinpah's *The Ballad of Cable Hogue* (1970) were shot in the area. The state highway department built a six-mile gravel road into Deadman's Canyon for *The Professionals,* which is set in Mexico. That road and a two-by-eight-foot piece of rock wall still remain.

Other films shot in the desert near Vegas are *The Hitcher* (1986), *Romancing the Stone* (1984), and Oliver Stone's *Salvador* (1986). *Vanishing Point* (1971), one of the all-time great road movies, zoomed through Nevada, shooting near the tiny towns of Lander, Nye, and Esmeralda. (Similar looking Utah locations included Thompson Springs, Cisco, and I-70.)

BOMBS AWAY!

Lots of top-secret military stuff gets filmed in Nevada. *Iron Eagle* (1986) soared above Nellis Air Force Base in Clark County, and *Top Gun* (1986) looked for bogeys above Fallon Military Base in Churchill County.

NEVADA'S GIFT TO THE LITTLE TRAMP

★ ★ ★ ★ ★ ★ ★ ★ ★ ★ ★ ★ ★ ★ ★ ★

Edna Purviance (Lovelock): Charlie Chaplin's Diane Keaton—his girlfriend and costar during his breakthrough years. She appeared in the two-reelers that made him the world's biggest star, as well as in his first feature, *The Kid*, and his noncomedic film, *A Woman of Paris*, the *Interiors* of 1923.

WHAT'S THERE

Elko: Bing Crosby's cattle ranch is off the Mountain City Highway (Highway 51), west of North Fork.

Eureka: Hamilton Ghost Town (between Eureka and Ely) is promoted as being "so well preserved it looks like a movie set," unlike most ghost towns, which "look like piles of rubble." It is 78 miles west of Ely on US 50, the World's Loneliest Highway.

Las Vegas: The American Museum of Historical Documents peddles stuff owned by famous people including Ingrid Bergman, Bruce Lee, and Walt Disney. 3200 Las Vegas Boulevard South, lower level of Fashion Show Mall.

WEDDING CHAPELS OF THE STARS

The Candlelight Chapel, "Where the Stars Are Wed," the "Number One Choice of Recording, Stage and Movie Personalities," has seen the likes of Whoopi Goldberg, Bette Midler, Patty Duke, and Michael Caine doing the deed. 2855 Las Vegas Boulevard South.

The Little White Chapel, "Where the Stars Are Married," offers a Joan Collins Special and has a sign out front screaming DYNASTY'S JOAN COLLINS WAS MARRIED HERE. As was Mickey Rooney—twice—along with Bruce Willis and Demi Moore, and Patty Duke, who is said to love rock & roll and to lose control under the influence of hot dogs. (Patty was *renewing* her vows, to be precise.) "Sincere and Dignified Since 1954," they invite you to "Meet the minister that married the stars—featured on 'Entertainment Tonite.'" 1301 Las Vegas Boulevard South.

The Chapel of the Bells is the current Mickey Rooney leader, having till-death-do-I-parted the runty Romeo

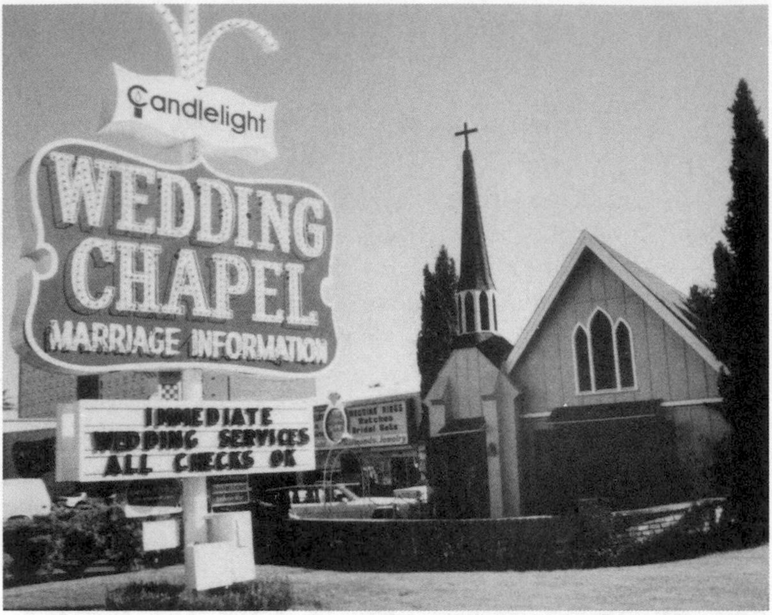

The Candlelight Chapel, "Where the Stars Are Wed."

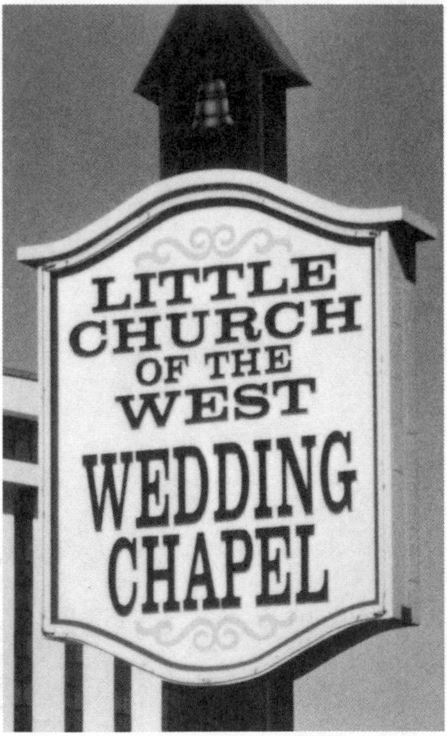

The Little Church of the West, the "Wedding Place of the Stars"

three times. Ernest Borgnine also got hitched here. 2233 Las Vegas Boulevard South.

At the Silver Bell Wedding Chapel, Don Johnson and tender young Melanie Griffith were wed (the first time around). 607 Las Vegas Boulevard South.

The Little Church of the West claims to be the "Wedding Place of the Stars," but will not divulge names, even though, "Since 1942, more celebrities have been married here than any other one place in the world." Our spies tell us, however, that this is where Judy Garland and, later, Dudley Moore tied the knot. 3960 Las Vegas Boulevard South.

Finally, there's the Chapel of the Stars, with the pithy slogan, "*Nobody* in Las Vegas Will Marry You for Less." 2019 Las Vegas Boulevard South.

Reno: The Harrah National Auto Museum displays cars of the famous: John Wayne's 1953 Corvette (the 51st one built; the Duke couldn't cram his tall frame inside, so he sold it); James Dean's 1949 Mercury from *Rebel Without a Cause*; Al Jolson's 1933 Cadillac Phaeton (with a V-16 engine); Jack Benny's 1923 Maxwell (it was often mentioned in his act); Lana Turner's 1941 Chrysler Newport; Frank Sinatra's 1961 Ghia (the first of its type sold in the United States); Bill Cosby's Aston; Elvis's 1973 Eldorado (he gave it to his karate instructor); and a 1948 Tucker, one of the four dozen or so remaining. The museum is located at 10 Lake Street South on 100,000 square feet of display space.

Searchlight: Clara Bow's retirement home, where she lived from 1931 to 1945 with her cowboy-star hubby, Rex Burns, is now the YKL Ranch, off US 95 near town. Burns became lieutenant governor of the state; Bow spent lots of time in sanitariums.

Table Mountain: This is the site where Carole Lombard's plane—flying her and others to a War Bond rally—crashed into a mountain. It's near Las Vegas.

NEW MEXICO

MADE IN NEW MEXICO

The earliest production in the state was probably Thomas Edison's *Indian Day School,* filmed at the Isleta Pueblo in 1898. Until the 1950s, New Mexico was almost exclusively a location for westerns. And there sure were a lot of 'em.

Las Vegas was the state's first film center: its Plaza Hotel was the base for producer Romaine Fielding, whose early silent westerns include *The Clod, The Rattlesnake, Toll of Fear,* and *The Golden Rod.* Tom Mix shot films like *The Rancher's Daughter, Local Color,* and *Never Again* in the area in 1914–15. Nowadays the most recognizable landmark is the firehouse, which is where Jack Nicholson

The famous Las Vegas, New Mexico, police station and firehouse, seen in *Easy Rider.*

decides to hit the road—mistake!—with Peter Fonda and Dennis Hopper in *Easy Rider.*

Gallup became the hub of the New Mexico film industry from the late twenties through the sixties: celebs would hang out at the still-existent El Rancho Hotel (see What's There). The first Gallup film was shot in 1928: Paramount's two-color production of *Redskin,* a Richard Dix western notable for its early sympathetic portrayal of Indians. More recently, exteriors for *Superman* (1980) were filmed here.

Except for Santa Fe and stunning vistas like White Sands and Shiprock, the fact is there aren't many locations in New Mexico that are all that distinctive. Many great films have been shot here that cannot be traced by today's location sleuth. They seem to break down into three categories: Westerns, Dusty Little Southwest Towns Where Evil Runs Rampant, and Cool B Movies.

WESTERNS of more recent vintage include *Streets of Laredo* (1949), *The Cheyenne Social Club* (1970), *Chisum* (1970), *Young Guns* (1988), which shot in Cerrillos, an old mining town, and the "Lonesome Dove" TV miniseries (1989), for which Black Lake, near Santa Fe, doubled as Montana.

DUSTY LITTLE TOWN movies include Billy Wilder's trenchant *Ace in the Hole* (1951), *Salt of the Earth* (1953), *Billy Jack* (1971), *The Ballad of Gregorio Cortez* (1982), and *The Milagro Beanfield War* (1988) (see What's There: Truchas).

COOL B MOVIES shot in New Mexico begin with *Easy Rider* (1969). Taos, where Dennis Hopper continues to hold forth, was where the boys got thrown in jail. Near town are the hot springs where they cavorted with commune chicks. See What's There. More groovy road movies were to follow, man: *Two-Lane Blacktop* (1971), *Truck Stop Women* (1974), *The Man Who Fell to Earth* (1976), and *Powwow Highway* (1989).

NEW MEXICO'S GIFTS TO HOLLYWOOD

★ ★ ★ ★ ★ ★ ★ ★ ★ ★ ★ ★ ★ ★ ★ ★

Bruce Cabot (b. Jacques Etienne de Bujac, Carlsbad): This high-born son of a Frenchman—no offense—attained fame in 1933 as the hero of *King Kong,* then played B-movie dudes for almost 40 more years. One of the Duke's cronies, and a notorious Hollywood stud.

John Denver (b. Henry Von Deutschendorf, Roswell): Denver abandoned the Land of Enchantment for a Colorado retreat when he hit it big. He's better known for his reedy recordings than for his work in *Oh, God!*

Kim Stanley (Tularosa): This overbearing Method actress won an Oscar nomination for 1964's *Seance on a Wet Afternoon* and played Frances Farmer's overbearing Method mother in *Frances.*

The El Rancho Hotel.

WHAT'S THERE

Cubero: The Villa de Cubero tourist courts, a roadside landmark, opened in 1937 on Route 66 (now NM 24). In 1942, Dennis Morgan and Bruce Cabot were here, along with camels and elephants, filming *Desert Song*. Oppenheimer and his pals came here in 1943 to relax from the tension of creating the atomic age in Los Alamos. Lucy came here after divorcing Desi. Hemingway supposedly wrote *The Old Man and the Sea* here. Owner Wallace Gunn was quoted on the subject of Hemingway in *Out West* magazine: "He was obnoxious as all get out. Went around partially dressed at all hours. All he did was type and drink wine."

Gallup: The El Rancho Hotel hosted a plethora of stars in its heyday, including Ronald Reagan; his name has been given to the fanciest room. Other names on rooms and in signed photos adorning the impressive beamed lobby include Kirk Douglas, Errol Flynn, Katharine Hepburn, Alan Ladd, Burt Lancaster, the Marx

Brothers, Tom Mix, Spencer Tracy, John Wayne, and Mae West.

The El Rancho was built in 1937 by Richard Griffith, D.W.'s brother; it even had a casino back then. A few years ago the place was going down the toilet, but Armand Ortega, who owns 13 Indian jewelry stores and "F-Troop's" Fort Courage, bought and refurbished it. It's located at 1100 East Old Highway 66. Reservations: 505/863-9311.

Santa Fe: J. W. Eaves Western Town, a location and tourist attraction, has two streets comprising 20 buildings or fronts. Its Mexican Village was seen in *Lust in the Dust* and *Silverado*. It's 14 miles southeast of town.

The Cook Ranch, Bill Cook's standing western set, was built for *Silverado* and also hosted shooting for "Lonesome Dove." It's 24 miles south of town (1¼ miles west of Galisteo).

The Santa Fe Center for Contemporary Arts has a soundstage that was used for *Outrageous Fortune, Lust in the Dust*, and *Silverado*. 291 East Barcelone Road.

Taos: Bryans Gallery, on Camino de la Placitas in the town square, occupies the former site of the town pokey. Art is exhibited in the actual jail cell where Fonda, Hopper, and Nicholson were incarcerated in *Easy Rider*. A photo display next to the cell commemorates its moment in the sun.

Truchas: Tafoya's General Store sells souvenirs from *The Milagro Beanfield War*, which was filmed here in 1988. Items emblazoned with the film's marketing image—a little man clicking his heels in the air—include coffee mugs, sweatshirts, and books. It's in the center of town, on the main street. The beanfield is 1½ miles north of the store on Highway 76. Ruby's Garage, seen in the film, is behind the store.

The filmmakers had wanted to shoot in Chimayo, but city fathers kept asking for more and more money, until finally Redford & Company pulled up stakes and headed for tiny Truchas, where they built adobe facades and gave an enormous boost to the local noneconomy.

MADE IN TEXAS

(Courtesy of Alamo Village, Home of Motion Pictures in Texas)

AUSTIN

The state capital (and main branch of the University of Texas) has a reputation as the most liberal town in the state. Which has nothing to do with anything, because you don't come to Texas to shoot a movie about a bunch of liberals.

***The Texas Chainsaw Massacre* (1974):** One of the scariest films ever, featuring the debut of Leatherface. Filmed in nearby Round Rock.

***Blood Simple* (1984):** Dynamic debut of filmmakers Joel and Ethan Coen. Filmed in Austin and Round Rock.

***Nadine* (1987):** Stars Kim Basinger, directed by Waxahachie's Robert Benton. Filmed in Austin.

***The Hot Spot* (1990):** Stars Don Johnson, directed by Dennis Hopper. Filmed in nearby Taylor.

PANHANDLERS

The film that evokes the most distinct images of the Texas panhandle is Terence Malick's beautiful *Days of Heaven* (1978). The film was shot, however, in Canada. *The Buddy Holly Story* (1978) did some filming in the proto-rocker's hometown, Lubbock.

The Buddy Holly statue in Lubbock.

DALLAS

Thanks to J. R. Ewing, Dallas is no longer a national synonym for "place where cool presidents are assassinated." And thanks to the spiffy new studios in suburban Las Colinas, Dallas can host films—like *Silkwood* (1983), *Streamers* (1983), *Robocop* (1987), and *Talk Radio* (1988)—that have nothing at all to do with Dallas.

Tough Enough (1981) stars Houston's Dennis Quaid and filmed two scenes at the Tarrant County Convention Center. David Byrne's condescending *True Stories* (1986) filmed the fictitious town of Virgil in the Dallas area. Errol Morris's historic *The Thin Blue Line* (1988), which resulted in an innocent man being released from prison, is based on the man's experience with justice, Dallas style. And *Born on the Fourth of July* (1989) was filmed in Dallas and surrounding communities.

Dallas's modern skyline inspires stories set in the future, such as *Logan's Run* (1975), which used the Dallas Market Center and Water Garden, and *Robocop,* in which the Dallas courthouse became OCP Headquarters—after a little matte work.

EL PASO

When someone in Hollywood says "El Paso," he isn't talking about this west Texas town; he's turning down your project—*passing* on it. But a few times "El Paso" *has* meant El Paso:

***The Bad News Bears in Breaking Training* (1977):** This, the first of two sequels, did some shooting at the Socorro Mission. I-10 east, Avenue of the Americas exit, south to Socorro Road.

The Socorro Mission, seen in *The Bad News Bears in Breaking Training. (Courtesy of El Paso Film Commission)*

***The Border* (1982):** Jack Nicholson is a corrupted border guard with a conscience.

***Paris, Texas* (1984):** German existentialist director Wim Wenders shoots a Sam Shepard script with surprisingly decent results. Also filmed in Houston.

***Fandango* (1985):** The Mexican wedding scenes were

filmed at the San Elizario Mission. I-10 east, Avenue of the Americas exit, nine miles past the Socorro Mission.

***Extreme Prejudice* (1987):** On the border again, this time with Nick Nolte and Powers Boothe. The Hueco Inn Cafe is the film's El Rincon bar. The inn features photos of Kevin Costner and Nolte playing on the 130-yard par-3 golf course out back. Highway 62/180, 30 miles east of town.

The Hueco Inn Cafe stands in as the El Rincon bar in *Extreme Prejudice. (Courtesy of El Paso Film Commission)*

HOUSTON

***Brewster McCloud* (1970):** Former cult film that looks kind of dippy today. Climax is when Bud Cort flies around the Astrodome.

***Urban Cowboy* (1980):** John Travolta and Debra Winger, who is totally hot in her first big role. Shot at the now defunct Gilley's, 4500 Spencer Highway, in Pasadena.

***Local Hero* (1983):** Peter Riegert is an unhappy Houston oil exec in Scotland, Burt Lancaster his boss back in Houston, in the best work of one of today's best directors, Bill Forsyth.

***Terms of Endearment* (1983):** The film office won't divulge the address of Aurora's house, so just cruise the nice neighborhoods. Also filmed at River Oaks, near Fort Worth.

SAN ANTONIO

The first best-picture Oscar went to *Wings* (1927), which was filmed at San Antonio's Carey Air Field. *I Wanted Wings* (1941), no relation, was shot at Randolph Air Field. *Viva Max!* (1969) exploits the town's most familiar landmark: it's about a nutty Mexican general out to recapture the Alamo. *Sugarland Express* (1974), a great road picture that was Steven Spielberg's first feature, was filmed here as well as in Floresville and the border town of Del Rio. *Piranha* (1978), a horror spoof written by so-called genius John Sayles, was shot in nearby San Marcos and Wimberley. In *Pee Wee's Big Adventure* (1985), Pee Wee searches for his stolen bicycle at the Alamo.

WAXAHACHIE: HOLLYWOOD ON THE SCRUB

This quaint small town—though they're hoping to win a huge underground atom smasher—south of Dallas has hosted more than two dozen features, some of them Oscar winners for local boys Robert Benton and Horton Foote:

***Bonnie and Clyde* (1967):** Cowritten by Benton, this influential postmodern gangster film also shot in Denton and Dallas.

***Tender Mercies* (1983):** Foote and Robert Duvall scored Oscars for this gentle look at a broken-down country singer.

***Places in the Heart* (1984):** Written and directed by Benton, who thanked the people of Waxahachie when he scooped up his best-screenplay Oscar. Sally Field did him one better with her "You like me, you really like me" speech accepting *her* Oscar for the pic.

***The Trip to Bountiful* (1985):** Geraldine Page pulled a surprising Oscar for her daffy portrayal of a senile woman, working off a Horton Foote screenplay. The low-budget hit was also shot at the old Dallas Railroad Terminal, which was dressed as the Houston bus station. Other towns visited were nearby Venus and Five Points.

DUSTY, ENDLESS TEXAS DIRTSCAPES

Forget the cities: this is the heart and soul of Texas filmmaking:

***Viva Zapata!* (Roma, Rio Grande City, 1952):** Marlon Brando as Zapata, Anthony Quinn as his brother, directed by Elia Kazan from a John Steinbeck script.

***Giant* (Marfa, Valentine, 1956):** Whoa! Rock Hudson and Elizabeth Taylor at the top of their form, James Dean at the end of his. The ranch house was constructed in Hollywood and transported to the location. *Come Back to the Five and Dime, Jimmy Dean, Jimmy Dean* (1982) is a fantasy about three James Dean fans who lived nearby during the filming of *Giant.*

***Hud* (Claude, 1963):** Paul Newman, Patricia Neal, and Melvyn Douglas on the Bannon Ranch, based on a Larry McMurtry novel. Shot at the abandoned Henderson Ranch near town.

***The Last Picture Show* (Archer City, 1971) and *Texasville* (Wichita Falls, Archer City, 1990):** A terrific Texas writer, McMurtry, adapted by a director, Peter Bogdanovich, doing what he does well.

***The Getaway* (Huntsville, San Marcos, San Antonio, El Paso, 1972):** Exciting Sam Peckinpah chase movie, starring Steve McQueen and Ali MacGraw, that was reportedly shot in continuity, a rarity.

***The Life and Times of Judge Roy Bean* (Langtry, 1972):** Paul Newman as the pistol-packin' judge and Ava Gardner as Lily Langtry, filmed in the town named after her (Langtry, not Gardner).

***The Great Waldo Pepper* (Elgin, Lockhart, Floresville, Kerrville, 1975):** George Roy Hill covers much of central Texas in this quirky look at early aviators. Starring Robert Redford and written by William Goldman.

TEXAS'S GIFTS TO HOLLYWOOD

★ ★ ★ ★ ★ ★ ★ ★ ★ ★ ★ ★ ★ ★ ★

Gene Autry (Tioga): Singing cowboy who got super-rich and bought the California Angels. Born on a ranch near town.

Tex Avery (Taylor): Major animator with a wildly kinetic style who helped create Bugs Bunny and other characters. He attended North Dallas High; you can see his early work in the school yearbook.

Carol Burnett (San Antonio): Best known for her TV variety show, a lightweight screen presence who continually tries to disprove it. The local tourist bureau wouldn't tell me the address of her childhood home: "It's in a bad part of town."

Gary Busey (Goose Creek): Totally insane person who rides motorcycles helmetless and turns in strong performances once in a while, highlights being the lead in *The Buddy Holly Story* and Mr. Joshua, the albino terrorist in *Lethal Weapon.*

Cyd Charisse (b. Tula Ellice Finklea, Amarillo): Hottest screen dancer ever, costar of Fred Astaire and Gene Kelly. Films include: *Singin' in the Rain, The Band Wagon, Silk Stockings.*

Dabney Coleman (Austin): Bad-guy specialist, the king of smarm. His hometown was Corpus Christi. Films include: *On Golden Pond, Tootsie, Nine to Five.*

Joan Crawford (b. Lucille Fay Le Sueur, San Antonio): Mommy Dearest, the quintessential movie star from the mid-1920s into the 1960s; her name was chosen in a national publicity contest. Films include: *Grand Hotel, The Women, Mildred Pierce, Johnny Guitar, What Ever Happened to Baby Jane?* Her family moved to Kansas City when she was three, so she's not much remembered here.

Josh Logan (Texarkana): Theater creature with a bigger film rep than his work warrants. Attended Princeton with Jimmy Stewart and Henry Fonda. Films include: *Picnic, Bus Stop, Camelot.*

Steve Martin (Waco): Top comedian of his generation who gradually but surely has become a first-rate comic leading man—the best since Cary Grant. He was raised in southern California. Films include: *The Jerk, All of Me, Roxanne, Parenthood.* See What's There: Austin.

Spanky McFarland (Fort Worth): Chubby little

leader of the Our Gang (aka Little Rascals) comedies, starting at age four.

Ann Miller (Chireno): Celebrated for maintaining her sensational dancing legs well into her sixties. Films include: *Stage Door, On the Town, Kiss Me Kate.*

Audie Murphy (Kingston): The most decorated hero of World War II; Hollywood capitalized on his fame by placing him in cheap westerns. He also appeared as himself in *To Hell and Back* (1955), based on his war memoirs. See What's There: Greenville.

Randy and Dennis Quaid (Houston): Randy made the first splash, playing poor slobs in *The Last Detail* and *The Apprenticeship of Duddy Kravitz.* Then Dennis and his vaunted stomach muscles, after a decade of bad roles, began grabbing romantic leads in *The Big Easy* and *Great Balls of Fire.* Like Jeff Bridges, Dennis is a major star whose films make no money.

Debbie Reynolds (El Paso): A 1950s nice-girl type, like Doris Day and Shirley Jones. Films include: *Singin' in the Rain, The Tender Trap, How the West Was Won.*

Tex Ritter (Murvaul): Singing cowboy with respectable music credentials. Father of TV slapstickmeister John Ritter. Born and raised near town. See What's There: Nederland.

Irene Ryan (El Paso): Granny of "The Beverly Hillbillies" was the star of many two-reel comedies in the thirties made by Educational Pictures.

Sissy Spacek (b. Mary Elizabeth Spacek, Quitman): Successfully specialized in spacey young girls in the 1970s, rougher going since then. Films include: *Badlands, Carrie, Coal Miner's Daughter.*

Patrick Swayze (Houston): Beefcake known for *Dirty Dancing* and *Ghost.* An eighties version of John Travolta.

Rip Torn (b. Elmore Torn, Temple): Came to prominence in an age of Tabs, Troys, and Rocks; at least his last name is real. Part of the "serious actor" bunch, he's the widower of Geraldine Page and cousin of Sissy Spacek. Films include: *Sweet Bird of Youth, Cat on a Hot Tin Roof, Cross Creek, Extreme Prejudice.*

WHAT'S THERE

Austin: The Steve Martin Collection and Gloria Swanson Archives are now part of the Harry Ransom Humanities Research Center at the University of Texas. Martin has donated several drafts of scripts for *Roxanne* and *Three Amigos*; more material is expected. The Swanson Archives include films, scripts, and other memorabilia. 21st Street and Guadalupe.

In a costume vault on campus is an even more valuable artifact: Scarlett O'Hara's green gown. It is considered priceless. You can't touch it.

Brackettville: Alamo Village is a movie set (*The Alamo*) that's been turned into a major tourist attraction, run by J. T. "Happy" Shahan. The many westerns shot

"Covered wagons and buckboards don't need no traffic lights" at Happy Shahan's Alamo Village. *(Courtesy of Home of Motion Pictures in Texas)*

Gunmen in front of the cantina at Alamo Village. *(Courtesy of Alamo Village, Home of Motion Pictures in Texas)*

here include *Two Rode Together* (John Ford directs Jimmy Stewart and Richard Widmark), *Bandolero!* (Stewart, Dino, and Raquel), *Arrowhead* (Charlton Heston, Jack Palance), *The Last Command* (about the Alamo), and *Barbarosa* (Willie Nelson, Gary Busey). A reenactment society rents the place out every year to do the Battle of the Alamo.

Highway 674, six miles north of town.

Greenville: There's an Audie Murphy Room (he was

Nederland is Tex Ritter Country.

born in a rural area a few miles north of here), displaying some of his medals and uniforms, at the W. Walworth Harrison Public Library, 3716 Lee Street.

Nederland: The Windmill Museum houses memorabilia from Tex Ritter's career, including his Grand Ole Opry outfit and personal photos. In Tex Ritter Park, 1500 block of Boston Avenue.

San Antonio: The Plaza Theater of Wax has a movie section, with exhibits including *Ben Hur, The King and I,* and *Doctor Zhivago.* Think it might have opened in the fifties? Across from the Alamo, 301 Alamo Plaza.

Weatherford: A Peter Pan statue honors Weatherford native Mary Martin. It's at 1214 Charles Street, in front of the library. Her childhood home still stands at 314 West Oak Street. Weatherford was also the hometown of Martin's son, Larry "J. R." Hagman.

U T A H

MADE IN UTAH

For the state with the least man-made excitement of all, an amazing number of major films have been shot here. Sweeping outdoor settings account for 99.9 percent of production.

PAPPY AND DUKE

Director John "Pappy" Ford didn't exactly discover Monument Valley and southeastern Utah, but he sure helped a lot of other people discover it. His trendsetting westerns virtually defined this awesome setting as the True West. He was known for shooting in one take, hoping for a "Frederic Remington look." With and without John Wayne, he returned again and again to make masterful westerns through the years.

Stagecoach (1939), a landmark western, was a breakthrough for the Duke and the first film Ford shot here; Monument Valley was an extremely remote area at the time. The site of filming is now the MacDonald Ranch, Highway 89. *My Darling Clementine* (1946) stars Henry Fonda as Wyatt Earp and Victor Mature as Doc Holliday and depicts the legendary shoot-out at the O.K. Corral.

Fort Apache (1948) is the first of three consecutive Pappy-Duke films about the U.S. cavalry. It costars Fonda and was filmed along the San Juan River at Mexican Hat. Ford shot a crucial scene with 700 Mormon extras in a driving rain rather than wait for good weather. *She Wore a Yellow Ribbon* (1949) was shot in Kanab and at the San Juan River. *Rio Grande* (1950) was filmed at White's Ranch, Ida Gulch, Professor Valley, and Onion Creek Narrows.

After this trilogy, Ford took a break from the Duke and shot *Wagon Master* (1950), which evolved into the TV show "Wagon Train." Locations included Professor Valley, the Colorado River, Spanish Valley, and Moab.

The next Pappy-Duke–Monument Valley collaboration was *The Searchers* (1956), a cinematic monument that is one of Martin Scorsese's favorite films. Ford once again captured on celluloid the beauty of the San Juan River at Mexican Hat. *Cheyenne Autumn* (1964) was a sympathetic portrayal of Indian resettlement. It was shot in Moab, Monument Valley, the George White Ranch, Onion Creek, and Arches National Monument. A wild Saturday night cast party in Moab featured Ricardo Montalban on bongos and Richard Widmark on chopsticks.

Duke's non-Pappy work in the area includes his debut as a forceful leading man, Raoul Walsh's *The Big Trail* (1930), which filmed in Zion National Park, and *The Comancheros* (1961), the final film of director Michael Curtiz (*Casablanca*). The latter was shot in Moab, Professor Valley, Dead Horse Point State Park, Kings Bottom, and the La Sal Mountains.

OTHERS WHO LIKED MONUMENT VALLEY

Ford never copyrighted Monument Valley, and he couldn't buy it because it's an Indian reservation. So a slew of productions followed his lead, including: *Kit Carson* (1940), *Billy the Kid* (1941), *The Harvey Girls* (1946), *How the West Was Won* (1962), *2001: A Space Odyssey* (1968), *Easy Rider* (1969), *The Trial of Billy Jack* (1974), and *National Lampoon's Vacation* (1983)—it's where Chevy Chase smashes up his car in the middle of nowhere. Clint Eastwood hasn't shot many westerns in Utah (only *The Outlaw Josey Wales*), but he did make *The Eiger Sanction* (1975) in Monument Valley and at Zion National Park.

MORE WILD WEST

There's more wild west in Utah than just Monument Valley. Other major westerns shot here include: *The Cisco Kid* (1931), Fritz Lang's *Western Union* (1941), *Jeremiah Johnson* (1972), which was filmed in Leeds, Vernal, Timpanogos, St. George, and Snow Canyon and stars Utahite Robert Redford; Redford again in *The Electric Horseman* (1979), filmed in St. George and Washington County, *Romancing the Stone* (1984), filmed in St. George, and *Indiana Jones and the Last Crusade* (1989). In the prologue, young Indy (River Phoenix) goes on a boy-scout trip to Arches National Park and Seven Mile Canyon. And although not strictly a movie, a memorable 1964 Chevy commercial, remade in 1973, was filmed at Castle Rock and featured a car atop a sheer tower of stone.

THE SCARY WEST

Utah isn't just westerns; many scary movies have been shot here. *The Car* (1977, about a car possessed by the devil), *Cujo* (1983), *Humanoids from the Deep* (1980), and *Silent Night, Deadly Night* (1984) don't look much like Utah, but they are. That last one, featuring a psycho Santa, is one of the most hated films of all time. For *The Car,* stuntman A. J. Bakunas set a world record for a prepared fall—195 feet, from a bridge near Zion Park.

The Executioner's Song (1982) tells the story of Gary Gilmore, a Utahite who was the first man to be executed in the modern era. It was filmed at the Utah State Prison, the State Capitol, and around Salt Lake and Utah counties. *Footloose* (1984), set in an ultrareligious Iowa hick town that bans dancing, was shot in Provo.

The scariest Utah production of all, however, is *The Conqueror* (1956), which was shot in Snow Canyon, near St. George. Starring John Wayne as Genghis Khan, it was not only one of the stupidest films of all time, it was also the deadliest. A nuclear test to the west during production caused radioactive fallout to be sprinkled liberally over the location. A majority of the cast and crew—including the Duke, his costars, and director Dick Powell—have since died of cancer. The government denies, denies, denies.

ANOTHER WORLD

Utah's desolation takes us to worlds not yet known to man: *Planet of the Apes* (1968) was filmed at Lake Powell, and *Spacehunter: Adventures in the Forbidden Zone* (1983), a rare Canadian production that required U.S. locations (because it isn't set on an ice planet, I guess), included the D&RG Railroad Spur in Moab and Cane Creek, Bull Canyon, and the Colorado River.

SALT LAKE CITY: BYOB

It's hard to picture puritanical Salt Lake City as the kind of place Hollywood types would want to go. And it's not. In *Melvin and Howard* (1980), Melvin Dummar attempts to corroborate Howard Hughes's so-called Mormon Will at the administration building of the Mormon church, on the 26th floor of the Beneficial Towers Building. The film also shot in St. George, Ogden, and Willard. Two boobish crimefighters, *Fletch* (1985) and Maxwell Smart, in *The Nude Bomb* (1980), pass through town in their investigations.

UTAH'S GIFTS TO HOLLYWOOD

★ ★ ★ ★ ★ ★ ★ ★ ★ ★ ★ ★ ★ ★ ★ ★

Hal Ashby (Ogden): Top film editor-turned-director of pseudo-counter-culture movies like *Harold and Maude, The Last Detail, Shampoo, Coming Home,* and *Being There.*

Roseanne Barr (Salt Lake City): A comer? Color me dubious: her film debut, *She-Devil* (1989), looks like a piece of candy, costars Meryl Streep, was released at the height of Roseanne's media ubiquity . . . and bombed.

Laraine Day (Roosevelt): Perky A-minus actress who, despite being a Mormon, married baseball's bad boy, Leo Durocher. Films include: *Foreign Correspondent, My Dear Secretary, Mr. Lucky.*

John Gilbert (Logan): Top post-Valentino romantic star of the silent era, supposedly Garbo's boyfriend. Never made it in talkies, either because of his voice or because his style was out of fashion. Garbo films include: *Flesh and the Devil, A Woman of Affairs, Queen Christina.*

Loretta (Gretchen) Young (Salt Lake City): Classy-looking dramatic actress who had a saintly image but is described by Kenneth Anger in the book *Hollywood Babylon 2* as Gretch the Wretch. Films include: *The Story of Alexander Graham Bell, Eternally Yours, The Farmer's Daughter.*

WHAT'S THERE

Grafton: Grafton is a deteriorating ghost town used as a location for *Butch Cassidy and the Sundance Kid* (which also filmed in St. George, Snow Canyon, and Zion National Park). The only building erected specifically for the film was Katharine Ross's house, visible in the famous "Raindrops" bicycle scene. Follow along the Virgin River, just outside Rockville, a few miles from the entrance to Zion. A good four-mile dirt road leads to town.

Kanab: Ray Lopeman's Frontier Movie Town and Western Heritage Museum. Films shot here or nearby go back to Tom Mix's *Deadeye Dick* (1922) and *Deadwood Coach* (1924). The lengthy list of productions includes, in addition to many of those mentioned in Made in Utah, *Drums Along the Mohawk* (1939), *Union Pacific* (1939), *Brigham Young* (1940), *Arabian Nights* (1942), which was Universal's first color film, *Pony Express* (1953), *The Rainmaker* (1956), *The Greatest Story Ever Told* (1965), *The Man Who Loved Cat Dancing* (1973), *In Search of Noah's Ark* (1976), and the "Death Valley Days" TV show. It's located at 297 West Center.

The Parry Lodge has 23 rooms named after stars who have filmed and stayed here, including Glenn Ford, Ava Gardner, Charlton Heston, Dean Martin, Frank Sinatra, Barbara Stanwyck, John Wayne, and Ronald Reagan (in his "Death Valley Days" days). $35–59/couple. Reservations: 801/644-2601. 89 East Center.

Moab: John Hagner's Hollywood Stuntmen's Hall of Fame, a great movie museum, has it all: over 200 footprints of stuntmen and stars; their costumes, saddles, and

The Hollywood Stuntmen's Hall of Fame and Museum in Moab features memorabilia, a gift shop, and more than 200 footprints of "Stunt People and Stars."

weapons; Jimmy Stewart's boots; Chuck Connors's Levis; John Wayne's boots from *The Man Who Shot Liberty Valance*; stunt equipment; paintings, posters, and many signed photos; and the Dave Sharpe Action Theater.

Hagner is a former stuntman who participated in the pie-throwing sequence in *The Great Race*. The museum is located in a former Mormon church, at 111 East 100 North.

Moab is a major production hub; the local film commission is the nation's oldest, in business more than 40 years. You can pick up an excellent driving tour of movie locations at the Moab Visitors Center, 805 North Main Street. A Moab Movie Jubilee is held in early September.

North Fork and Provo Canyon: The Sundance Institute is Robert Redford's great cause, a twice-annual powwow of filmmaking elite and teacher's-pet young talent. You can gaze as the stars graze: in winter on the slopes, year-round in Sundance Resort's Tree Room and Grill Room. The walls feature photos of Redford, Paul Newman, and other cronies. T-shirts, postcards, and caps are for sale.

Ogden: The National Western Film Festival takes place in mid-July. 801/629-8288.

WYOMING

MADE IN WYOMING

TETONS OF FUN

***The Big Trail* (Jackson, 1930):** John Wayne's first big role, and with a top director, Raoul Walsh, to boot. Locations for the recently restored 70mm epic ranged from Wyoming's Snake River all the way to Oregon.

***The Big Sky* (Jackson, 1952):** Howard Hawks adventure with Kirk Douglas, based on A. B. Guthrie's novel.

***Shane* (Jackson, Grand Teton National Park, 1953):** Shane (Alan Ladd) rides off into the Tetons as Brandon de Wilde whines, "Come back, Shane!"

***Spencer's Mountain* (Moose, 1963):** The prototype for "The Waltons," it stars Henry Fonda and Maureen O'Hara and was shot on the Triangle X Ranch, at the northern end of Grand Teton National Park.

***Any Which Way You Can* (Jackson, 1980):** The *Every Which Way But Loose* sequel lives up to the original, as Clint bare-knuckle brawls his way to fun with Clyde the Orangutan. Locations included the Cowboy Bar (25 North Cache) and the town square.

***Rocky IV* (Jackson, 1985):** Sly trained here for his bout with the Russkie—it was supposed to be Siberia. The site was east of Blacktail Butte and north of Jackson. Jackson Hole Airport was also a location.

***Ghosts Can't Do It* (Jackson, 1990):** Bo Derek and Anthony Quinn in a nutty, nutty sex farce shot in Grand Teton (!) National Park. Donald Trump makes a cameo.

THE REST . . .

***Wyoming Roundup* (Rock River, 1904):** Shot in the days when most people would never get to see Wyoming in person.

***Charge of the Light Brigade* (Cheyenne, 1912):** A production of the Edison Film Company.

***Close Encounters of the Third Kind* (Devils Tower National Monument, 1977):** See What's There.

***Powwow Highway* (Sheridan, 1989):** This Native American road film shot at the top of the Big Horn Mountains and in downtown Sheridan.

WYOMING'S GIFT TO HOLLYWOOD SQUARES

★ ★ ★ ★ ★ ★ ★ ★ ★ ★ ★ ★ ★ ★ ★ ★

JM J. Bullock (Casper): Filling Paul Lynde's white loafers is a daunting challenge, but the effervescent Bullock seems up to the task.

WHAT'S THERE

Devils Tower National Monument: This dramatically exposed volcanic core was the central image in *Close Encounters.* Steven Spielberg refused to shoot with a studio mock-up. Locals were reportedly so inhospitable to the filmmakers that they doubted real aliens would want to land here.

Devils Tower, the destination of those tune-happy aliens in *Close Encounters of the Third Kind. (Photo by Butch McFarland).*

Rosebud
KIRBY

Chapter 4

NORTHERN PLAIN JANES

- Minnesota •
- Montana •
- North Dakota •
- South Dakota •
- Wisconsin •

MINNESOTA

MADE IN MINNESOTA

THE COLD EARTH

***Airport* (Minneapolis-St. Paul, 1970):** Filmmakers found the hazardous winter flying conditions they required at the International Airport. The biggest film of 1970, it started a disaster-film cycle.

***Ice Castles* (St. Paul, 1979):** Lynn-Holly Johnson—a real-life skater—goes blind, but luckily Robby Benson is there to catch her.

***Wildrose* (Mesabi Iron Range, 1981):** Lisa Eichhorn plays a female iron-pit worker. Not exactly *Flashdance.*

***Patti Rocks* (1988):** A nighttime drive through chilly Gopher State bleakness.

NORDIC BLONDS

***The Heartbreak Kid* (Bloomington, 1972):** Cybill Shepherd is the Nordic blond object of newlywed Charles Grodin's affection. He chases her to the University of Minnesota.

***The Personals* (Minneapolis, 1981):** Independent romantic comedy about Nordic blonds shot in summertime, when there is minimal snow in Minneapolis.

ALSO . . .

***Slaughterhouse Five* (Lake Minnetonka, 1972):** Directed by Minnesotan George Roy Hill.

MINNESOTA'S GIFTS TO HOLLYWOOD

★ ★ ★ ★ ★ ★ ★ ★ ★ ★ ★ ★ ★ ★ ★ ★

James Arness (Minneapolis): The "Gunsmoke" hero, brother of Peter Graves, appeared in several films in the early fifties, including (in the titular role) *The Thing.* He was discovered by John Wayne.

William Demarest (St. Paul): "My Three Sons' " Uncle Charley knocked out some great character work in the movies, particularly in the comedies of Preston Sturges.

Judy Garland (b. Frances Gumm, Grand Rapids): Singing child star (*The Wizard of Oz,* Mickey Rooney movies) who lived fast and hard, leaving a legacy for her cultists. See What's There: Grand Rapids.

Terry Gilliam (Minneapolis): He was the American-born member of Monty Python—don't get too excited, he was the one who did that animation. Directed *Time Bandits, Brazil,* and *The Adventures of Baron Munchausen.*

Tippi Hedren (Lafayette): Known primarily for two things: *The Birds* and her daughter, Melanie Griffith. Hitchcock was said to be obsessed by her; at the time, he was a puckered, putrescent old crank.

Jessica Lange (Cloquet): King Kong's bauble suddenly gained major credibility with passionate work as the scheming adultress in *The Postman Always Rings Twice* and as Frances Farmer in *Frances.*

Tom Laughlin (Minneapolis): Financially supersuccessful auteur of four Billy Jack films, each more bloated and self-righteous than the last. *The Trial of Billy Jack* runs almost three hours and features Sacheen Littlefeather, who turned down Brando's Oscar for *The Godfather.*

E. G. Marshall (Owatonna): A news announcer–politician type who starred in such serious efforts as *Twelve Angry Men, Interiors,* TV's "The Defenders" and *Superman 2,* in which he played the president. (His was also the voice of the Pres in *The Day After.*)

Prince (Minneapolis): A motorcycle-riding outsider (like Billy Jack) whose films get progressively more self-indulgent (like Billy Jack). Hmmm—*Prince Goes to Washington*? Not yet.

Jane Russell (Bemidji): Paul Bunyan country reared this bountiful star, best known for the publicity surrounding her breasts in Howard Hughes's *The Outlaw.*

Winona Ryder (Winona): Good thing this talented young comer wasn't born in, say, Cle Elum.

Richard Widmark (Sunrise): Sandy Koufax's father-in-law, Widmark became noted for his work as edgy, violent heroes and villains in such films as *Kiss of Death* and *Pickup on South Street* and as Jim Bowie in John Wayne's *The Alamo*.

WHAT'S THERE

Center City: Hazelden Clinic, the up-and-coming drug clinic of the stars. 15245 Pleasant Valley Road.

Chanhassen: Site of Prince's Paisley Park Studios, location for his *Sign O' the Times*. They would not divulge the address, so you can conclude it's a great place. I urge you to pay a visit.

Grand Rapids: Here in Judy Garland's hometown, every June brings a Judy Garland Festival. In 1989, for the film's 50th anniversary, the festival brought in a pair of Judy's ruby slippers from *The Wizard of Oz*, valued at a cool million. 1990's festival celebrated the 50th anniversary of the "Golden Team," Judy and Mickey Rooney, and included an Andy Hardy Ice Cream Social and Dance and photo opportunities with some of the original Oz munchkins, posing on the town's yellow brick road.

Like the yellow brick road in Liberal, Kansas, this one offers you the opportunity to have your own personal message inscribed on your own personal brick. The current tariff for this is $55.

The yellow brick road leads to the Central School, an 1895 structure that now houses the Itasca County Historical Society, which boasts the world's largest Judy Garland collection: here are *Wizard of Oz* memorabilia, photos, Judy's cradle and scarf, childhood family portraits done by a local photographer, scripts, and more. It's all at 10 Fifth Street N.W.

The town is working on an official WELCOME TO GRAND RAPIDS, HOME OF JUDY GARLAND sign for its

The Central School, which houses the Judy Garland collection, and Yellow Brick Road in Grand Rapids. *(Courtesy of the Judy Garland Festival)*

1991 centennial. Garland's childhood home has been moved to 727 Second Avenue N.E. For information on the festival or museum, call 218/326-6431.

The Best Western of Grand Rapids is known as the Rainbow Inn, and houses the Judy Garland Room, the biggest meeting room in town. Portraits and pictures of Garland and *The Wizard of Oz* hang in the room. For reservations, call 800/528-1234. 1300 Highway 169 East.

The First Avenue club from *Purple Rain.* It's real. *(Courtesy of Andrew Peterson)*

Minneapolis: The First Avenue club from *Purple Rain* is an actual nightspot, located at 701 First Avenue North. In Eden Prairie, a suburb, is the famous Graffiti Bridge, inspiration for the Prince movie and album.

St. Paul: The world's largest movie projector is at the 3M William L. McKnight Omnitheater, Science Museum of Minnesota, 30 East 10th Street.

MONTANA

MADE IN MONTANA

***The Thing* (Glacier National Park, 1951):** Temperatures dropped to 30 below during filming of Howard Hawks's horror masterpiece.

***Little Big Man* (Crow Agency, Lame Deer, Custer Battlefield National Monument, 1970):** Dustin Hoffman plays a survivor of Custer's Last Stand; shooting occurred at the actual site, which is now a popular tourist attraction—especially popular with Indians.

***The Missouri Breaks* (Billings, Red Lodge, 1976):** Arthur Penn, director of *Little Big Man,* returns to the Treasure State with Marlon Brando and Jack Nicholson and gets something on film, but no one's sure quite what it is he got. The Breaks is where the Missouri River begins, near Great Falls.

***Heaven's Gate* (Kalispell, 1980):** The rugged Kalispell area, near Glacier National Park, was the principal location for the Film That Destroyed United Artists. The commodious Outlaw Inn (on Highway 93) was home base for the principals of the cast and crew. Director Michael Cimino bought 156 acres of land here, then attempted to write off as production expenses improvements to and rent for the property—the naughty scamp.

***Runaway Train* (1985):** Filmed somewhere in the wilds of Montana, this arty action flick was directed by a Russian émigré, Andrei Konchalovsky, and based on a screenplay by samurai-meister Akira Kurosawa.

***The Untouchables* (Great Falls, 1987):** The shootout with rum runners near the bridge at the Canadian border was shot at Hardy Bridge, near town.

MONTANA'S GIFTS TO HOLLYWOOD

★ ★ ★ ★ ★ ★ ★ ★ ★ ★ ★ ★ ★ ★ ★ ★

Dana Carvey (Missoula): This "Saturday Night Live" comic might have a film career if he'd just stop doing that Church Lady bit. His first feature was *Opportunity Knocks* (1990).

Gary Cooper (b. Frank James Cooper, Helena): Mr. Stolid Man of Action for over 30 years. See What's There.

Myrna Loy (Radersburg): Best known for her charming portrayal of Nora Charles in the Thin Man comic mysteries. Voted the Queen of Hollywood in 1939. (Gable was the King.) Loy was born in Radersburg and moved to Townsend and later to Helena. See What's There: Helena.

Steve Reeves (Glasgow): The muscular Reeves found fame—and made producer Joseph E. Levine rich—in period Italian action flicks with roles like Hercules.

What's There

Anaconda: The Washoe Theater, at 305 Main Street, is a lovingly preserved remnant of the small-town movie palace. Films are still unspooled here nightly.

The Washoe Theatre in Anaconda. *(Courtesy of Julie Kuehndorf)*

Big Timber: This small town north of Yellowstone National Park is lately a lure to "privacy-seeking" Hollywoodites—including Mel Gibson, Brooke Shields, Michael Keaton, Dennis Quaid and Meg Ryan, Jeff Bridges, and Peter Fonda—who have spreads here and want to be alone together.

Helena: Gary Cooper's 1901 birthsite, at 730 11th Avenue, still stands. Other childhood homes were at Fifth Avenue and Beatty Street, 15 Shiland Street, and 712 Fifth Street.

In the fifties, there was a Cooper Gallery in the museum of the local historical society. He would come to town and help plug a pal's Frontier Town–type tourist attraction. Both are gone.

The Myrna Loy Fine Arts Center, a refurbished old jail, is now under construction on Ewing Street. You can buy a brick on the Sidewalk of the Stars; call 800/67-MYRNA.

Silver Star: *Roadside Hollywood* salutes the greatest film lovers of all time: in 1925, this town had a population of 75, but had two movie theaters with a total of 126 seats.

NORTH DAKOTA

NORTH DAKOTA'S GIFT TO HOLLYWOOD
★ ★ ★ ★ ★ ★ ★ ★ ★ ★ ★ ★ ★ ★ ★

Angie Dickinson (b. Angeline Brown, Kulm): Ageless Angie was born here and grew up in Edgelev, North Dakota, about as unlikely an origin for a leggy Rat Pack bauble as could possibly be. That's America for you.

What's There
◄ ◄ ◄ ◄ ◄ ◄ ◄ ◄ ► ► ► ► ► ► ► ►

Fargo: The Fargo Theatre, at 314 Broadway, is a restored 1926 art moderne movie palace with live organ accompaniment on weekends. For the program, call 701/235-4152.

MADE IN SOUTH DAKOTA

(Courtesy of the South Dakota Department of Tourism)

BUFFALO STAMPEDES

***The Last Hunt* (Custer State Park, 1956):** For the film's great buffalo stampede, 1,000 buffalo were herded by eight jeeps. Cameras were placed behind barricades and marksmen were stationed at strategic spots. Director Richard Brooks carried a pistol strapped to his side. Also filmed at Sylvan Lake and the Badlands.

***How the West Was Won* (Custer State Park, 1962):** The first film shot in Cinerama. Three directors took the helm over a who's who cast. Shooting here included the linking of the transcontinental railroad and, yes, a buffalo stampede.

Mount Rushmore, South Dakota. *(Courtesy of the South Dakota Department of Tourism)*

DEAD PRESIDENTS

***North by Northwest* (Keystone, 1959):** The classic scenes at Mount Rushmore were shot here—sort of. National Park Service policy specifies that no acts of violence and no death scenes are permitted to be filmed at Mount Rushmore, so Hitchcock & Company cheated by shooting the violence elsewhere, then editing it in.

IT'S SO . . . DAKOTA-Y

***A Man Called Horse* (Custer State Park, 1970):** Remembered for the brutal scene in which Richard Harris is hung by his nipples. Second-unit shots only were done here. Originally the filmmakers were going to film in South Dakota, and even consulted the Rosebud Sioux, but they ended up filming in Mexico.

***Dances with Wolves* (Rapid City, Pierre, 1990):** Filming of Kevin Costner's directorial debut took place near Fort Pierre, north of Rapid City along the Belle

Custer State Park, host to *A Man Called Horse* second-unit camera crews. *(Courtesy of the South Dakota Department of Tourism)*

Fourche River. During filming, wags referred to the film as "Kevin's Gate."

SOUTH DAKOTA'S GIFTS TO HOLLYWOOD

★ ★ ★ ★ ★ ★ ★ ★ ★ ★ ★ ★ ★ ★ ★ ★

Cheryl Ladd (Huron): The poor man's Farrah Fawcett kicks off a trio of vivacious SoDak blondies . . .

Dorothy Provine (Deadwood): . . . including the poor man's Shirley Jones . . .

Mamie Van Doren (b. Joan Lucille Olander, Rowena): . . . and the poor man's Jayne Mansfield, who was, of course, the poor man's Marilyn Monroe. See What's There.

WHAT'S THERE

Rowena: Still-smokin' Mamie Van Doren was raised in this tiny town—there are no street addresses—near Sioux Falls. Her birthplace still stands, and has recently been remodeled. It's the first house you'll encounter entering town from the west, on the south side of Highway 38.

WISCONSIN

Not a lot of film production here, but an amazing collection of major film figures have hailed from the Cheese State.

MADE IN WISCONSIN

***Stroszek* (Plainfield, 1977):** Weirdo German director Werner Herzog heard about this little town, where murderer Ed Gein hailed from, and decided he *had* to make a film here. See What's There.

***Damien: Omen II* (Eagle River, 1978):** Scary *Omen* sequel starring William Holden. There's a brutal ice-skating murder of old Lew Ayres.

***F.I.S.T.* (Mineral Point, 1978):** Stallone's first after *Rocky*, written by Joe Ezsterhaus, one of the highest-paid writers in the biz. Also filmed in Dubuque, Iowa.

***Mrs. Soffel* (North Freedom, 1984):** Although the

The Midcontinent Railroad Museum, featured in *Mrs. Soffel*. *(Photo: Wisconsin Tourism Development—Film Office)*

film was set in Pennsylvania, the Midcontinent Railroad Museum was used because there wasn't enough snow back east.

Back to School **(Madison, 1986):** The only successful Rodney Dangerfield vehicle to date, shot at the University of Wisconsin.

Bascom Hall at the University of Wisconsin–Madison was featured in *Back to School. (Photo: Wisconsin Tourism Development—Film Office)*

Major League **(Milwaukee, 1989):** Milwaukee County Stadium stood in for Cleveland Municipal Stadium; as many as 25,000 extras appeared in these scenes.

Milwaukee County Stadium, home to those zany underdogs in *Major League. (Photo: Wisconsin Tourism Development—Film Office)*

WISCONSIN'S GIFTS TO HOLLYWOOD

★ ★ ★ ★ ★ ★ ★ ★ ★ ★ ★ ★ ★ ★ ★ ★

Don Ameche (Kenosha): An actor synonymous with a role: "ameche" became slang for "telephone" after he appeared in *The Story of Alexander Graham Bell.* If this sort of thing happened today, what would a "stallone" be?

Eddie Cline (Kenosha): Talented comedy writer and director who worked with Buster Keaton, W. C. Fields, and many others.

Ellen Corby (Racine): Grandma Walton.

Ben Hecht (Racine): The most prominent of the journalists who migrated to Hollywood in the 1930s, he was uncredited for his script-doctoring of a slew of classics, including *Gone with the Wind, Lifeboat,* and *Stage-*

coach. His massive credits include *The Front Page, Scarface, Twentieth Century, Nothing Sacred, Gunga Din, Wuthering Heights,* and *Notorious.* An underappreciated giant of film. See What's There.

Carole Landis (b. Francis Lillain Mary Ridste, Fairchild): Very attractive blond actress whose films include *Topper Returns* and *Four Jills in a Jeep.* She committed suicide at the age of 29 over unrequited love for Rex Harrison.

Joseph Losey (La Crosse): One of those American directors who is better appreciated in Europe. He probably feels the same way; he was blacklisted in 1951 and exiled to England. His films include *The Servant* and *Modesty Blaise.*

Fred MacMurray (Beaver Dam): The man who bought up much of Los Angeles County and brought up "My Three Sons" grew up here before going to Hollywood for a Ronald Reagan–style career. His best film by far is *Double Indemnity.* And *Son of Flubber.* Born in Kankakee, Illinois.

Fredric March (b. Ernest Frederick McIntyre Bickel, Racine): Classy leading man who won Oscars for *Dr. Jekyll and Mr. Hyde* and *The Best Years of Our Lives.* Other films include *A Star Is Born, Nothing Sacred,* and *Anna Karenina.*

Pat O'Brien (Milwaukee): Childhood friend of Spencer Tracy who played Irish cops and priests, plus the title role in *Knute Rockne, All American.*

Nicholas Ray (La Crosse): Quintessential fifties cult director. His work includes *They Live by Night, Johnny Guitar,* and *Rebel Without a Cause.* Ray went to the same high school as Joseph Losey.

Gena Rowlands (Cambria): Emotive star of films by her late husband John Cassavetes, especially *A Woman Under the Influence,* and Woody Allen's *Another Woman.*

Spencer Tracy (Milwaukee): Yet another classy, highly respected Wisconsin film figure with an incredible résumé. His includes *Captains Courageous, Boys Town, Northwest Passage, A Guy Named Joe* . . . all the way through to *Guess Who's Coming to Dinner,* his last film.

Orson Welles (Kenosha): One of the most brilliant actor-directors ever. *Citizen Kane.* See What's There.

Gene Wilder (b. Jerry Silberman, Milwaukee): Mel Brooks gave Wilder a leg up (*The Producers, Blazing Saddles, Young Frankenstein*), but he also scored on his own (well, with Richard Pryor) in *Silver Streak* and *Stir Crazy.*

WHAT'S THERE

Kenosha: Orson Welles was born in a house, still standing, on Seventh Avenue just off 61st Street. The current occupants are unrelated to the behemoth talent. Also, there are many Ameches still in the area, and I don't mean "telephones."

Milwaukee: Spencer Tracy's childhood homes: 2970 South Kinnickinnic Avenue and 2447 South Graham Street.

Racine: Ben Hecht homes are at 1635 College, Bickle Street, and 827 Lake Avenue (later 823 Lake). At 827 was the barn where he performed acrobatics.

Plainfield: Ed Gein's farmhouse, south of town, was burned down by locals. Gein's weird 1957 ritual murders were the inspiration for *Psycho, The Texas Chainsaw Massacre, Silence of the Lambs,* and *Deranged.*

Chapter 5

HEARTLAND

- Illinois
- Iowa
- Kansas
- Nebraska

It's almost astonishing that in a state this big, 99 percent of the movies shot here were filmed in less than 2 percent of the surface area, that being Chicagoland. This is a state that, outside of Chicago, has no identity—except perhaps for Hollywood studio films about Abraham Lincoln.

For the purposes of this book, in fact, Chicago is a special case. The Gifts to Hollywood section is supposed to demonstrate what a great melting pot Hollywood has always been for good-looking white people with a modicum of talent, turning Midwestern hicks into glamorous, sophisticated idols. But until 25 years ago, Chicago was the second-largest, second-most-sophisticated city in the country. So learning that your favorite stars come from Chicagoland should not be all that surprising. Therefore, the Gifts to Hollywood section has been abridged.

MADE IN ILLINOIS

There have been three types of movies shot in Chicago over the years: movies about crime, movies not about crime, and movies by John Hughes:

"CHEE-CA-GO: AL CAPONE, RAT-A-TAT-TAT"

Chicagoans traveling in Europe still endure this refrain whenever they divulge their hometown; Hollywood's gangster movies of the 1930s have left an indelible international impression.

The Front Page (1931), based on the play by Charles MacArthur and Chicago journalist Ben Hecht, evokes the sharp nastiness of Chicago in the 1920s and 1930s. But it was *Scarface* (1932), also cowritten by Hecht and based on Al Capone, that equated Chicago with mobsters and tommy guns.

It was probably "The Untouchables" TV series of the

1950s more than anything that reinforced this image. Brian DePalma's *The Untouchables* (1987), written by Chicagoan David Mamet, adopts the same setting, evokes the same Chicago, and was a massive hit. The climactic scene with the baby carriage on the train station stairs, an homage to the Odessa Steps sequence in Eisenstein's *Potemkin,* was filmed at Union Station, 210 South Canal Street. (The station was also seen in *The Sting* [1973].) Mamet's *Things Change* (1988) is a lighthearted peek at Chicago mobsters.

Nowadays, Chicago crime films concentrate on overblown car chases and clever new ways of fighting on the el, Chicago's system of elevated trains:

***The Blues Brothers* (1980):** Mayor Jane Byrne allowed Dan Aykroyd and Chicagoan John Belushi to take over the city: filming of an obscenely excessive car chase shut down Lake Shore Drive for days, and the film's exorbitant finale takes place outside the mayor's office, Daley Plaza, Washington and Dearborn streets. Jake and Elwood's apartment was at 22 West Van Buren Street.

***The Hunter* (1980):** Steve McQueen's last film contained an el homage to his *Bullitt* chase. Also, a car is driven out of Marina Towers, 300 North State Street, and into the Chicago River. There's a similar scene in *The Blues Brothers,* as a matter of fact.

***Code of Silence* (1985):** Chuck Norris is a tough, loner Chicago cop. There's a fight scene that begins atop an el train and ends in the Chicago River at the Wells Street Bridge.

***Running Scared* (1986):** Gregory Hines and Billy Crystal are two wacky, violent cops. This one *combines* car chases and el tracks: there's a car chase *on* the el tracks! The weird-looking atrium for the film's climactic shoot-out is at the State of Illinois Center, 100 West Randolph Street.

Finally, the exterior of the station house from "Hill Street Blues," which is set in Anytown, is at the corner of 14th and Morgan streets.

URBAN, BUT NOT NEW YORK

Sometimes Chicago is used simply because it's a big city that hasn't been overexposed on film. *About Last Night* (1986), based on David Mamet's play *Sexual Perversity in Chicago,* was probably only shot here because of Mamet (although the distributor *had* considered—briefly—releasing the film under Mamet's title). *Nothing in Common* (1986), with Tom Hanks and Jackie Gleason, showed the same modern, bright city as *About Last Night.* As did *Class* (1983): Jacqueline Bisset performs a love scene with young Andrew McCarthy in a glass elevator at snazzy Water Tower Place, 835 North Michigan Avenue. On the seamier side, Paul Newman gets hustled in a pool room at the North Center Bowling Alleys, 4017 North Lincoln Avenue, in *The Color of Money* (1986).

JOHN HUGHES

Until finally heading to Hollywood, Hughes made his home in comfy north suburban Glenview. His films are all set in the northern suburbs, which are notable for their cleanliness, affluence, and racial monotony: *Sixteen Candles* (1984), which was shot at Skokie's shuttered Niles East High School, Lincoln Avenue; *The Breakfast Club* (1985), the first brat package, for which a set was constructed from scratch; *Ferris Bueller's Day Off* (1986), which features a parade downtown, on Dearborn between Madison and Washington; *She's Having a Baby* (1988), which, for the first half, offers a peek at what Hughes is *really* thinking; and *Uncle Buck* (1989), in which John Candy leaves his choice apartment (across from Wrigley Field) to tend the kids in the suburbs.

The same environment is conveyed much better in *Risky Business* (1983), in which Tom Cruise sets up a whorehouse in his parents' Glencoe home. (His dad's Porsche slips into the marina at Belmont Harbor, Belmont at Lake Michigan.) *Ordinary People* (1980) was shot in Lake Forest, one of the nicest suburbs of them all, but the people in that movie don't have nearly so much fun.

Northwestern University, in Evanston, is the local

favorite for Halls of Ivy. (The University of Chicago looks pretty collegiate, too, but it's in a bad neighborhood.) Films shot here include *Nothing in Common* (1986), *Class* (1983), *Doctor Detroit* (1983), and the scene with Tom Berenger in the library in *Major League* (1989).

If you want to see a different side of Chicago (i.e., the South Side), try *Stony Island* (1978) or *Cooley High* (1975), which has the dubious distinction of inspiring TV's "What's Happening!"

ILLINOIS'S GIFTS TO HOLLYWOOD

★ ★ ★ ★ ★ ★ ★ ★ ★ ★ ★ ★ ★ ★ ★ ★

CHICAGOLAND CLOWNS

Chicago is America's Number One source of comedy. Between funny people who grew up here and those who performed in the famous Second City troupe, no other town has provided so many fresh, funny slants. One reason is that wise guys on the coasts think of the Midwest as a vast wasteland of farmers and their mules, so they trot out the same old shtick. In Chicago, wise guys know better, and they attempt to *challenge* middle America. Sometimes.

Chicagoans who have had a comic impact in the movies include: John and James Belushi, from Wheaton; Jack Benny (b. Benjamin Kubelsky), from Waukegan; Edgar Bergen; John and Joan Cusack; Chic Johnson, of the comedy team Olsen & Johnson; Bill Murray, from Evanston; Bob Newhart; and *Ghostbuster* Harold Ramis.

CHICAGO AUTEURS

Walt Disney: His youth is more closely associated with Missouri. His birthplace, at 1249 Tripp Avenue, is no longer standing.

Bob Fosse: A hard-charging director and choreographer. His work includes *The Pajama Game, Damn Yankees, Cabaret, Lenny,* and the pseudoautobiographical (that's three prefixes plus two suffixes) *All That Jazz.*

Preston Sturges: A comic director of genius who experienced a free hand in his snappy, cynical films of the early 1940s, including *The Lady Eve, Sullivan's Travels, The Palm Beach Story, The Miracle of Morgan's Creek.*

CHICAGOLAND ACTORS

Chicago's first contributions to motion pictures were silent queens Gloria Swanson and Blanche Sweet. The next generation included Ralph Bellamy and Robert Young, followed by a wave of Bruce Dern and Rock Hudson, both from suburban Winnetka, Charlton Heston (from Evanston), Kim Novak, and Jason Robards, Jr. More recently minted stars include Harrison Ford, Daryl Hannah, and young Fred Savage.

"DOWNSTATE"

Roger Ebert (Urbana): The cocreator of the "thumbs" system of film criticism and, more importantly, screenwriter of Russ Meyer's *Beyond the Valley of the Dolls.*

William Holden (b. William Beedle, O'Fallon): Longtime movie good guy, a favorite of Billy Wilder. Europeans consider him the quintessential good-looking American. His boyhood home, unmarked, is on North Cherry Street. Films include: *Golden Boy, Sunset Boulevard, Born Yesterday, Stalag 17, The Wild Bunch.*

John Malkovich (Christopher): Pretentious actor who was involved with Chicago's Steppenwolf Theater (see What's There) before making it as a wild-eyed character actor. Films include: *The Killing Fields, Places in the Heart, Dangerous Liaisons.*

Louella Parsons (Freeport): Powerful Hearst newspaper gossip columnist in the old days.

Ronald Reagan (Dixon): An actor who *always* needed a script. He was born in Tampico, Illinois, but raised here. See What's There.

Carl Switzer (Paris): The freckle-faced, off-key Alfalfa in the "Our Gang" series.

Greg Toland (Charleston): A master cinematographer who employed deep-focus technique (foreground and background simultaneously in focus; see *The Little Foxes*) and odd angles (look at all the ceilings in *Citizen*

Kane). Other films include: *Wuthering Heights, The Grapes of Wrath, The Best Years of Our Lives.*

Dick Van Dyke (Danville): The center of his own classic 1960s TV show. His best film work, *Mary Poppins,* was detested by Poppins's creater, P. L. Travers; he has been banned from the sequel. Also in *Bye Bye Birdie* and *The Comic.*

WHAT'S THERE

Chester: A mighty Popeye statue overlooks the Mississippi in Segar Memorial Park. It honors Elzie Crisler Segar, a Chester native who created the spinach-chomping cartoon hero in 1929.

The Popeye statue. *(Photo by Mike Coles)*

Chicago: A plaque commemorates the site where, in July 1934, John Dillinger, betrayed by Anna Sage, the "woman in red," was shot after seeing *Manhattan Melodrama* at the Biograph Theatre. The beautifully restored first-run theater is a National Historic Landmark. 2433 North Lincoln Avenue.

Second City was the beginning for Alan Arkin, Mike Nichols, Elaine May, Gilda Radner, John Belushi, and many, many more. 1616 North Wells Street. Reservations: 312/337-3992.

The Steppenwolf Theatre, John Malkovich's old turf, is located at 2851 North Halsted. Information: 312/472-4141.

And the Goodman Theatre, David Mamet's old hang-out, is at 200 South Columbus Drive. Information: 312/443-3800.

Dixon: Ronald Reagan's boyhood home is open for tours. 816 South Hennepin Avenue.

Forest Park: Mike Todd's grave is in the Waldheim/Forest Home Cemetery, 863 South Des Plaines Avenue. Todd, a flamboyant producer (*Around the World in 80 Days*), was married to Elizabeth Taylor when he died in a plane crash. Also buried there are preacher Billy Sunday and commie Emma Goldman (played by Maureen Stapleton in *Reds*).

Galena: Belvedere Mansion and Gardens is a 22-room Italianate mansion built in 1857 by steamboat magnate J. Russel Jones. It contains art items from Liberace's estate, plus oil paintings and the famous green drapes from *Gone with the Wind.* Open 11–5, Memorial Day–October. 1008 Park Avenue.

Metropolis: This is Superman Town. The town boasts a Superman billboard, Superman water tower, Superman phone booth, and Superman statue (Market Street at Superman Square), a street called Lois Lane, a display of green kryptonite (safely behind glass in the Chamber of Commerce office), and a Burger Queen with a Superman motif. The local paper is the *Planet.*

Welcome to Metropolis, Illinois. *(Courtesy of Julie Kuehndorf)*

The Superman statue in Superman Square, Metropolis. *(Courtesy of Julie Kuehndorf)*

The town, the only Metropolis in America with a post office, hosts annual Superman Days in mid-June, where you can see the Little Miss Supergirl contest, the Superman Tug-o-War, and a simulated bank robbery.

Sparta: This town is where the real story behind *In the Heat of the Night* took place. It was transformed into Sparta, Mississippi, in the movie so it would seem more southern.

Waukegan: This is a town that knows how to treat a famous son. Jack Benny has several boyhood homes here: an apartment over a butcher shop on Glendon Street, 224 South Genesee Street, and 518 Clayton Street, which is the accepted boyhood home. Jack Benny Drive leads to a park, where you'll find the Jack Benny Center for the Arts (at 39 [!] Jack Benny Drive). The Benny statue in the center is described as "comical." Jack Benny Junior High School is at 1401 Montesano Avenue. The historical society (1917 North Sheridan Road) has his old costume trunk, letters, scrapbooks, clippings, and photos. It's open Wednesdays through Fridays, and Sundays.

Woodstock: Paul Newman and Orson Welles began their careers at the still-open 1890 Opera House, at 121 Van Buren, in the old-timey, red-brick town square. Schedule: 815/338-5300.

IOWA

MADE IN IOWA

CORN

***Children of the Corn* (Whiting, 1984):** A town of evil farm kids, based on a Stephen King novel, with TV stars Peter Horton ("thirtysomething") and Linda Hamilton ("Beauty and the Beast").

***Country* (Waterloo, 1984):** At the height of the farm

crisis, Sam Shepard and Jessica Lange pitched in with this entry in the 1984 Farm Filmathon.

***Miles from Home* (Cedar Rapids, 1988):** Richard Gere and Kevin Anderson become folk heroes when they burn down their farm rather than let the bank have it.

***Field of Dreams* (Dyersville, 1989):** Reviews were mixed, but this sentimental father-son baseball movie obviously got to people. See What's There.

FILMS THAT CUT THE CORN

***Union Pacific* (Council Bluffs, 1939):** A Cecil B. DeMille epic.

***Cold Turkey* (Winterset, Greenfield, 1971):** A Norman Lear film with Dick Van Dyke as an antismoking minister.

***Pennies from Heaven* (Dubuque, 1981):** Steve Martin took a chance in this daring Depression-era lip-sync musical written by Dennis Potter.

IOWA'S GIFTS TO HOLLYWOOD

★ ★ ★ ★ ★ ★ ★ ★ ★ ★ ★ ★ ★ ★ ★ ★

William Frawley (Burlington): A burly character actor in well over a hundred films who struck gold as Fred Mertz on "I Love Lucy."

Harry Langdon (Council Bluffs): A man-child silent comedian who ranked just below Chaplin, Keaton, and Lloyd for a while. Unfortunately, he couldn't figure out what was funny and what wasn't. Some of his descendants still live in Council Bluffs, but nobody's quite sure in which house he was born or where he lived. The town bears no tributes or remembrances.

Cloris Leachman (Des Moines): This Miss America runner-up won an Oscar for *The Last Picture Show* (1971) and appeared in Mel Brooks's *Young Frankenstein* and *High Anxiety,* but she really hit it big as Phyllis in "The Mary Tyler Moore Show." She is the mother of actors Annette O'Toole and Robert Englund (Freddie Krueger).

Donna Reed (Denison): Famous for her TV show—and for replacing, then giving way again to Barbara Bel Geddes on "Dallas"—but had big roles in *From Here to Eternity* and *It's a Wonderful Life.* See What's There.

George Reeves (Woodstock): Superman came from Smallville, and the actor who played him did, too. He appeared in *From Here to Eternity,* but at previews the audience shouted for Superman—many of his scenes were cut. Also remembered as Brent Tarleton in *Gone with the Wind* and as the scarred villain in *Rancho Notorious.*

Jean Seberg (Marshalltown): A small-town girl who won a national search to star in *Saint Joan.* She never really made it in America, but managed to appear in Jean-Luc Godard's French New Wave classic *Breathless* as well as *The Mouse That Roared* and *Lilith.* See What's There.

John Wayne (b. Marion Michael Morrison, Winterset): The Duke. See What's There.

WHAT'S THERE

Denison: Donna Reed's hometown boasts a Donna Reed Drive and the Donna Reed Center for the Performing Arts; plans eventually call for a museum. Her childhood home, a farmhouse, burned down recently. Every June, Denison hosts a Donna Reed Festival. The first, in 1986, was kicked off with the presentation of Reed's *From Here to Eternity* Oscar to Crawford County. You can see the little fella at the W. A. McHenry House, 1428 First Avenue North. 1990's five-day festival had workshops, screenings, a classic car parade, a picnic for 4,000 to 5,000 people, and a minitribute to Reed. For info call 712/263-3334.

Dyersville: The *Field of Dreams* field is now a tourist attraction. Farmer Don Lansing retained the part of the film's 3½-acre field that sat on his property. His neighbor Al Ameskamp, however, plowed *his* part of the field.

Donna Reed Festival brochure. *(Courtesy of The Donna Reed Foundation for the Performing Arts)*

Ameskamp caved in and restored his portion when he saw the thousands of pilgrims streaming to the site. (For the film's climax, 1,500 cars paraded to the field at night with their headlights on.)

The local chamber of commerce—which previously was stuck promoting the National Farm Toy Museum—peddles *Field of Dreams* T-shirts ($8-12) and sweatshirts ($20). There's a box on the field for contributions. The farm is four miles northeast of town, off Highway 136. You can get a map in town. When you get close, a TO FIELD OF DREAMS sign guides you in.

Marshalltown: Seberg's Pharmacy was owned by Jean Seberg's parents, but they've recently sold it. 236 North 13th Street.

Riverside: When in 1983 a member of the town council learned that *Star Trek*'s Captain Kirk was ostensibly from "a small town in Iowa," he convinced the council that Riverside should be that town. A spot behind what used to be the town barbershop was designated the official site of the blessed event, scheduled for March 26, 2228. A sign reading "Future Birthplace of Captain James T. Kirk" went up along the interstate, but was soon ordered removed by the Department of Transportation; it was replaced with "Riverside: Where The Trek Begins."

A 20-foot-long *USS Riverside* float, built to resemble the *Enterprise*, docks beside the interstate on US 218S, east of town. The town hosts Kirk's future birthday party every March 26, and in late June holds a full-blown Trekfest. The enterprising council is now trying to finance a $10,000 bronze statue of Kirk to place beside the *Riverside*.

Winterset: Even Ronald Reagan has visited the birthplace of John Wayne, one of the few movie-star homes to merit an official brown historical sign on the interstate. The street through town is John Wayne Drive and bears a drawing of the Duke.

The house, restored to its 1907 appearance (Duke's

The birthplace of John (Duke) Wayne. (John Wayne Birthplace, Winterset, Iowa).

birth year), contains memorabilia, including a *True Grit* eye patch, his suitcase from *Stagecoach*, and the doctor's bag of the man who delivered him. Souvenirs for sale include *Stagecoach* kitchen magnets and wood shingles taken from the house's old roof. An annual **John Wayne Festival** takes place every Fourth of July. 224 South Second Street.

KANSAS

MADE IN KANSAS

YOU WANT FLAT, YOU GOT IT

***Picnic* (Halstead, Hutchinson, Salina, 1955):** In Hutchinson, 2,000 townsfolk served as extras in the picnic scene—just as a tornado hit. In Salina, the distraught director, Joshua Logan, was having trouble getting Kim Novak to cry during a romantic waterfall scene. It's not clear whether she asked Logan to pinch her or whether he simply showed initiative in this regard; in any case, she cried.

***Carnival of Souls* (Lawrence, 1962):** Outstanding, stylish little horror movie. Lawrence is used effectively for its dullness, as a contrast with the weird phantoms visiting our Jayhawk heroine. Director Herk Harvey, a local, shot two weeks in Lawrence, then one week at the abandoned Saltair amusement park near Salt Lake City. (He had driven past the park's Moorish towers and decided it would be great setting for a horror film.) The film was screened in Lawrence in 1961 to lukewarm response, was shelved, and then re-released in 1989 to highbrow acclaim.

***In Cold Blood* (Holcomb, also Kansas City, Kansas, 1967):** Holcomb was the actual site of the 1959 Clutter family slaughter, upon which Truman Capote's book and this movie are based. In fact, the film was shot at the actual Clutter house (River Valley Farm, River Road). Brrrr! The film's trial scene was shot at the same Finney County Court House, in Garden City, where the actual trial was held, and cast the same actual jury.

***Bad Company* (1972):** Jeff Bridges and Barry Brown play two rascally Civil War–era drifters in Robert Benton's underrated adventure based on the name of a popular 1970s rock group.

***Prime Cut* (Kansas City, also Kansas City, Missouri, 1972):** An entertaining, grisly look at the Midwestern Meat Mafia and the beautiful women—including Sissy Spacek—they sell into slavery.

***Paper Moon* (Hays, 1973):** A terrific *Ryan O'Neal* movie? The black-and-white photography of Depression-era Kansas is totally convincing.

***The Day After* (Lawrence, 1983):** Again, Lawrence is utilized for its absolute averageness, in this case demonstrating how unfortunate an atomic attack would be for normal people. One of the highest rated TV programs ever.

KANSAS'S GIFTS TO HOLLYWOOD

★ ★ ★ ★ ★ ★ ★ ★ ★ ★ ★ ★ ★ ★ ★ ★

Kirstie Alley (Wichita): The *Star Trek II* beauty, also seen in *Look Who's Talking, Madhouse,* and a little show called "Cheers."

Roscoe "Fatty" Arbuckle (Smith Center): Fatty was the comic juggernaut of the late teens. Unfortunately, he was implicated—but never convicted—in the bawdy death of Virginia Rappe, a hanger-on. The Shoeless Joe Jackson of the film industry, he was scapegoated to appease those who disapproved of the overindulgent ways of Hollywood folk.

Hugh Beaumont (Lawrence): Beaver's dad played solid citizens and private-eye Mike Shayne in B pictures of the forties and fifties.

Louise Brooks (Cherryvale): A shrewd, defiant beauty whose strong will truncated a promising career. Her hairstyle and manner as Lulu in *Pandora's Box* is still aped today: Melanie Griffith's character in *Something Wild* wears a Brooksy wig and calls herself Lulu. She was working as a shopgirl years after setting the screen afire, and spent her last years in Rochester, New York, near the George Eastman Center. See What's There.

Dennis Hopper (Dodge City): Hopper debuted at 19 in *Giant,* then found solid work until after 1969's *Easy Rider.* The success of that film was followed by a spiral downward, with a few exceptions, until his apotheosis in the mid 1980s as the Brat Pack's eccentric uncle.

Joseph Francis "Buster" Keaton (Piqua, aka Pickway): Keaton grew up on the road, as a human mop in his family's vaudeville act, so it's fitting he was born on the road. According to his amazingly unbitter autobiography, *My Wonderful World of Slapstick,* the town of Pickway was soon thereafter blown away by a cyclone.

Hattie McDaniel (Wichita): Reportedly the first black woman to sing on American radio, she's best known for her Oscar-winning role in *Gone with the Wind.*

Gordon Parks (Fort Scott): A professional photographer, he worked for *Life* magazine for 20 years before directing his first feature. The second time out of the box, Parks hit it big with *Shaft,* the granddaddy of blaxsploitation—and what a great theme song.

Vivian Vance (Cherryvale): Lucy's sidekick, whose heft was mandated by the carrot-topped comedienne. See What's There.

WHAT'S THERE

Cherryvale: The childhood homes of Louise Brooks (324 West Main Street) and Vivian Vance (309 West Sixth

Street) are found here. Distant relatives of Vance still live there. The Cherryvale Public Library maintains a collection on both favorite daughters.

Independence: The William Inge Collection harbors records, tapes, and books from the private cache of this Pulitzer-winning playwright and Oscar-winning screenwriter, an Independence native. Inge's movies include *Come Back Little Sheba, Picnic,* and *Splendor in the Grass.* The collection is within Independence Community College, College Boulevard. For info call 316/331-4100.

Kansas City: The renovated Granada Theatre, 1015 Minnesota, hosts occasional film presentations. The Granada houses the only theater organ in the area.

Lawrence: Some claim that the restored Liberty Hall, which still shows art movies, was the first movie theater west of the Mississippi. Since I phrased it this way, you can tell I'm a doubter. It opened in 1912 as the Jayhawker, a vaudeville house. It's at 642 Massachusetts Street.

Liberal: Dorothy's House is located at 567 East Cedar Street. Kansas bills itself as the Land of Ahs, and US Route 54 from Wichita to Liberal is officially designated The Yellow Brick Road. At the end of the road tens of thousands of pilgrims have found a 1907 farmhouse (1907 is the year L. Frank Baum wrote *The Wizard of Oz*) refashioned as a replica of the movie's Gale home. At its 1981 dedication, the governor of Kansas proclaimed Dorothy's House "the gateway to fantasy, fun and the good life in Kansas."

A fake storm cellar door leads nowhere. Dorothy's bedroom is adorned like in the movie: a photograph documents the similarity. The pinafore hanging in the bedroom is said to be one of 10 made for Judy Garland. Also in Dorothy's room are a stuffed Toto, replica ruby slippers, and a painting on a fake window showing a twister on the horizon.

Three Munchkins have visited; height marks on a

wall demonstrate how tiny they really are. The actual model of the house that was seen blowing around in the movie is here; it broke in shooting but has been restored.

Out front is a yellow brick road comprising individual bricks sponsored by fans. You can buy a brick with your message on it for $50, like "Bud & Bettye Brixey, Hooker, OK," "Hi-Grade Cleaners," "Liberal Elks Lodge #1947," "The Ooley Family," "Cast of Up With People 82–83," and "Spudnuts" have done. There are over a thousand bricks and counting.

On summer afternoons, local high school girls impersonate Dorothy. A gift shop in the kitchen pantry sells dolls, $3 ruby slippers, and fancy farm hats. Open year-round, Tuesday–Saturday 9–5, Sunday 1–5.

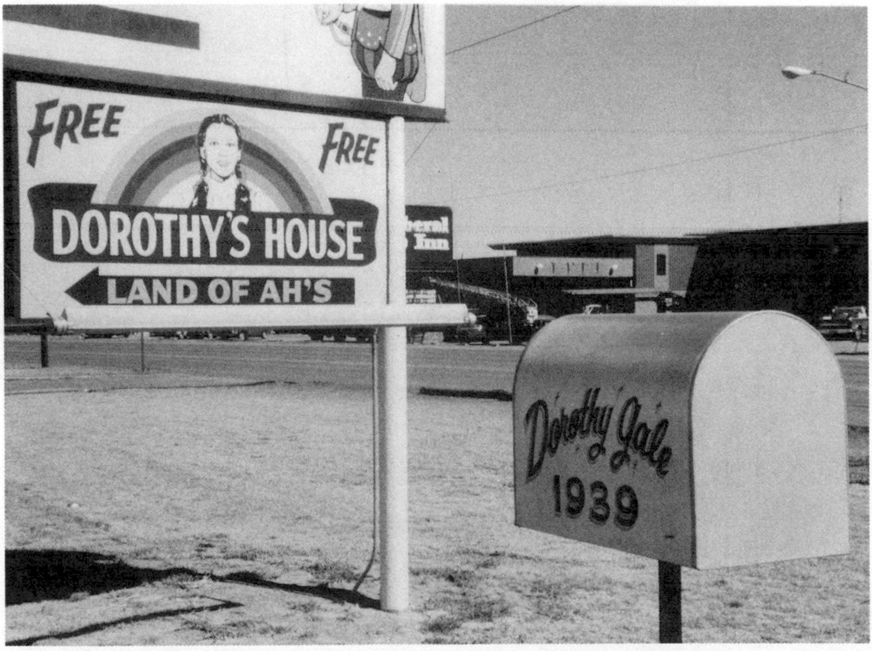

Welcome to Dorothy's House. *(Courtesy of Julie Kuehndorf)*

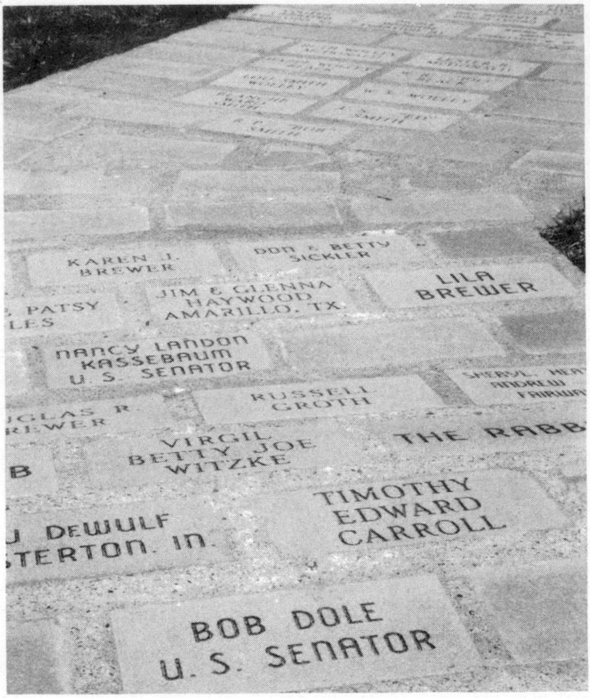

Welcome to the Yellow Brick Road. *(Courtesy of Julie Kuehndorf)*

NEBRASKA

A state that has given far more than it's gotten from Hollywood. The east end of Nebraska has produced more big stars per capita than anywhere else on earth.

MADE IN NEBRASKA

***Boys Town* (Boys Town, 1938):** The story of the "reformatory without walls" founded by Father Flanagan. See What's There.

***Terms of Endearment* (Lincoln, 1983):** Debra Winger met and carried on with Nebraska's (bachelor) Governor, Bob Kerrey, during filming and for a short time thereafter.

NEBRASKA'S GIFTS TO HOLLYWOOD

★ ★ ★ ★ ★ ★ ★ ★ ★ ★ ★ ★ ★ ★ ★ ★

Fred Astaire (b. Fred Austerlitz, Omaha): Suave hoofer extraordinaire. See What's There.

Marlon Brando (Omaha): Master of The Method who influenced three generations of actors. His mother was a leader of the legendary Omaha Community Playhouse. See What's There.

Montgomery Clift (Omaha): Intense, good-looking actor who was far more intense and far less good-looking after a car accident, causing his spirits and career to plummet swiftly.

Sandy Dennis (Hastings, also Lincoln): Twitchy, neurotic whiner from *Who's Afraid of Virginia Woolf, The Out of Towners,* and *Up the Down Staircase.*

Henry Fonda (b. Henry Brace, Grand Island): The American ideal—or at least a guy who played lots of characters who were. See What's There.

Swoosie Kurtz (Omaha): One of those character actresses who play someone in their late thirties, early forties for about 50 years. Films include: *Bright Lights, Big City* and *The World According to Garp.*

Harold Lloyd (Burchard): Ranked below Keaton and Chaplin by critics, but his films made more money than theirs, and he built the grandest Hollywood mansion of them all—Greenacres. See What's There: Burchard, Pawnee City.

Nick Nolte (Omaha): Gravel-voiced, large-bodied hard guy who's enlivened testosterone epics aplenty, including *48 HRS, North Dallas Forty,* and *Who'll Stop the Rain.* He lives in West Virginia.

Darryl F. Zanuck (Wahoo): The founder of Twentieth Century Studios, Zanuck was a giant of the industry for many years. He crusaded for "message" pictures like *The*

Grapes of Wrath and *Gentleman's Agreement.* His son Richard is a major player today. See What's There.

WHAT'S THERE

Boys Town: Spencer Tracy's Oscar from *Boys Town* (1938), which was shot on location here, is on display in the Hall of History. Off Flanagan Boulevard, west of Omaha via Highway 6 (West Dodge Road).

Burchard: Harold Lloyd's birthplace, at 24 Pawnee Street, is still standing. Well, leaning. Streets don't appear to be named in this town, nor the houses numbered. You might find the seemingly abandoned house one block east of Route 99, in the middle of this teeny (population 120) burg an hour southeast of Lincoln. Ask for directions at the Golden Nugget Saloon.

Grand Island: Henry Fonda's Grand Island birthplace has been relocated to the excellent Stuhr Museum of the Prairie Pioneer. The preserved house is part of Old Railroad Town, a stroll-through village of transplanted vintage buildings. 3133 West Highway 34, four miles north of I-80 exit 312.

Henry Fonda's birthplace.

Omaha: Inside the Omaha Community Playhouse, where Henry, Peter, and Jane Fonda and Dorothy McGuire started out, is the Fonda-McGuire Theater. Henry Fonda and Dorothy McGuire performed together here in the early 1930s. One floor below, in the Educational Common, is a photo display of the many stars who have played here. It's at 6915 Cass Street.

Birthplaces of the stars:

Fred Astaire: 2326 South 10th Street
Marlon Brando: 1026 South 32nd Street
Montgomery Clift: 3527 Harney Street

Henry Fonda attended Omaha's Central High School.

Pawnee City: Harold Lloyd's boyhood home, a major improvement over his birthplace, is a big white clapboard home at 1008 Eighth Street. It's one block north of Highway 8 (Seventh Street).

Wahoo: The Legrande Hotel, Fifth and Broadway, is empty now (the town "hopes to restore it" someday) but it was home to Darryl F. Zanuck till age seven. His grandfather owned it and his father was the night watchman.

Zanuck's daughter has contributed funds to the town's Zanuck Memorial Square over the years. An addition is planned that will include a collection of Zanuck's films, artifacts, Oscars, and other awards.

A commemorative plaque in front of Zanuck (that's *Darryl F.* Zanuck) Center. *(Photo courtesy of the Wahoo Chamber of Commerce)*

NASHVILLE
NO ELVISES
WITHOUT PERMIT
TCB
XXX

Chapter 6

'BILLIES 'N OKIES

- Arkansas
- Kentucky
- Missouri
- Oklahoma
- Tennessee

MADE IN ARKANSAS

ARMY MEN

***A Soldier's Story* (Fort Smith, Little Rock, 1984):** Fort Chaffee is the Southern black military camp in the film. Little Rock's Lamar Porter Baseball Field was used for the ball-game scenes.

Fort Chaffee in Fort Smith, Arkansas, seen in *A Soldier's Story* and *Biloxi Blues*. *(Courtesy of the Arkansas Film Commission)*

***Biloxi Blues* (Fort Smith, Van Buren, 1988):** Fort Chaffee is a white post this time in one of Neil Simon's more tolerable works.

THE FOUKE MONSTER!

***The Legend of Boggy Creek* (Fouke, 1972):** This successful docudrama about the Fouke Monster was shot here. *Return to Boggy Creek* (1977) and *The Barbaric Beast of Boggy Creek, Part 2* (1983) also spent a little production money here.

ALSO . . .

***End of the Line* (Benton, Little Rock, North Little Rock, 1987):** Little Rock native Jay Russell's first feature stars fellow Little Rockian Mary Steenburgen (who also produced) along with Levon Helm and irascible Wilford Brimley hisself. Shooting took place at Benton's train yard and police station; Little Rock's Atikins Building, Rogers Building, and First Commercial Building; and the Union Pacific track from North Little Rock to Carlisle.

***Rosalie Goes Shopping* (Stuttgart, 1990):** This German sleeper, starring chubby charmer Marianne Sagebrecht, was set in Stuttgart, Arkansas, because of the hilarious parity of its name and the German auto-making city of the same name. Locations in Stuttgart (Arkansas) include the municipal airport, the Stuttgart Public School, Prairie Acres Ranch House, Riceland Mill, and the Stuttgart Agricultural Museum.

ARKANSAS'S GIFTS TO HOLLYWOOD

★ ★ ★ ★ ★ ★ ★ ★ ★ ★ ★ ★ ★ ★ ★ ★

Alan Ladd (Hot Springs): This stoic shorty was a serviceable action hero best remembered for his titular role in *Shane*. He also starred in *The Glass Key* and *This Gun for Hire*. His son, Alan, Jr., is an industry biggie who scored with *Star Wars* and is known as Laddie. Ladd's boyhood home, partially made of logs, was in a rural section, south of town off Highway 7. The land has become part of a subdivision and the structure is no longer there.

Dick Powell (Mountain View): A singer (*Forty-Second Street, Gold Diggers of . . .* films) turned actor (*Christmas in July; Murder, My Sweet*) who later directed the multiply disastrous *The Conqueror* (See Utah). See What's There.

Jean Yarbrough (Marianna): Comedy director who worked with Hal Roach and Abbott & Costello. He's also responsible for such nutty cult movies as *Hillbillys in a Haunted House, The Devil Bat, The Brute Man,* and *The Creeper*.

WHAT'S THERE

Hot Springs: Lorne Greene, decked out in "Battlestar Galactica" finery, welcomes one and all to the Josephine Tussaud Wax Museum, a hotbed of fun. Alfred Hitchcock

The Josephine Tussaud Wax Museum in Hot Springs National Park. "THEY SEEM ALIVE."

ushers those who dare into the Chamber of Horrors, and biker chick Nancy Sinatra snuggles up to Steve McQueen on the back of his hog. The "Stairway to the Stars" section features stars standing on a stairway: Liz Taylor, Mae West, Clark Gable from *GWTW,* and Sophia Loren. 250 Central Avenue.

Mountain View: There aren't any street addresses in town, but everybody knows Dick Powell's boyhood home. It's next to the telephone office.

The Old Mill in North Little Rock. *(Courtesy of the Arkansas Film Commission)*

North Little Rock: The Old Mill, an authentic re-creation of an old water-powered grist mill, was used as a backdrop during the credits in *Gone with the Wind.* It's in the Lakewood residential district, Lakeshore Drive and Fairway Avenue.

Russellville: Jimmy Lile's Knife Shop, on Route 6, features "knives similar to those made for Sylvester Stallone in the Rambo movies."

KENTUCKY

MADE IN KENTUCKY

MOONSHINE COUNTRY

***The Flim Flam Man* (Versailles, 1967):** Breezy George C. Scott comedy of a traveling backwoods con man.

***Coal Miner's Daughter* (Whitesburg, Jenkins, 1980):** Sissy Spacek copped an Oscar for this bio of country singer Loretta Lynn.

ALSO . . .

***The Asphalt Jungle* (Lexington, 1950):** A John Huston crime caper, with a young Marilyn Monroe. The film's climactic scene was shot here.

***Goldfinger* (Fort Knox, 1964):** This is where the gold is, so it was a natural temptation to Mr. Auric Goldfinger, the man with the Midas touch—a spider's touch.

***Stripes* (Louisville, Fort Knox, Elizabethtown, 1981):** Lots of Kentucky shooting for the film that showed how Bill Murray—for whom this was a launching pad—can enliven mundane material.

***Eight Men Out* (Latonia, Louisville, 1988):** This 1919 period film based on the Black Sox scandal was lensed throughout the mid-South. The location in Latonia was the Railway Exposition Company; in Louisville it was Churchill Downs and the railroad station.

***Rain Man* (Melbourne, Newport, 1988):** St. Anne's Convent in Melbourne was Walbrook, Raymond's home. Pompilio's Bar and Restaurant in Newport was the atmospheric diner where Charlie and Raymond have breakfast and Raymond exhibits his genius for numbers with a box of toothpicks. Pompilio's is at 600 Washington. The cemetery scene was also shot in Newport. Timothy Rolf, a local tombstone artist, created the stone for Charlie and Raymond's father, and displays the priceless prop at his place of business.

KENTUCKY'S GIFTS TO HOLLYWOOD

★ ★ ★ ★ ★ ★ ★ ★ ★ ★ ★ ★ ★ ★ ★ ★

Ned Beatty (Louisville): Porcine, prolific character actor who will never outlive the "squeal like a pig" scene from *Deliverance.*

Tod Browning (Louisville): Cult director of the twenties and thirties who would surely have a long-running horror series if he were working today. Films include: *Dracula, Freaks, The Devil Doll.*

Irene Dunne (Louisville): Classy star of drama and sophisticated comedies of the thirties and forties. Films include: *The Awful Truth, My Favorite Wife, I Remember Mama.*

David Wark Griffith (Crestwood): Practically invented movies. Cofounder of United Artists who directed *The Birth of a Nation, Intolerance, Broken Blossoms, Orphans of the Storm.* Incredibly, beset by financial woes, he washed out of the business at age 46. See What's There.

Victor Mature (Louisville): Muscle man who was not much of an actor—the Stallone of his day. Films include: *Samson and Delilah, My Darling Clementine, Kiss of Death.*

Patricia Neal (Packard): Tragedy-crossed actress who appeared in some great films, including *The Fountainhead, The Day the Earth Stood Still, A Face in the Crowd, Hud.*

WHAT'S THERE

BIRTH OF A FILM GUY

Centerfield: D. W. Griffith's grave is located here. Impressively, there's an official state historical marker indicating the eternal presence of Mr. Movies—beneath a modest gravestone—on the roadside outside the Mount

Tabor church graveyard. Reportedly, the grave was originally in a family plot, but the Screen Directors Guild moved Griffith and gave him a new stone. Highway 22, west of town, near La Grange.

Crestwood: D. W. Griffith's birthplace has been razed and is now the Ray Deible farm. Highway 22, three miles east of town.

La Grange: D. W. Griffith's home from 1920 to 1939, hardly a palace, is at 206 West Fourth, at the southeast corner of Madison Street. There might be occasional tours—contact the City of La Grange, 121 West Main Street, La Grange, Kentucky 40031.

Louisville: D. W. Griffith's boyhood home was at 421 West Chestnut Street. The building now hosts the Show 'n Tell Topless-Bottomless Lounge.

Paducah: Chez Tomlin. Here's one of the biggest boohoos in *Roadside Hollywood.* Just a few years back, you could have met Lily's brother and mother at their restaurant/tearoom/gift shop. Lily's Gallery featured a sculpture of Ernestine the Operator (executed by the daughter of Gene Shalit), Edith Ann's rocking chair, a giant pencil from *The Incredible Shrinking Woman,* and the nurse doll from *All of Me.* Wow! But guess what? It's gone.

There is still one pilgrimage for Lily lovers to make in Paducah, however. Starnes Barbeque has Lily's picture on the wall; she used to go there. 4008 Joe Clifton Drive.

MISSOURI

MADE IN MISSOURI

LIFE ON THE MISSOURI

***Huckleberry Finn* (Arrow Rock, Lupus, 1974) and *Tom Sawyer* (Arrow Rock, Lupus, 1973):** Arrow Rock filming was at a state park on the Missouri, rather than the Mississippi River. The cave scenes for *Tom Sawyer* were shot at Meramec caverns—Jesse James's 19th-century hideout.

LAW-DERIDING CITIZENS

***Jesse James* (Pineville, Lake Ozark, 1939):** Tyrone Power and Henry Fonda played Jesse and Frank James, native sons of Clay County. During filming, a stunt horse died going over a cliff. Public outcry led to the American Humane Association's monitoring of all productions using animals.

***Paper Moon* (St. Joseph, 1973):** Depression-era film found well-preserved structures in the town where Jesse James was shot, including the Missouri Valley Trust Company Bank and the old St. Charles Hotel.

***Escape from New York* (St. Louis, 1981):** John Carpenter turned the streets of St. Louis into a burnt-out, futuristic New York City where demented thugs reign. He could have simply shot in the South Bronx but was probably too afraid.

EBONY AND IVORY

***The Intruder*, aka *I Hate Your Guts!* (Charleston, 1961):** A serious Roger Corman integration movie with William Shatner as a racist fomenter. Charleston citizens played most of the supporting roles. "During the climax of the film," Corman says, "when people started to catch on to what the movie was *really* about, we began to have problems. We were to shoot for two days in front of a high school in Eden Prairie, Missouri. After the first day, we were thrown out of town." They were thrown out of Charleston, too. To top it off, it was the first time a Corman film lost money.

SHOW ME . . .

***Shepherd of the Hills* (Branson, 1940):** The play is performed here every summer to this day. The 1964 remake was also shot here and included filming at Branson's Silver Dollar City tourist attraction.

***Dreamer* (St. Louis, Alton, Illinois, 1979):** This bowling *Rocky* was filmed in a town that boasts one of

America's two bowling halls of fame. (The other is in Milwaukee.)

Chuck Berry: Hail! Hail! Rock 'n' Roll **(St. Louis, Wentzville, East St. Louis, 1987):** The film features two filmed concerts at St. Louis's historic Fox Theatre, perfor-

Berry Park in Wentzville, seen in the film *Chuck Berry: Hail! Hail! Rock 'n' Roll.*

mances at the Cosmo Club in East St. Louis, and a visit to Berry's home at Berry Park, 691 Buckner Road in Wentzville.

Mr. and Mrs. Bridge **(Kansas City, 1990):** This Merchant-Ivory production (*Room with a View*) starring Paul Newman and Joanne Woodward was shot at Union Station and the Liberty Memorial.

MISSOURI'S GIFTS TO HOLLYWOOD

★ ★ ★ ★ ★ ★ ★ ★ ★ ★ ★ ★ ★ ★ ★ ★

Robert Altman (Kansas City): Quirky director known for cross-cutting and overlapping dialogue. Films include: *M*A*S*H, McCabe and Mrs. Miller, Nashville.*

Stan Brakhage (Kansas City): Major figure in the avant-garde for many years. His short films are concerned with evocative, experimental images.

Joan Crawford (Kansas City): The Hollywood glamour queen was born in San Antonio but raised in Kansas City. She lived at the New Midland Hot, 407 East Ninth Street, and worked as a laundress at the Gate City Laundry, 403 East Ninth. Neither still exists.

Walt Disney (Kansas City): The king of family entertainment was born in Chicago but raised on a farm in Marceline and in Kansas City. See What's There: Kansas City, Marceline.

Friz Freleng (Kansas City): Influential, longtime Warner Brothers animator who, like Ub Iwerks, worked for Walt Disney in Kansas City in the late 1920s. Freleng also helped create the Pink Panther cartoon series.

Betty Grable (St. Louis): World War II pinup girl who insured her legs for $1 million but hasn't left much of a celluloid legacy. She lived at the Forest Park Hotel in St. Louis and attended the Mary Institute.

Jean Harlow (b. Harlean Carpentier, Kansas City): The famous platinum blonde had a brief but explosive career in the 1930s before dying of illness at age 26. Films include: *The Public Enemy, Red Dust, Dinner at Eight.*

John Huston (Nevada): Self-styled Hemingway, son of actor Walter Huston. Responsible for some classics, but overrated on the whole as a stylist. Films include: *The Maltese Falcon, The Treasure of the Sierra Madre, The African Queen, Prizzi's Honor.* See What's There.

Ub Iwerks (Kansas City): Cocreator of Mickey Mouse who spearheaded many technical advances and worked on Disney projects for 40 years but got the shaft from Uncle Walt.

Kevin Kline (St. Louis): Overspirited, classically trained dramatic and comic presence. Films include: *The Big Chill, A Fish Called Wanda, I Love You to Death.*

Steve McQueen (Slater): Rugged, regular guy who specialized in action pix, including *The Blob, The Great Escape, Bullitt, Papillon.* See What's There.

Geraldine Page (Kirksville): Dotty Method actress. Films include: *Sweet Bird of Youth, Interiors, The Trip to Bountiful.*

William Powell (Kansas City): Powell was born in Pittsburgh, but his family moved here when he was a teen. They lived at 3116 Tracy, in a house that no longer exists. He was a classmate of Casey Stengel's at the old Central High; Stengel, a jock, would mercilessly heckle the young thespian.

Vincent Price (St. Louis): Country Day High grad who became the movies' horrormeister. Films include: *House of Wax, The Fly, The Abominable Dr. Phibes.*

Ginger Rogers (b. Virginia Katherine McMath, Independence): Formed the all-time great cinematic dancing partnership with Fred Astaire. Fredless films include: *Kitty Foyle, The Major and the Minor.* See What's There.

Kathleen Turner (Springfield): Sultry soap-opera actress who made an impression in *Body Heat* and has gone on to dramatic and comedic stardom. Films include: *The Man with Two Brains, Romancing the Stone, Who Framed Roger Rabbit* (voice of Jessica Rabbit).

Dianne Wiest (Kansas City): Emotive New York actress whose films include *Parenthood* and *Hannah and Her Sisters.*

Shelley Winters (b. Shirley Schrift, St. Louis): Tell-all cow whose career is totally incomprehensible. Films include: *A Place in the Sun, The Night of the Hunter, Lolita, The Poseidon Adventure.*

Jane Wyman (b. Shara Jane Fulks, St. Joseph): Former wife of Ronald Reagan whose credits include *The*

Lost Weekend, The Yearling, Johnny Belinda, and *Magnificent Obsession.*

WHAT'S THERE

Independence: Ginger Rogers's birthplace still stands at 100 West Moore Street, one block north of US 24, at Main Street. She grew up at 3306 Bellefontaine Avenue, just three blocks from Walt Disney, although Diz was 10 years older.

Kansas City: One of Walt Disney's boyhood homes, 3028 Bellefontaine Avenue, is now the Disney Home National Historic Landmark. Perversely, however, it is not marked. Another still-standing residence is at 3415 Charlotte. His first, failed cartoon company, Laugh-O-Gram, was based in a now-crumbling building at 1127 East 31st Street. Disney attended the Kansas City Art Institute; this is where Mickey Mouse was born.

Jean Harlow's childhood home and birthplace was at 3344 Olive Street. She also lived at 4409 Gillham Road and at 79th and Tracy, and attended the Barstow grade school at 15 Westport Road. All still exist, though the Barstow school has relocated.

Color films from the MGM and Columbia vaults are stored a hundred feet below Worlds of Fun Amusement Park, in an old limestone quarry. 13 miles northeast of town on I-435.

Jeanne Eagel's grave is at Calvary Cemetery, 6901 Troost. She's in Block 9, Section 183.

Marceline: Walt Disney's boyhood farm is located here. His family moved here from Chicago when he was five; he would return for visits later in life. Highway 5 and West Broadway.

Nevada: John Huston's birthplace, a neat brick house that is unoccupied but is used to store antiques, is at 404 South Adams Street. His father, actor Walter Huston, managed the local utilities. Huston, ever the raconteur, invented several boasts about his family and Nevada that city historians vehemently deny. One is that his grandfather won the whole town in a poker game. Another is that his dad burned the whole town down. Lies, lies, lies.

Slater: Steve McQueen's childhood home is on Thompson Lane. East of town, just past the city limits sign, take the first right onto Thompson. It's known as the Old Thurman House, and it's not in the bestest of condition.

St. Louis: One of the five known pairs of ruby slippers from *The Wizard of Oz* is sometimes displayed in a glass case in the gallery of St. Louis art dealer Philip Samuels. He paid $165,000 for the pair in 1988. 8112 Maryland Avenue.

OKLAHOMA

MADE IN OKLAHOMA

***The Grapes of Wrath* (McAlester, 1940):** The John Ford–Henry Fonda adaptation of John Steinbeck's great Okie saga was a credit to all involved.

***Tex* (Bixby, 1982):** The first of three S. E. Hinton adaptations—Matt Dillon appeared in all—and one of the first "sophisticated" Disney productions.

***The Outsiders* (Skiatook, Tulsa, 1983):** Francis Coppola's adaptation of Tulsa native S. E. Hinton's book that's such a hit with sensitive, self-pitying, *Breakfast Club*–ish high schoolers. Dream cast of heartthrobs: Rob Lowe, Tom Cruise, Ralph Macchio, Patrick Swayze, Emilio Estevez, C. Thomas Howell, Matt Dillon. Also a bomb-o 1990 Fox TV show.

***Fandango* (Tulsa, 1985):** This rowdy, unsuccessful road movie—presenting Judd Nelson at his most annoying—was shot all over the Midwest, but unfortunately

The burned house from *The Outsiders.* This site is now completely underwater.

preceded costar Kevin Costner's fame. In the film, an airplane cruises down a highway, Tulsa's Broken Arrow Expressway.

***Rain Man* (Cogar, El Reno, Guthrie, Hinton, 1988):** The Cogar location of this well-traveled Oscar winner was the APCO service station at the intersection of State Highways 152 and 37. Tom Cruise and Dustin Hoffman stop here to make a phone call.

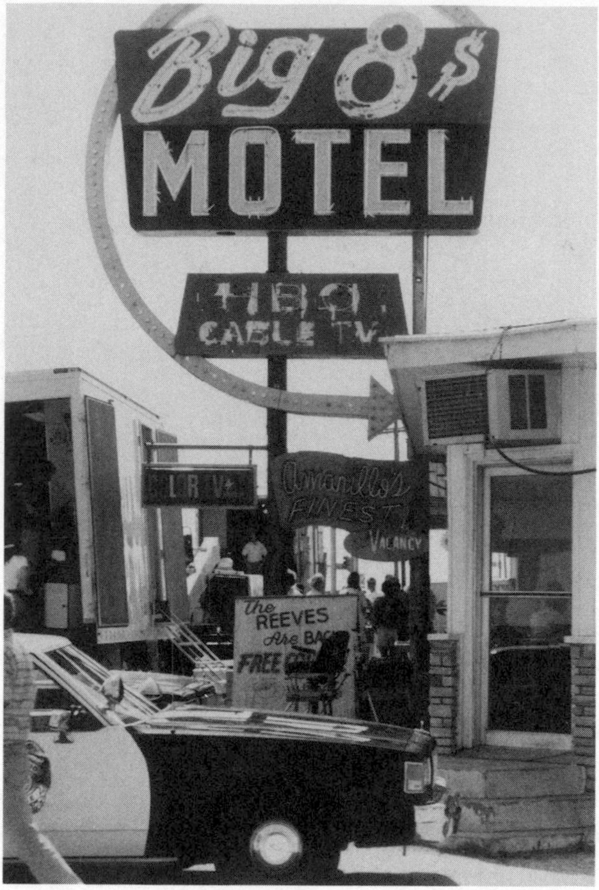

The Big 8 $ Motel in El Reno, seen in *Rain Man.*

The Big 8 $ Motel in El Reno was supposed to be set in Amarillo, Texas, so a neon sign was added: AMARILLO'S FINEST. Motel owners Kneles and Louise Reeves plan to keep the sign as it is. The motel was crucial to the plot; here Cruise learns that Hoffman was "Rain Man."

In Guthrie, Hoffman visits the doctor at the "Guthrie Clinic" at the corner of Oklahoma and Division streets. The garrulous 89-year-old man in the waiting room gabbing about the pony express was a local who was allowed

Rain Man's "Wapner" farmhouse in Hinton.

to babble, Robin Williams–like, while the cameras rolled.

The farmhouse where Cruise and Hoffman stop to watch "Wapner" is two miles southeast of Hinton on Highway 37.

OKLAHOMA'S GIFTS TO HOLLYWOOD

★ ★ ★ ★ ★ ★ ★ ★ ★ ★ ★ ★ ★ ★ ★ ★

Lon Chaney, Jr. (b. Creighton Chaney, Oklahoma City): The junior half of history's greatest father-son monster tandem. Junior played Son of Dracula, Frankenstein, the Mummy, and the Wolfman.

Blake Edwards (Tulsa): Hyperpretentious farceur director who started strong (*Breakfast at Tiffany's, The Pink Panther*), rode the Panther series into the ground—including one that starred Peter Sellers after he was dead—and finally went to Self-Love Hell (*Blake Edwards's That's Life, Blake Edwards's A Fine Mess.*)

James Garner (b. James Baumgarner, Norman): It's said that nobody can dislike this guy, except maybe vegetarians. Films include: *The Great Escape, The Americanization of Emily, The Skin Game, Murphy's Romance.*

Ron Howard (Duncan): Opie (and Richie Cunningham) turned out to be not a curiosity but a director and producer of no mean vision. Films include: *Grand Theft Auto, Night Shift, Splash, Willow, Parenthood.*

Jennifer Jones (b. Phyllis Isley, Tulsa): Protégé of powerful David O. Selznick who got some plum roles: *The Song of Bernadette, Duel in the Sun, Tender Is the Night.*

Vera Miles (Boise City): Janet Leigh's nosy sister in *Psycho* also appeared in *The Searchers* and Hitchcock's *The Wrong Man.*

Will Rogers (Oologah Lake): Rogers's film career is not remembered much today because: 1) for some reason Fox won't release his 21 talkies; and 2) his films are pretty unwatchable today. But he made 75 altogether and was a top box office attraction of the 1930s. Films include: *Judge Priest, Steamboat 'Round the Bend, David Harum.*

The Will Rogers statue in Claremore. *(Courtesy of Julie Kuehndorf)*

WHAT'S THERE

Claremore: The Will Rogers Memorial is the biggest thing in this part of the country, except for the world's largest McDonald's, in Vinita. The impressive museum displays, among many items, his tunic and ball and chain from *A Connecticut Yankee in King Arthur's Court,* his hat and ropes from *The Ropin' Fool* (Rogers's silent classic), and the contents of his pockets the day in 1935 that he crashed in the Alaskan tundra. The film archive shows videos of about 40 of his films, and is working to transfer the original prints from nitrate to safety stock.

Note the shoes of the Will Rogers statue: they've been burnished by admirers for luck. (At the Tulsa Airport is a bust of Rogers—there they rub his nose. At Will Rogers High in Tulsa, they also rub the nose.) One mile west of town on Route 88. Open 8–5 daily, year-round.

The region also has a turnpike, schools, and many other parts of the superstructure dedicated to its favorite son (though some now clamor for Ron Howard).

Dewey: Tom Mix Museum. Mix was a marshal here for a few years before beginning his movie career. The

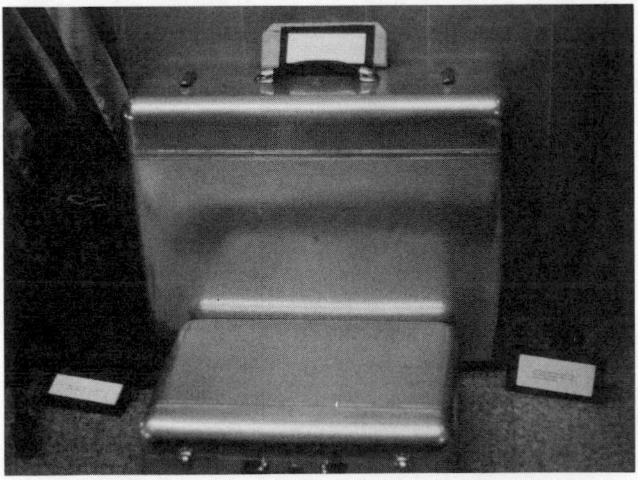

Tom Mix's suitcase of death at the Tom Mix Museum. *(Courtesy of Roadside America)*

museum, which displays his suitcase and boots of death, started in 1968 as a way of bringing tourism to Dewey. John Wayne visited here the following year.

There's a replica of Mix's horse, Tony, near the entrance. Some of his serial westerns are shown here in scratchy prints with broken sprocket holes. 721 North Delaware, at Don Tylor Avenue.

The Will Rogers statue at the Cowboy Hall of Fame.

Oklahoma City: The superslick Cowboy Hall of Fame has within it a Hall of Fame of Western Film. Here are portraits and saddles of western heroes: Rex Allen, Gene Autry, Walter Brennan (by Norman Rockwell), Gary Cooper, Glenn Ford, William S. Hart, Jack Hoxie, Joel McCrea (looking old and puffy), Tom Mix, Slim Pickens, Roy Rogers and Dale Evans, Barbara Stanwyck, James Stewart, and Robert Taylor.

The collection also features Tex Ritter's hat, Dale Robertson's 1873 Colt .45 revolver, a memorial coffee cup presented by Duke to Walter Brennan during *Rio Bravo*

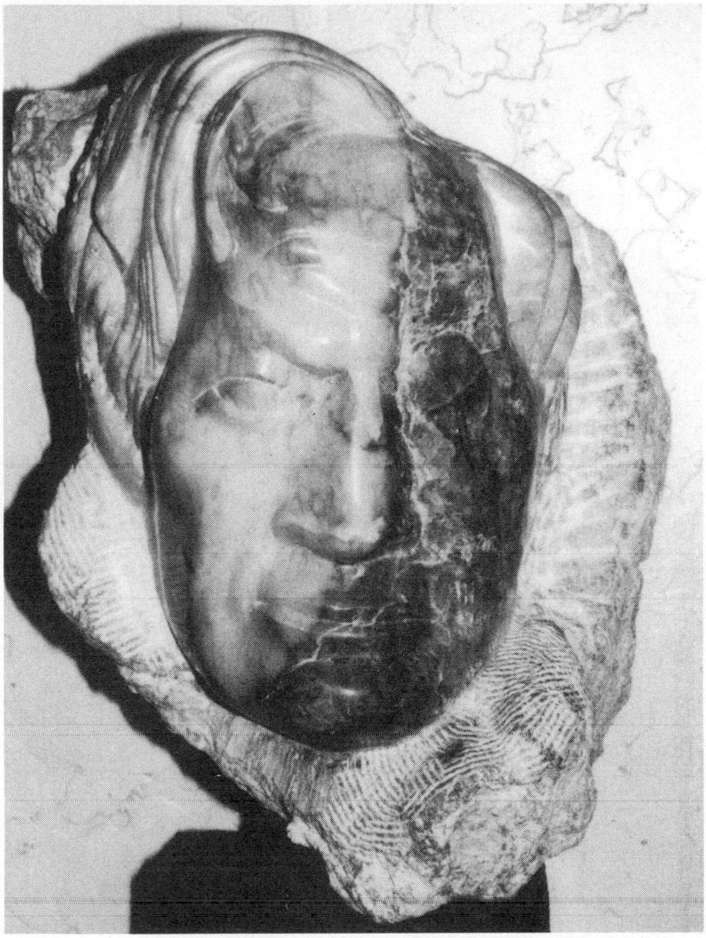

Scary statue of "The Duke" at the Cowboy Hall of Fame.

(WALTER FROM DUKE it says; the other side has a bad drawing of Brennan and a caption: "Which one of you b—— killed my dog"), and Smiley Burnett's hat and scarf.

An entire room is devoted to the valuable John Wayne Collection, which includes a slew of Hopi Kachina dolls; a statue of Duke zooming by on a horse; Duke's Buddhas and Chinese earthenware pigs; the Great Western Arms .45 used in *The Shootist*; the *True Grit* Colt .45, belt, holster, and rifle; a bust of John "Pappy" Ford; and a bizarre "artistic" bust called The Duke. A theater within the room shows film clips. 1700 N.E. 63rd Street.

Oologah Lake: Will Rogers Birthplace: the preserved home is open to the public. The home was originally on a less picturesque site, so it was moved here for the tourists. But it's still in the middle of nowhere off a dirt road, one mile north of Oologah on US 109, then one mile east on State Highway 88.

Shawnee: Wheels-Deals-Antiques has 110 vehicles from 1903 to 1941, including a Carole Lombard car. State Highway 18, north of I-40.

TENNESSEE

MADE IN TENNESSEE

***Raintree County* (Reelfoot Lake, 1956):** This was the setting for the film's dramatic ending. Reelfoot Lake is in the northwest part of the state.

***Walking Tall* (1972), *Part 2, Walking Tall* (1974),** and ***Final Chapter, Walking Tall* (1976):** The series was shot in McNairie County, where real-life sheriff Buford Pusser cleaned house and was, in the end, assassinated. *Final Chapter* is about Hollywood coming to make the first film. See What's There: Pigeon Forge.

***At Close Range* (1985):** The first great Sean-Madonna collaboration. (Madonna wrote and sang the film's theme song, "Live to Tell.") Christopher Walken is a snake-eyed thief who kills his son. Set in rural western Pennsylvania.

MEMPHIS '89

***Great Balls of Fire* (1989):** This nutty, underappreciated bio of Jerry Lee Lewis used many historic locations, including the newly remodeled Orpheum Theater and the exterior of Sun Studio (706 Union Street). The interior of the legendary recording studio, however, was duplicated elsewhere. Also filmed in Marion, Arkansas, and at the Jet Center in West Memphis.

Mystery Train **(1989):** Cool-school-grad-summa-cum-laude Jim Jarmusch shot at Sun Studio and a bunch of defunct locales: the Arcade Hotel, on Chaucer Street (defunct but re-dressed for the film); the Arcade Diner, also on Chaucer; the city's original train station (near the hotel and diner, now defunct); Stax Studios (defunct, defunct, defunct, but the facade is to be moved into the jazzy new multimillion-dollar Memphis Pyramid). The film's Shades Bar was built on the site of an old optometrist's office.

NASHVILLE: "I KNOW—LET'S SHOOT IN RYMAN AUDITORIUM!"

Nashville **(1975):** The film's climax occurs at The Parthenon, the world's only full-scale model of the foreign one. It's in Centennial Park, West End Avenue and 25th Avenue North, and was built from 1920 to 1931. The film also shot in Ryman Auditorium, former home of the Grand Ole Opry (hillbilly slang for "Grand Old Opera").

Coal Miner's Daughter **(1980):** Scenes for this bio of Loretta Lynn were shot in . . . Ryman Auditorium.

Honkytonk Man **(1982):** Clint dies, but at least he gets to play . . . Ryman Auditorium.

Sweet Dreams **(1984):** Jessica Lange plays Patsy Cline singing in . . . Ryman Auditorium.

TENNESSEE'S GIFTS TO HOLLYWOOD

★ ★ ★ ★ ★ ★ ★ ★ ★ ★ ★ ★ ★ ★ ★ ★

James Agee (Knoxville): Probably the most highly regarded film critic in history. Yes, even more than Rex Reed. He was also involved in writing two great scripts: *The African Queen* and *The Night of the Hunter.*

Dolly Parton (Sevierville): Really a singer who appears in movies, but impossible to dislike. Films include: *Nine to Five, Steel Magnolias, The Best Little Whorehouse* *in Texas,* and *Rhinestone.* See What's There: Pigeon Forge.

Cybill Shepherd (Memphis): Top model cast by Peter Bogdanovich to great effect in the *The Last Picture Show.* Her career sank in the 1970s as she made one bad Bogdanovich too many, then was revived by the hit TV show "Moonlighting." The kind of celeb who figures to go in and out of the limelight for years. Films include: *The Heartbreak Kid, Chances Are, Texasville.*

WHAT'S THERE

Adamsville: The Buford Pusser Home and Museum, at 342 Pusser Street, contains personal artifacts of the *Walking Tall* sheriff, and is open for tours.

Crossville: Talavera Club is a dinner house owned by Amy Brissler, a former Hollywood costume designer (1935–1970) who will display her old sketches and photos of stars, a rehearsal costume from *Gone with the Wind,* a Bette Davis Queen Elizabeth costume, or a beaded black lace Mae West dress if you ask. West of town, take exit 311 off I-40. Go one mile south on Plateau Road, then one mile west on US 70, then three miles north on Jim Garrett Road. Reservations required: 615/277-3749, dinner only.

McMinnville: Here's the only place anywhere you can watch a movie 300 feet underground. Cumberland Caverns, the second largest cave system in the United States, boasts the Hall of the Magic King, the largest cave room in the East; it's 600 feet long, 150 feet wide, and 140 feet high. Besides a dining room that seats 500, a 15-foot, 1,500-pound chandelier (from a Brooklyn theater), and a theater pipe organ, the room has a stage, equipped for live shows and movies. It's seven miles southeast of town, 30 stories below Highway 8. 615/668-4396.

Memphis: Elvis stuff. Ask around.

The Heartbreak Hotel restaurant in Memphis. No, it's not down at the end of Lonely Street.

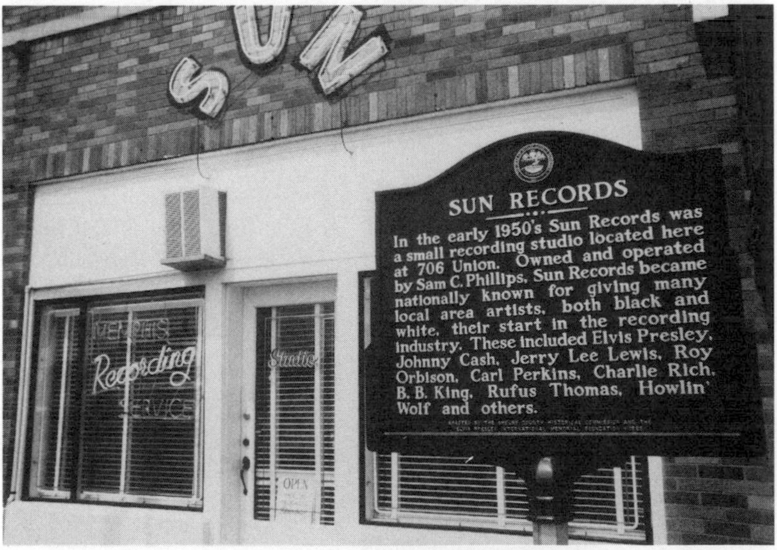

Sun Records in Memphis. Elvis played here.

Nashville: If you want to see the ever-popular Ryman Auditorium, home of the Grand Ole Opry from 1943 to 1974 and site of numerous location shoots, you can take a tour for $2. 116 Fifth Avenue North.

Pall Mall: Alvin York's grave is located at Alvin York's Farm and Grist Mill. York was a pacifist who became a much-decorated World War I hero. Gary Cooper won an Oscar for portraying him in *Sergeant York* (1941). Highway 127.

Pigeon Forge: The Smoky Mountain Car Museum has the real James Bond Aston-Martin used in *Goldfinger*

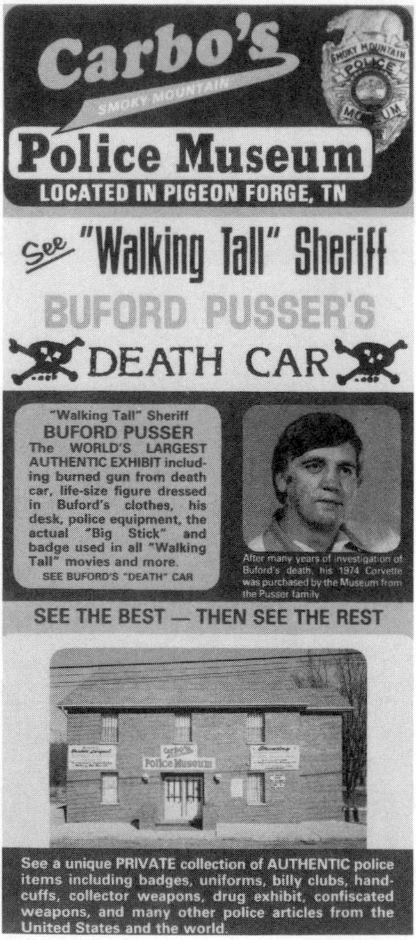

Carbo's Smoky Mountain Police Museum. *(Courtesy of Dr. and Mrs. B. C. Carbo, Carbo's Police Museum, Pigeon Forge, Tennessee 37863)*

and *Thunderball,* an Elvis Mercedes, Buford Pusser's 1968 Toronado patrol car, and Billy Carter's service truck. Highway 441.

Carbo's Police Museum loudly advertises the fact that they have Buford Pusser's death car. They also possess Pusser's burned gun from the death car, life-sized figures dressed in his clothes, his desk, and the actual big stick and badge used in the movies. Highway 441.

"Dolly's First Hamburger . . . You Too Can Enjoy One of These at Mountain Dan's," Dollywood.

Dollywood is a disappointing theme park that uses Dolly Parton—who does not own it—as a front person. Off Highway 441.

Sevierville: Not only does this Smoky Mountain Stripville have tourist attractions based on Fred Flintstone's Bedrock *and* a Hee-Haw City, but it also boasts a bronze, life-sized statue of favorite daughter Dolly Parton.

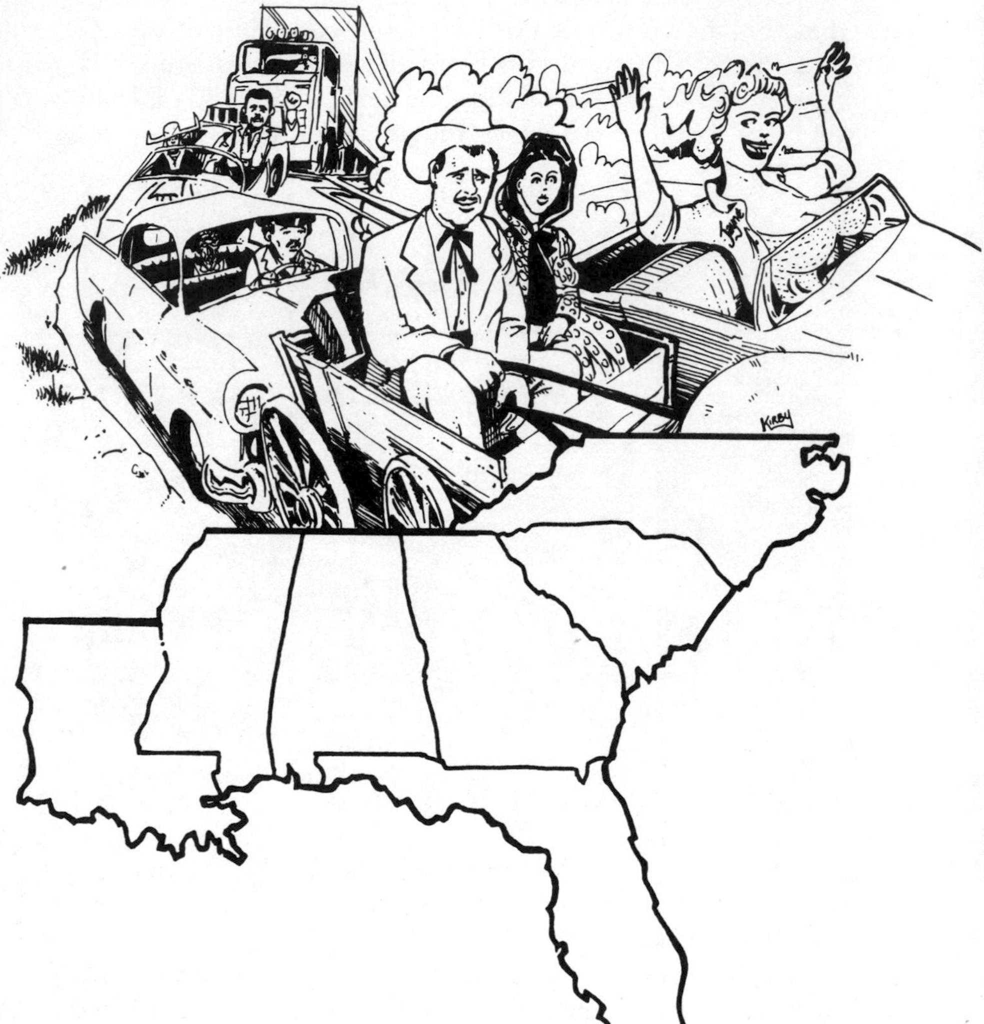
KIRBY

Chapter 7

DIXIE

- Alabama
- Florida
- Georgia
- Louisiana
- Mississippi
- North Carolina
- South Carolina

MADE IN ALABAMA

BURT AND SALLY

***Stay Hungry* (Birmingham, 1975):** Sally and Jeff Bridges in Bob Rafelson's low-key, episodic narrative about bodybuilders, including Arnold Schwarzenegger.

***Hooper* (Tuscaloosa, 1978):** Burt's stunt boss, Hal Needham, took the reins for this movie about Hollywood stuntmen starring Burt and Sally.

***Norma Rae* (Opelika, Auburn, 1978):** Sally really, really gained credibility—with an Oscar—from this pot-stirrer.

***Back Roads* (Mobile, 1981):** Sally is anticute in this, the first production of CBS Pictures—and not surprisingly one of the last. Also shot in Brownsville, Texas.

***Stroker Ace* (Talladega, 1983):** Sally's given way to Loni now, but that's not the problem with this car-chase epic. The Burt film that caused his public to say enough is enough. Great title, eh?

ALSO . . .

***The Phenix City Story* (Phenix City, 1955):** Phil Karlson's cult film about lawyer who returns to small town to take on corruption.

***To Kill a Mockingbird* (Monroeville, 1963):** Gregory Peck won an Oscar as a lawyer defending a black in the rabid South. Robert Duvall plays the mentally deficient guilty party.

***The Heart Is a Lonely Hunter* (Selma, 1967):** Nice use of small-town South as Alan Arkin plays a too-perfect deaf-mute, helping all and sundry with their problems.

***Close Encounters of the Third Kind* (Mobile, 1977):** Spielberg filmed some major scenes in a World War II dirigible hangar here, reputedly the largest indoor set ever constructed. Scenes included the UFO base, the Indiana roadway, and the side of Devils Tower. The production also bought a house here for domestic scenes.

Space Camp **(Huntsville, 1986):** Huntsville's Space Center, which actually hosts a real-life space camp for kids, was the location for this incredibly ill-timed feature—it was in production when the *Challenger* exploded.

ALABAMA'S GIFTS TO HOLLYWOOD

★ ★ ★ ★ ★ ★ ★ ★ ★ ★ ★ ★ ★ ★ ★ ★

Tallulah Bankhead (Huntsville): A dangerously witty theater actress whose best film by far was *Lifeboat.* Her father was Speaker of the House William Brockman Bankhead.

Louise Fletcher (Birmingham): After copping an Oscar in 1975 for *One Flew Over the Cuckoo's Nest,* Fletcher thanked her deaf parents in sign language. At least, it's *assumed* they're deaf. Often confused with Ellen Burstyn, who won the Oscar in 1976.

Dean Jones (Decatur): Unbelievably limp star of Disney's *That Darn Cat* and *The Love Bug* who is now a born-again Christian cable performer.

ALABAMA IS TV COUNTRY

Pat Buttram (Addison): The inimitable Mr. Haney of "Green Acres," and Gene Autry's western sidekick.

Kate Jackson (Birmingham): An original "Charlie's Angel," also starred in "Dark Shadows," "The Rookies," "Scarecrow and Mrs. King."

George Lindsey (Jasper): Goober from "The Andy Griffith Show" and "Hee Haw."

Jim Nabors (Sylacauga): Gomer from "The Andy Griffith Show" and later "Gomer Pyle, U.S.M.C." Now growing macadamia nuts in Hawaii.

Wayne Rogers (Birmingham): Trapper John from the TV "M*A*S*H." Like fellow cast member MacLean Stevenson, when he struck out on his own he struck out but good, except for the semihit sitcom "House Calls."

MADE IN FLORIDA

COULD BE ANYWHERE

You might think "Miami" when you think of Florida, but the truth is that "Miami Vice" has overexposed the town, and little location filming has gone on there in the past decade, despite its favorable climate and the state's big push for film production.

A trend in Sun Belt filmmaking is to shoot a film in a specific locale even though the story has nothing to do with that locale; the filmmakers simply like the weather here. This is the kind of production that state film commissions try desperately to woo, and sort of the whole point to Orlando's Disney and Universal Studios. Two films fitting this bill, besides the Disney productions (see What's There: Orlando), are *Absence of Malice* (1981) and *Making Mr. Right* (1987), both shot around Miami.

THE SUN BELT'S MATCHING WHITE SHOES

Some films, like *Cocoon,* make use of Florida because of its preponderance of old people. Others, such as *Married to the Mob* or *The Palm Beach Story,* play off its image as a vacationland. *Jaws 3-D,* which was shot at Orlando's Sea World, was not only the one chance you'll ever get to see Dennis Quaid in 3-D, but also used a well-known location with great promotional value.

Surprisingly, though, most films set in the state have nothing to do with the traditional Florida clichés. The productions make use of the varied terrain and dependable climate, and the spectrum of films produced in the state—dating back to a 1923 D. W. Griffith melodrama, *The White Rose,* which he filmed in Hialeah—is fairly astonishing.

EVIL UNDER THE SUN

Florida's tropicality offers filmmakers the exoticness of an African adventure with the convenience of water you don't have to boil before drinking.

***Wild Harvest* (Homestead, 1947):** *Grapes of Wrath* clone set during a San Joaquin Valley harvest. The sadistic foreman makes female migrants eat dirt; he is later mutilated with pruning shears. Narrated by Walter Winchell.

***2,000 Maniacs* (St. Cloud, 1964):** Perhaps the greatest achievement of the cartoonishly gory Herschell Gordon Lewis, the film is about a defunct Rebel stronghold that arises, Brigadoonlike, to wreak havoc on Yankee tourists. Not recommended by the state tourist bureau.

***Body Heat* (1981):** William Hurt is bamboozled by Kathleen Turner in this highly atmospheric Palm Beach–area film noir.

***Licence to Kill* (Key West, Monroe County, 1989):** One of the least anticipated James Bond adventures, and a box-office disappointment.

SPRING BREAK

Where the Boys Are* (1960) and *Where the Boys Are '84 were shot in the deposed spring break capital of America: Fort Lauderdale. Crackdowns on rowdyism have led miffed collegians up to Daytona Beach or to South Padre Island, Texas.

ALSO . . .

***Thirty Seconds over Tokyo* (Pensacola, 1944):** A manly cast in a WWII actioner about the first raid of Japan. Shot at Hurlburt Field at Eglin Field Naval Air Station.

***Honky Tonk Freeway* (Mount Dora, 1981):** The entire town was painted pink for this film, about a Florida town bypassed by a new freeway. This watchable bomb is credited with the largest budget-to-box-office ratio of all time, but there are lots worse films than this—the next one, in fact.

Rude Awakening **(Wekiwa State Park, 1989):** The South American jungle scene was filmed here.

FLORIDA'S GIFTS TO HOLLYWOOD

★ ★ ★ ★ ★ ★ ★ ★ ★ ★ ★ ★ ★ ★ ★ ★

Faye Dunaway (Bascom): Ms. Cheekbones, star of *Bonnie and Clyde, Chinatown, Network,* and *The Handmaid's Tale.*

Buddy Ebsen (Orlando): Jed Clampett used to be a movie hoofer, appearing in *Broadway Melody* films in the thirties and other light fare over the years. He attended Howard Middle School in Orlando.

Stepin Fetchit (b. Lincoln Theodore Monroe Andrew Perry, Key West): Fetchit, who presaged the trend of blacks renouncing their plantation names by about 45 years, took his stage name from a racehorse he won some money on. (Amazingly, in 1969, basketball star Lew Alcindor won $1,000 on a horse named "Kareem Abdul Jabbar.") Fetchit played character roles in the twenties and thirties, not all of them racially insulting.

Butterfly McQueen (Tampa): Famous as Prissy, the squeaky-voiced slave in *Gone with the Wind.* She was unable to obtain roles that extended her range much, so she left the business.

Sidney Poitier (Miami): This sophisticated actor and director was raised in the Bahamas. Films include: *The Defiant Ones, Porgy and Bess, A Patch of Blue, In the Heat of the Night, To Sir with Love,* and *Guess Who's Coming to Dinner,* in which he plays a flawless, perfect man engaged to Katharine Hepburn's average-looking daughter, supposedly causing great consternation. Also directed the hit comedy *Stir Crazy.*

Burt Reynolds (Palm Beach): Reynolds played football at Florida State and was raised in Palm Beach, but he was born in Georgia. His directorial debut was *Gator,* based on his experiences in the Sunshine State.

WHAT'S THERE

Cypress Gardens: *Easy to Love,* an Esther Williams vehicle, was shot at this longtime tourist attraction that sadly lacks mermaids. Off Highway 540.

Hawthorne: Marjorie Kinnan Rawlings's Cross Creek Homestead, a state historic site supported by decaying pilings, is open for tours. It was a location for *The Yearling,* which was based on her novel, and *Cross Creek,* which was based on her life. Route 3.

Jupiter: In the lobby of the Burt Reynolds Dinner Theater are photos of stars who've appeared here: Farrah Fawcett, Sally Field, Charles Nelson Reilly. Burt has performed in and directed productions here. 1001 East Indian Town Road. Info: 305/747-5261.

Key Largo: The original *African Queen* is docked by Holiday Inn owner James Hendricks. The boat was built in 1912 in England and christened *The Livingston,* then commissioned in 1951 for the film. It had fallen on hard times when Hendricks, in 1982, bought it in northern Florida and proceeded to restore it. He's since run it all over the world.

Unfortunately, he was forbidden by law to carry tourists on the boat because of its foreign roots. So he appealed to Congress and in 1989 received special dispensation to give rides on the *African Queen.* Yay! Info: 305/451-2121.

Lake Buena Vista: Disney and Universal Studios movie theme parks. No surprises here, except when the Universal rides are actually working. Films shot at Disney Studios: *Splash Too, Ernest Saves Christmas. Parenthood,* set in St. Louis, was shot at Universal.

Miami: Our Lady of Mercy Cemetery has Jackie Gleason's mausoleum. The Greek-style crypt has "And away we go!" chiseled into the marble steps leading to the tomb. It's on a slope overlooking the water, resembling a golf course. 11411 N.W. 25th Street.

HMS Bounty. This tourist attraction, based on *Mutiny on the Bounty,* used to be in St. Petersburg, where it featured the salty voices of Clark Gable and Charles Laughton. The *Bounty* is undergoing renovation in Savannah at this writing, so call first: 305/375-0486. If it's closed, just head on down to Key Largo for the *African Queen* instead.

North Miami: The Mulholland Drive Cafe is co-owned by Patrick Swayze. 3599 N.E. 207th Street.

St. Augustine: The Tragedy in U.S. History Museum, a truly unique attraction, displays two vehicles that have played major roles in our nation's history: Jayne Mansfield's death car and the death car from the movie *Bonnie and Clyde.* It's at 7 Williams Street, across from the Old Jail, at the turnoff for the Fountain of Youth.

Silver Springs: A popular tourist attraction—even though it doesn't have mermaids—that has also been a popular movie location through the years. It was a setting for the Johnny Weissmuller Tarzan movies, three James Bond films (*Thunderball, Never Say Never Again,* and *Moonraker*), *The Creature from the Black Lagoon* and *Revenge of the Creature,* and many more. One mile east of Ocala on Route 40.

Wakulla Springs: *The Creature from the Black Lagoon* was also filmed at this low-key swamp resort that features swamp tours and a pole-vaulting fish named Henry. The secluded lodge has simple, inexpensive rooms. South of Tallahassee, off Route 267. Reservations: 904/640-7011.

Weeki Wachee: Mermaids at last! *Neptune's Daughter,* starring Esther Williams, was shot here, which is as good an excuse as any to visit this classic roadside attraction, where mermaids drink R.C. Cola underwater. At the junction of Routes 19 and 50.

West Palm Beach: The Hanley-Hazelden Center: spot the celebs! 5200 East Avenue.

MADE IN GEORGIA

ATLANTA, BURNING AND NOT

***Gone with the Wind* (Atlanta, 1939):** See What's There.

***Sharkey's Machine* (Atlanta, 1981):** Burt Reynolds shows the world that Atlanta is now an urban area. Rachel Ward's first big film.

***The Slugger's Wife* (Atlanta, 1985):** Neil Simon shows the world that he now has no shame.

***Driving Miss Daisy* (1989):** Miss Daisy's home was at 822 Lullwater Road, in the Druid Hills section of town. The Biltmore Hotel was the site of the Martin Luther King Banquet. Several companies offer "Driving Miss Daisy" tours of the city to cash in on this surprise hit and Oscar winner. These things come and go; check with the Atlanta Tourist Bureau.

AND . . .

***Deliverance* (Tallulah Falls, Chattooga River, 1972):** Jon Voight and Burt Reynolds in a gripping backwoods adventure based on the novel by Georgian James Dickey, who plays a sheriff. The film was shot in sequence, and dialogue was looped—recorded without sync sound and dubbed later. Following the film's release, the county enjoyed a major influx of tourists wanting to relive the adventure (or squeal like pigs); this economic boon led to the creation of a state film commission.

***Conrack* (Saint Simons Island, 1974):** Jon Voight is a white teacher at a black school on this isolated island, the childhood home of Jim Brown.

***Glory* (Savannah, Jekyll Island, 1989):** This historic old town stood in for Boston in the film; troops parade down River Street. Battle scenes were shot on Jekyll Island.

GEORGIA'S GIFTS TO HOLLYWOOD

★ ★ ★ ★ ★ ★ ★ ★ ★ ★ ★ ★ ★ ★ ★ ★

Kim Basinger (Athens): A lippy blond whose star continues to ascend. Films include: *Batman, The Natural, Never Say Never Again.*

Melvyn Douglas (b. Melvyn Edouard Hesselberg, Macon): Gruffly suave, Douglas starred opposite some of Hollywood's top leading ladies, including Greta Garbo in *As You Desire Me, Ninotchka,* and *Two-Faced Woman.* Other films include *Being There, Mr. Blandings Builds His Dream House, Hud,* in which he played Paul Newman's father, and *The Candidate,* in which he played Robert Redford's father.

Oliver Hardy (Harlem): One-half of one of the greatest comedy teams ever, Hardy started his career in the

Historical marker honoring Oliver Hardy's birthplace, Harlem. *(Courtesy of the City of Harlem)*

1910s but didn't really click until being teamed with Brit Stan Laurel in 1926. See What's There.

Nunnally Johnson (Columbus): A journalist wooed by Hollywood, Johnson enjoyed a long, successful screenwriting career. Films include: *The Grapes of Wrath, The Three Faces of Eve, The Man in the Gray Flannel Suit, The Dirty Dozen.*

Stacy Keach (Savannah): Tough fireplug type of actor with flashes of intelligence. Films include: *Up in Smoke, Fat City, The Long Riders.*

DeForest Kelley (Atlanta): *Star Trek* Dr. "Bones" McCoy used to have a real film career, appearing in *Raintree County* (as a Southern officer who dies), *Gunfight at the O.K. Corral,* and others.

Burt Reynolds (Waycross): Reynolds, the second biggest box office star of the 1970s, was born here but grew up in Palm Beach, Florida. True to his roots, he's done a lot of filming in the southeast.

Alice Walker (Eatonton): Walker and other celebs attended the premiere of Steven Spielberg's adaptation of her novel *The Color Purple* when it opened in 1985 at Eatonton's Pex Theatre.

Joanne Woodward (Thomasville): This actress broke into the biz with a bang, winning an Oscar at age 27 for *The Three Faces of Eve.* Other films include *Rachel, Rachel* (the first film directed by her husband, Paul Newman) and *Mr. and Mrs. Bridge.*

WHAT'S THERE

WHERE'S TARA?

Clayton County, Georgia, is the setting for the Tara mansion in Margaret Mitchell's *Gone with the Wind.* For years the county has been trying to raise funds to build a Tara that would be exactly like the movie Tara and would display genuine artifacts from the film. A few years back, a 1 percent Tara sales tax was voted down, and boosters are still reeling. Jonesboro, in the heart of Clayton County, features a Tara Boulevard and an old dwelling called Ashley Oaks. The Jonesboro Chamber of Commerce (8712 Tara Boulevard) offers a walking tour that includes the 1898 courthouse where Mitchell researched her novel.

Meanwhile, Georgia's Coweta County was cruising along with its own Tara. An investment group purchased the facade from the movie's Tara and the home of the Fitzgeralds, who were Mitchell's grandparents—this was said to be inspiration for her Tara. All was fine until around the 50th anniversary of the film's release, when plans inexplicably collapsed.

Herb Bridges, a prominent *GWTW* specialist, has offered to contribute his priceless collection—including Rhett's top hat and Scarlett's Paris bonnet—to any Tara that can get it together. So far, no takers.

So, Tara lovers, you might ask yourselves, "With all the movie-related tourist attractions out there, how come there's no Tara near Atlanta?" Answer: Don't ask me. One place that offers up *GWTW* memorabilia is the Atlanta Museum, a one-man operation inside an old house at 537–39 Peachtree Street NE. Unfortunately, the proprietor, J. H. Elliott, Jr., is more than likely to be away from the premises, so you'd better phone ahead: 404/872-8233.

The most reliable *GWTW* experience in Atlanta—as of this writing—is at the CNN Centre 6 theater, which unspools *Gone with the Wind* twice a day, every day, on Screen 6. 100 Techwood Avenue SW.

Atlanta: The Fox Theatre, a 1929 Oriental-style movie palace, is perhaps the grandest of all existent Fox theaters. Tours, run by the Atlanta Preservation Center, are given Mondays, Thursdays, and Saturdays. 660 Peachtree Street NE at Kimball (Ponce de Leon).

The downtown Atlanta Hilton and Towers is a recent movie shrine—this is where Rob Lowe had video fun (Room 2845) and got caught. Corner of Courtland and Harris N.E. Reservations: 800/HILTONS. He met his

Brochure from Atlanta's Fox Theatre. *(Courtesy of Atlanta Landmarks, Inc.)*

femmes fatales at Rio's nightclub, which is now closed but was on Luckie Street N.W.

Braselton: Kim Basinger bought this small town (population 500) 53 miles northeast of Atlanta in 1989 for $20 million. Possibilities included turning it into a film center and tourist attraction. (Kenny Rogers was in town in 1982 filming *Six Pack.*) But so far, there's nothing to indicate the movie star has any connection to the town at all. There's not even a movie theater. All you can do is go there and hope for one of her infrequent visits.

Carrollton: Actress Susan Hayward's grave is in Our Lady's Memory Garden at the Cemetery of Our Lady of Perpetual Help Church. Her tombstone reads Mrs. F. E. Chalkley, but a nearby sign translates. It's on Center Point Road, off Highway 113, north of town.

Harlem: Oliver Hardy's birth site is now Barton's Coin-Operated Laundry, on South Hicks Street, behind City Hall. There's a state historical marker in front of City Hall. His father's buried in the local cemetery. In October 1989 the town hosted the first annual Oliver Hardy Festival. None of his boyhood homes in Madison and Milledgeville still exists.

LOUISIANA

MADE IN LOUISIANA

FAULKNER

***The Long Hot Summer* (1958):** Based on Faulkner's short story *The Hamlet.* The cast, directed by Martin Ritt, includes Paul Newman, Joanne Woodward, and Orson Welles.

***The Sound and the Fury* (1959):** Ritt and Woodward returned a year later to try Faulkner again in Louisiana, this time with Yul Brynner.

NORTON

***Mandingo* (1975):** Boxer Ken Norton was on top of the world in the mid seventies, and he truly shines in this slave adventure.

***Drum* (1976):** More Norton means more KERPOW!

SCARY MUTANTS

***Easy Rider* (Morganza, New Orleans, 1969):** The boys run into a little trouble in Morganza, and Jack Nicholson ends up staying.

The restaurant in *Easy Rider*, with local stars of the film, including the Cat Man, out front.

***Return to Boggy Creek* (1977):** Sequel Number One, starring Dawn Wells of "Gilligan's Island."

***Southern Comfort* (1981):** Lost National Guardsmen get wiped out by spooky, inbred swamp Cajuns.

***Steel Magnolias* (Natchitoches, 1989):** Arrggh! Shirley MacLaine and Sally Field are coming to get you! Natchitoches, famous for its meat pies, is the hometown of the film's writer, Robert Harling (and also of meat pie Rex Reed).

A MOVIE TOUR OF NEW ORLEANS

***Angel Heart* (1987):** Mildly controversial voodoo film noir shot in the Maple Leaf Club, also up and down Magazine Street. Location shooting outside town, in rural Louisiana, took the filmmakers to Napoleanville and Laurel Valley (near Thibodeaux), which was the voodoo-daffy plantation village in the film.

***The Big Easy* (1987):** The climactic shootout takes place at Blaine Kern's warehouse, where new Mardi Gras floats are assembled and old ones are stored. It's at the Mississippi River, First and Tchoupatoulis. Dennis Quaid wines and dines Ellen Barkin at Tipitina's, where the Neville Brothers hold court. The Cajun band party, where Quaid plays from the porch, was shot at Bruning House, at West End, in Bucktown, behind Bruning's restaurant. Soon after the filming of *The Big Easy*, which deals with police corruption, the state film commission was nailed in a major kickback scandal.

***Blaze* (also Baton Rouge, Winnfield, 1989):** Based on the romance between Louisiana governor Earl Long and flamboyant stripper Blaze Starr, the production shot along St. Louis Street pretending it was Bourbon Street. It was simply much easier to get permission from merchants on St. Louis than it would have been on legendary, heavily trafficked Bourbon.

GREAT FOOD, GREAT MUSIC, GREAT VOODOO

Other New Orleans films through the years include:

***Birth of the Blues* (1941):** This Bing Crosby vehicle featured great jazz, thus capturing the essence of New Orleans better than any actual location shooting could. Well, sort of.

***Panic in the Streets* (1950):** A gangster on the lam unwittingly carries a deadly, supercontagious disease. This gripping film noir, directed by Elia Kazan, shot extensively in New Orleans. An irony of the film is that among the cast is Zero Mostel, who was blacklisted in the McCarthy era; his director, Kazan, snitched and got off scot-free.

***A Streetcar Named Desire* (1951):** Stool pigeon Kazan returned to town a year later for Tennessee Williams's "ode" to Elysian Fields lowlifes, with landmark performances by Marlon Brando and Vivien Leigh.

***The Buccaneer* (1958):** The last film produced by Cecil B. DeMille, who had earlier directed the 1938 version, celebrates the region's number one legend, Jean Lafitte, and the War of 1812, with Charlton Heston as Andrew Jackson.

***King Creole* (1958):** Arguably Elvis's best movie, it costars Carolyn "Morticia" Jones, Vic Morrow, and Walter Matthau.

***Mardi Gras* (1958):** Arguably Pat Boone's best movie. Oh boy.

***The Cincinnati Kid* (1965):** Pete Rose, a hustling, crewcut youngster from . . . No, it's Steve McQueen in a high-stakes pokerathon.

***Pretty Baby* (1978):** Louis Malle lovingly directs his babe, Susan Sarandon, and 12-year-old Brooke Shields is sold to Keith Carradine. The production was also filmed in Hattiesburg, Mississippi.

***Cat People* (1982):** It was billed as a remake of the great 1942 horror film, but instead director Paul Schrader, like some pinhead Mardi Gras reveler, chose to use the New Orleans location as an excuse for pointless weirdness.

***Tightrope* (1984):** This tense Clint Eastwood vehicle was shot mostly at night, for that rain-slicked-street-on-the-sleazy-side-of-town look.

***Down by Law* (1986):** After a New Orleans prologue, Jim Jarmusch's nutty version of "Streetcar '86" takes his oddball characters into the swamps and backwoods of southern Louisiana.

***No Mercy* (1986):** An unfunny *Down by Law* with Richard Gere and Kim Basinger, this also ends up in the swamps.

***Miller's Crossing* (1990):** Joel and Ethan Coen chose New Orleans not for the romantic Vieux Carre ambience but for the decaying industrial superstructure that hasn't been much modified over the years—specifically since 1929, when the film is set.

Also see What's There.

AND . . .

***Bellizaire the Cajun* (1986):** Authentic-feeling but slow look at nineteenth-century Cajun life.

***The Blob* (Abbeville, 1988):** Better special effects, but not a better film, than the original.

***Everybody's All American* (Baton Rouge, 1988):** Dennis Quaid eases off on the *Big Easy* accent a tad playing a faded Louisiana State football hero. Real LSU games were used for filming: they'd shoot before games and at halftime.

LOUISIANA'S GIFTS TO HOLLYWOOD

★ ★ ★ ★ ★ ★ ★ ★ ★ ★ ★ ★ ★ ★ ★ ★

Dorothy Lamour (b. Mary Leta Dorothy Kaumeyer, New Orleans): Former Miss New Orleans who played object of lust in numerous Hope-Crosby "Road" pictures.

John Larroquette (New Orleans): Overacting multiple Emmy winner who insists on appearing in Blake Edwards movies.

Ben Turpin (New Orleans): Cross-eyed Mack Sennett comedy cast member who reputedly insured his eyes against uncrossing with Lloyds of London.

Ray Walston (New Orleans): Offbeat oeuvre includes *Damn Yankees, The Happy Hooker Goes to Washington,* and *Fast Times at Ridgemont High,* but best loved as Uncle Martin in "My Favorite Martian."

Carl Weathers (New Orleans): Action Jackson, Apollo Creed, Fortune Dane—sounds like the cast of an adult movie. Former NFL player with the Oakland Raiders.

WHAT'S THERE

Baton Rouge: *sex, lies, and videotape* (1989) filmed at the Bayou Bar, on Chimes Street. This is where Andie McDowell's totally hot sister, Laura San Giacomo, tends bar. Zeezee Gardens, on Perkins Road, is the fern restaurant where McDowell opens up (figuratively) to James Spader.

Louisiana was a French colony, and this film is very much in the style of Frenchman Eric Rohmer.

Burnside: Houmas House is the setting of *Hush, Hush Sweet Charlotte.* Built in 1840, it's on the National Register of Historic Places. The plantation is open for tours; guides, presumably female, wear antebellum dresses. Route 1.

Morgan City: The first Tarzan movie, *Tarzan of the Apes* (played by Elmo Lincoln), was shot here at the Atchafalaya River delta in 1917. There's a display about this at Swamp Gardens, a touristy swamp in the middle of an

The Tarzan display at Swamp Gardens.

urban area (so to speak). A Tarzan mannequin hangs from a vine: his legs, however, are shapely and feminine—they come from a female figure. A recording begins with the Tarzan yell, then details the film series' history. There's another dummy—the cameraman, who wears a beret. Buster Crabbe, a popular Tarzan, dedicated the display in the 1970s. It's at 725 Myrtle Street. The silent Tarzan movie can be seen at Turn-of-the-Century House, 715 Second Street, Monday–Friday 9–5, Saturday–Sunday 1–5.

New Orleans: The most common and efficient establishing shot for New Orleans is Jackson Square, in the heart of the Vieux Carre, which features the Cabildo arcade seen in *King Creole*, and the Presbytere.

The Vieux Carre (French Quarter) is crammed with memorable houses. At the corner of Chartres and Esplanade is a large home seen in *Cat People*, among other films. On the corner of Third and Prytamia is a beautiful structure seen in films including *Obsession* and *Tightrope*.

At the superpopular Antoine's Restaurant (713 St. Louis Street), the Annex Room features photos of celebrities who have passed through its portals.

Jayne Mansfield's decapitating car crash occurred near New Orleans, on the northeast side of Lake Ponchartrain, toward the Mississippi border. She wiped out on the old road from Slidell to Biloxi. (Her death car is on display at the Tragedy in U.S. History Museum, in St. Augustine, Florida.) There's some dispute as to in which state the decapitation actually occurred. This sounds like the set-up to a sick joke, but it's not.

MADE IN MISSISSIPPI

SCREWY SOUTHERNERS

***Baby Doll* (Benoit, 1956):** A racy film condemned by the Legion of Decency—hey, no cutting in line! Based on a story by Tennessee Williams, it was shot at the Old Burras Place, which had been vacant for 25 years. Benoit's population at the time was 444, many of whom got bit roles.

***Ode to Billy Joe* (Greenwood, 1976):** Set in 1953, Max "Jethro" Baer's adaptation of Bobbie Gentry's hit song—explaining why Robby Benson takes a brody off the Tallahachie Bridge—uses its location well.

***Miss Firecracker* (Yazoo City, 1989):** Written by Beth Henley (*Crimes of the Heart*), a Mississippi native, the film has a great ensemble cast . . . and, unfortunately, a Beth Henley script.

SCARY SOUTHERNERS

***Intruder in the Dust* (Oxford, 1949):** A Faulkner adaptation shot in his hometown. The real-life Lowe twins, Ed and Eph, played the Gowrie twins in the film; one can still see them together, at 68, dressed exactly alike. Locals didn't think much of Faulkner until the MGM crew arrived here to film.

***Nightmare in Badham County* (Greenwood, Carrollton, 1976):** Scary Southern sheriff Chuck Connors is everyone's idea of a bad time in this made-for-TV movie.

***Mississippi Burning* (Jackson, Braxton, Vaiden, Canton, Port Gibson, Vicksburg, 1988):** The title of the film refers to the name of the FBI file on the murders of three civil rights workers. The filmmakers did *not* do any shooting in Philadelphia, the town where the murders occurred. Some people can't take a little constructive criticism.

THE BLACK "EXPERIENCE"

***The Autobiography of Miss Jane Pittman* (Natchez, Woodville, 1974):** This award-winning TV movie chronicles the life of a 110-year-old former slave, played by Cicely Tyson.

***Crossroads* (Natchez, Greenville, Vicksburg, Port Gibson, 1986):** Ralph Macchio searches for the blues in a film suggested by the myth that Robert Johnson, the legendary bluesman of the 1930s, met the Devil at a Mississippi crossroads and traded his soul for his talent.

ANOTHER CENTURY

***Raintree County* (Natchez, 1957):** Liz Taylor, Montgomery Clift, and the Civil War—an attempt to outdo *Gone with the Wind.* Clift had his face-mangling car accident during filming.

***Horse Soldiers* (Natchez, 1959):** The true story of a Civil War doctor, directed by John Ford and starring John Wayne and William Holden, who received the highest salary to that date for doing the film.

ALSO . . .

***Home from the Hill* (Oxford, 1960):** Family conflict in the South, with Robert Mitchum blowing everybody else off the screen.

***The Reivers* (Greenville, Carrollton, 1969):** An enjoyable, Faulknerian cross-country spree with Steve McQueen and the kids.

***Thieves Like Us* (Jackson, Canton, 1974):** Nice location and period work in Robert Altman's culty remake of *They Live by Night,* with Shelley Duvall and Keith Carradine.

MISSISSIPPI'S GIFTS TO HOLLYWOOD

★ ★ ★ ★ ★ ★ ★ ★ ★ ★ ★ ★ ★ ★ ★ ★

Jim Henson (Greenville): Unbelievably successful muppeteer whose premature death in 1990 took away one of the few true creative masters in the biz.

James Earl Jones (Arkabutla): Jones grew up in Manistee, Michigan; nobody in Arkabutla seems to recall him, but then his voice wasn't what it is now.

Elvis Presley (Tupelo): Born here. There's some stuff here. See What's There.

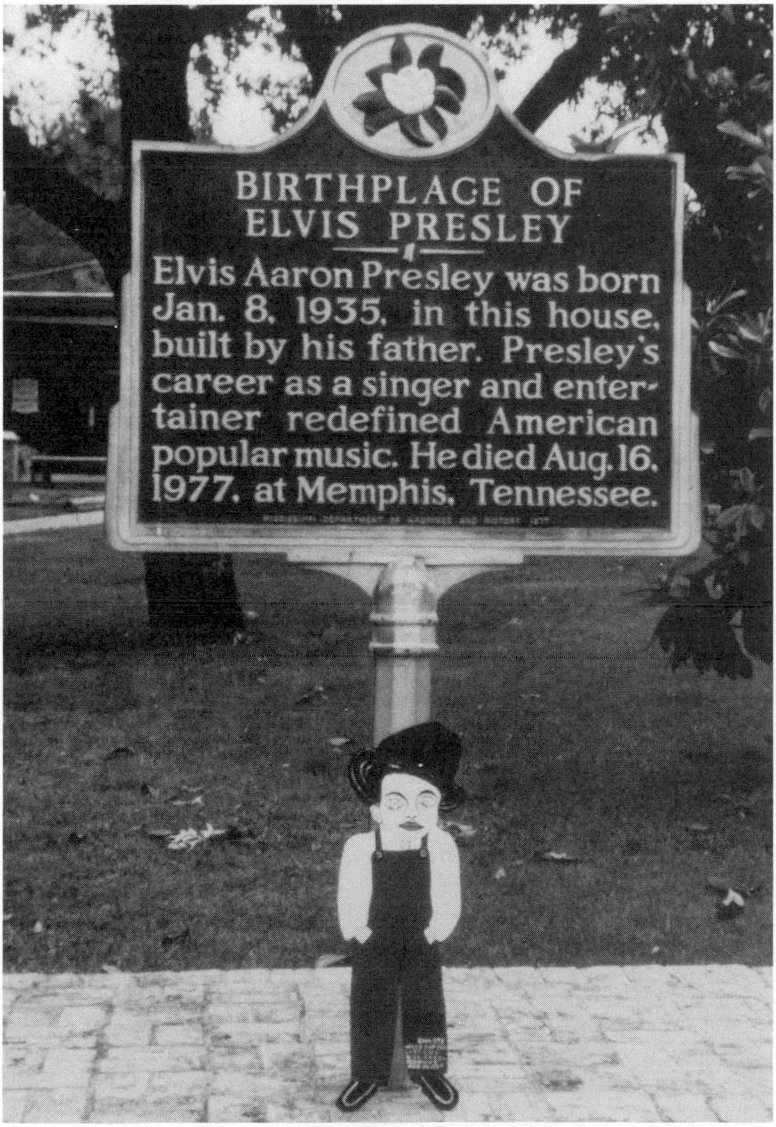

Tupelo, Mississippi, the birthplace of the King.

Stella Stevens (b. Estelle Egglestone, Hot Coffee): The yummy star of *The Nutty Professor* and other pleasant sixties froth is a contender for *Roadside Hollywood*'s Best Hometown Name award.

WHAT'S THERE

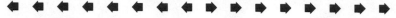

Meridian: The Hanasa Temple, now a Shriner-run variety theater, is a beautifully restored 1928 movie theater with a unique organ. Corner of 8th Street and 24th Avenue.

Tupelo: Elvis Presley driving tour brochures are available in town. The tour includes his birthplace on Elvis Presley Drive, Tupelo Hardware, where he bought his first guitar, Milam Junior High School, the Elvis-themed McDonald's, Elvis Presley Lake, and much, much more.

Elvis in Tupelo brochure. *(Material provided by the Tupelo Convention and Visitors Bureau)*

NORTH CAROLINA

MADE IN NORTH CAROLINA

North Carolina has more production complexes than anywhere outside California: DEG in Wilmington, Earl Owensby Studios in Shelby, Carolina-Atlantic in High Point, Caswell Studios in Providence, and Magder Entertainment in Yanceyville. The state is definitely on the way up, movie-wise. Wilmington is probably the most filmed city per square mile in the U.S.A. The downside is that few of the films shot here have any sense of regionality. In fact, an inordinate number of outright bombs have come from Wilmington—the Los Alamos of moviemaking.

***Thunder Road* (Asheville, 1958):** Robert Mitchum at his best, playing an intrepid moonshiner.

***Three in the Attic* (Chapel Hill, 1968):** Three girls lock one lucky guy in the attic *to do with as they please.* Shot at the women's residence halls, University of North Carolina campus.

***Brainstorm* (Research Triangle, Pinehurst, Outer Banks, 1983):** Natalie Wood died during production, but it's not all that bad. Good look at the New South.

***Reuben, Reuben* (Shelby, 1983):** Set in a New England college town, shot in hospitable North Carolina. Kelly McGillis's screen debut.

***The Color Purple* (Marshville, Ansonville, Lilesville, 1985):** Spielberg's notorious Oscar loser (ask him about it sometime) was shot here, though set near Eatonton, Georgia.

***Crimes of the Heart* (Southport, Wilmington, 1986):** Jessica, Diane, and Sissy—but there's no movie here. Set in Beth Henley's Mississippi, but shot at Harper House in Southport.

***Critical Condition* (High Point, 1987):** A now-razed wing of the High Point Regional Hospital was closed off for shooting this limp Richard Pryor vehicle.

***Bull Durham* (Durham, Raleigh, Greensboro, Asheville, Burlington, Wilson, 1988):** Ex–minor leaguer Ron Shelton's dream pairing of sex and baseball. Game scenes were filmed at Durham Athletic Park, home of the real-life Durham Bulls, who participated as extras.

***The Handmaid's Tale* (Durham, 1989):** This vision of "the near future" was shot in town and at the classically collegiate Duke University campus.

WILMINGTON

***Year of the Dragon* (1985):** Vivid New York City locations, the underbelly of Chinatown, created on a back lot. From the 'Nam Movie Guys: directed by Michael Cimino from an Oliver Stone script.

***Blue Velvet* (1986):** Ookiest David Lynch since *Eraserhead,* shot at the Carolina Apartments on Market Street, Sunset Park, New Hanover High School, and Wilmington Police Department headquarters.

***King Kong Lives* (1986):** Dino de Laurentiis, not satisfied with his 1976 remake, used his studio here to make a sequel to the remake. Scenes were also shot at the Wilmington campus of the University of North Carolina.

***Hiding Out* (1987):** A grownup hides out at a high school, proverbially "knowing then what he knows now." Directed by Bob "Beat It" Giraldi. Shot at the Old Tileston school building and Topsail Senior High.

***Raw Deal* (1986):** Schwarzenegger on the rampage. Shot at the Old Wilmington Light Infantry Armory and at the Independence Shopping Mall.

***Track 29* (1988):** Totally warped Nicolas Roeg film with Theresa Russell, Gary Oldman, Christopher Lloyd, and Sandra Bernhard as The Nurse.

***Weeds* (1987):** Nick Nolte plays a San Quentin lifer who forms a theater troupe. Shot at historic Thalian Hall.

***Teenage Mutant Ninja Turtles* (1990):** New York City was re-created down here for this comic–book based box-office bonanza.

STEPHEN KING IN WILMINGTON

Perhaps the reason Stephen King projects work so well shooting in Wilmington is that his stories benefit from a vague sense of place. Of course, it's hard to say, because his Wilmington films actually don't work at all: *Firestarter* (1984), which was also shot at the Orton Plantation and Lake Lure; *Cat's Eye* (1985); *Silver Bullet* (1985), which also filmed in Burgaw; and *Maximum Overdrive* (1986), which King directed, so he has no excuse.

NORTH CAROLINA'S GIFTS TO HOLLYWOOD

★ ★ ★ ★ ★ ★ ★ ★ ★ ★ ★ ★ ★ ★ ★ ★

Ava Gardner (Smithfield): Top sex symbol in the late 1940s and early 1950s who got involved with the kind of guys who get involved with lots of gals. Films include: *The Killers, The Sun Also Rises, Night of the Iguana, The Barefoot Contessa.* She married Frank Sinatra and Mickey Rooney. See What's There.

Andy Griffith (Mount Airy): Typecast by his great TV show *after* his 1957 role-of-a-lifetime screen debut in *A Face in the Crowd.* (His later show, "Matlock," was also a hit.) His other major film role was in the adaptation of the play that made him famous, *No Time for Sergeants.* See What's There.

WHAT'S THERE

Asheville: Biltmore Estate was Melvyn Douglas's fabulous mansion in *Being There* (1979). It was also seen in *The Private Eyes* (1980), with Tim Conway and Don Knotts as bumbling detectives—does the word *bumbling* ever not appear in a description of these guys' movies?;

The Swan (1956), a Grace Kelly film that was partially shot here; and *Mr. Destiny* (1990), starring Jim Belushi and Michael Caine. South of town, off the Blue Ridge Parkway or I-40.

Mount Airy: Mount Airy was the basis for Andy Griffith's Mayberry, and vestiges of both Griffith and Mayberry remain. There's the Andy Griffith Playhouse, on Rockford Street, near downtown. His boyhood home is at 711 East Haymore Street.

The barber shop and Snappy Lunch on Main Street might ring a note of familiarity to Mayberry seekers, but the Bluebird Cafe has disappeared. The office of the Mount Airy Chamber of Commerce, at 134 South Renfro Street, displays the Mayberry Collection, a series of oil paintings by artist Mike Johnson that includes the Swimmin' Hole, Wally's Service Station, the Sheriff's Car, and the Barber Chair. The office, which still fields inquiries about the idyllic life seen in the sitcom from people looking to relocate, is open Monday through Friday, 8:30–5:00.

Shelby: Earl Owensby Studios, where Owensby cranks out such Southern drive-in grist as *Hit the Road Running* and *Wolfman,* is located at 1048 Old Boiling Springs Road.

Smithfield: Ava Gardner Museum (aka The Teacherage): Gardner lived in this boardinghouse, run by her parents, from age two to age 13. The structure has been preserved in its vintage state, and since the early 1980s has contained the biggest collection of Gardnerabilia in the world: posters, videos, scripts, 10,000 stills, letters, a dozen movie costumes, and a dozen oil paintings done by Dutch artist Bert Pfeiffer, *who paints only Ava!*

Gardner was born about a mile from the site. In the 1950s there was a road sign indicating Smithfield's status as the HOME OF AVA GARDNER, but it deteriorated. Local boosters are "hoping for a new sign soon." The museum is on SR 1007 (Brogdon Road), seven miles east of Smithfield. Phone ahead before visiting: hours are uncertain, and the collection might be relocated within town. Info: Doris Cannon, 919/934-2176.

Gardner is buried at Sunset Memorial Park, on Highway 70 just west of town. There's a "steady stream to the grave," according to Ms. Cannon. Soon after Gardner's death in late 1989, residents reported seeing Frank Sinatra, who was madly in love with Gardner in the 1950s. There have been no confirmed sightings.

SOUTH CAROLINA

MADE IN SOUTH CAROLINA

***The Great Santini* (Beaufort, 1979):** A memorable Robert Duvall performance as a marine who's mean to his son. Filmed at the Tidalholm Mansion, 1 Laurens Avenue.

***Swamp Thing* (Charleston, 1982):** This comic-book adventure, which spawned a sequel, was Adrienne Barbeau's only major non-John Carpenter film.

***The Big Chill* (Beaufort, 1983):** Kevin Kline's house was the Tidalholm Mansion, seen in *The Great Santini*. The most notorious aspect of the shoot—not including the overexposure of Motown music and the media's use of the title phrase out of context, e.g., "Big Chill generation"—was that during production William Hurt cohabited with his girlfriend Sandra Jennings, which, she claimed, made them common-law mates in the eyes of South Carolina. She lost her suit in a New York court; much of the cast testified at the 1989 trial.

***The Lords of Discipline* (Charleston, 1983):** Set in a 1964 military school and, like *Santini*, based on a Pat Conroy novel. Most of the filming took place in England.

Another Conroy story, "The Water Is Wide," a nonfiction look at Daufuskie Island, became the film *Conrack* (1974).

Shag, the Movie **(Myrtle Beach, Georgetown, 1989):** Second-generation Hollywood—Tyrone Power, Jr., Phoebe Cates, Bridget Fonda, Carrie Hamilton, Page Hannah—in fluff about a quartet of cuties cruising a great beach town in 1963. Based on the official state dance of South Carolina.

The Abyss **(Gaffney, 1989):** An underwater epic that cost big bucks but disappointed at the box office. See What's There.

Days of Thunder **(Darlington, Daytona, 1990):** Tom Cruise car-racing flick shot at Darlington Motor Speedway and at the Daytona Speedway in Florida, where NASCAR officials allowed Cruise's movie car to roll around the track *during* the Daytona 500. NASCAR people are bummed at the way they are portrayed in the movie, which reeks anyway.

Sleeping with the Enemy **(Abbeville, 1990):** After returning to civilization, star Julia Roberts called Abbeville "horribly racist" and "living hell." Townsters responded with a *Variety* ad that read, "Pretty Woman? Pretty Low." Presumably, this was meant as a rebuttal of her charges.

SOUTH CAROLINA'S GIFTS TO HOLLYWOOD

★ ★ ★ ★ ★ ★ ★ ★ ★ ★ ★ ★ ★ ★ ★ ★

Stanley Donen (Columbia): This Gamecock choreographer struck gold when he hooked up with Gene Kelly to codirect some of the greatest musicals ever, including *Singin' in the Rain* and *On the Town.* He scored on his own as well, with *Charade, Two for the Road,* and many others.

Lauren Hutton (Charleston): The Cybill Shepherd factor: an impulsive model-turned-actress. Films include: *American Gigolo, Gater, Viva Knievel!*

Bo Hopkins (Greenwood): This glaze-eyed big guy was favored by Sam Peckinpah, but he is no Bo Svenson. Films include: *The Wild Bunch, American Graffiti, The Day of the Locust.*

WHAT'S THERE

Gaffney: The never-completed Cherokee Power Station is the first movie studio to be built out of an abandoned nuclear reactor containment building. The grueling production of *The Abyss* took place here in 1988 inside the two largest freshwater filtered tanks in existence: they hold 7.5 million and 2 million gallons of water.

Mount Pleasant: Boone Hill Plantation, a tourist attraction dating back to 1681, boasts nine original slave cabins and was a location for *Gone with the Wind.* Highway 17 North.

KIRBY

Chapter 8

THE RUST BELT

- Indiana
- Michigan
- New Jersey
- Ohio
- Pennsylvania
- West Virginia

MADE IN INDIANA

Johnny Holiday **(Plainfield, 1949):** Juvenile delinquent film shot near Indianapolis.

Some Came Running **(Madison, 1958):** Frank Sinatra, Dean Martin, and Shirley MacLaine in a small midwestern town. Ring-a-ding-ding!

Winning **(Indianapolis, 1969):** A Paul Newman car-racing film set in the racing capital of America.

Breaking Away **(Bloomington, 1979):** This well-received bicycle-race dramedy was filmed entirely in Indiana. It was set and shot at the Indiana University campus and at the Woolery Stone Mill.

Hoosiers **(central Indiana, 1985):** This Cinderella drama about Indiana's fervent passion for high school basketball was filmed entirely within the state.

INDIANA'S GIFTS TO HOLLYWOOD

★ ★ ★ ★ ★ ★ ★ ★ ★ ★ ★ ★ ★ ★ ★ ★

Anne Baxter (Michigan City): Frank Lloyd Wright's granddaughter found her way into some meaty roles in such films as *The Razor's Edge, All About Eve,* and *The Ten Commandments.*

Scatman Crothers (Terre Haute): A black Andy Devine, Scatman might be best remembered for his role as the caretaker who comes to the rescue in *The Shining.*

Howard Hawks (Goshen): One of the top all-time directors, Hawks crossed genres to create such classics as *Scarface, Twentieth Century, Bringing Up Baby, His Girl Friday, The Big Sleep,* and *The Thing.*

Carole Lombard (b. Jane Alice Peters, Fort Wayne):

Sparkling comedienne without peer, a cousin of Howard Hawks who married Clark Gable and died in a plane crash on a War Bond tour. Her many top-flight films included *Twentieth Century, My Man Godfrey, Nothing Sacred,* and *To Be or Not To Be.* See What's There.

Shelley Long (Fort Wayne): "Cheers" star who seems to be having trouble getting untracked in the movies, mainly because she chooses lame scripts. Still worshipped by Chicagoans for her legendary furniture commercials.

Karl Malden (b. Mladen Sekulovich, Gary): American Express spokesman who used to take on difficult roles in such Elia Kazan films as *A Streetcar Named Desire, On the Waterfront,* and *Baby Doll.*

Ole Olsen (Wabash): Half the comedy team of Olsen and Johnson, who starred in such anarchic thirties and forties comedies as *Hellzapoppin* and *Crazy House.*

Sydney Pollack (South Bend): Director of star vehicles like *The Way We Were, Tootsie,* and *Out of Africa.*

Richard Pryor (Gary): Peter Sellers Syndrome: big talent who ends up in moronic movies. Pryor's better efforts include *The Bingo Long Traveling All-Stars and Motor Kings, Stir Crazy,* and *Nashville.* He was born in Peoria, Illinois, but raised in Gary.

Red Skelton (Vincennes): Goofy comic whose films include *Bathing Beauty* and *The Fuller Brush Man.* A recent survey found that most Americans think Skelton is dead, although he was alive at the time of the survey.

Robert Wise (Winchester): Film editor (*Citizen Kane, The Magnificent Ambersons*) turned director whose work includes *The Day the Earth Stood Still, West Side Story, The Sound of Music,* and the first *Star Trek* film.

Dick York (Fort Wayne): The first Darrin from "Bewitched" was, as a youth, the Olivier of the educational film, playing unsafe drivers and teens with attitude problems.

WHAT'S THERE

Burlington: The actual location of William Frawley's childhood home is a matter of dispute, but you can cover your bases by visiting *both* 1203 North Sixth Street (the house has been demolished) and 604 North Street (still standing).

Chesterton: Yellow Brick Road Gift Shop & Oz Museum. An array of *Wizard of Oz* memorabilia and a fantasyland await travelers to the town where L. Frank Baum allegedly penned the book that started it all. 109 East Yellow Brick Road. Open Monday–Saturday, 10–5, Sunday 11–4.

Fairmount: James Dean's Hometown. At the James Dean Grave and Memorial a bust that Dean himself had commissioned was mounted on a pedestal shortly after his burial, but was sawed off soon afterward and never seen again. At first, cultists were blamed, but now it seems to have been the work of veterans who resented Dean for dodging the draft by pleading homosexuality; they claim he was straight. Park Cemetery, County Road 150E.

James Dean's grave. *(Courtesy of Julie Kuehndorf)*

James Dean Museum sign. *(Courtesy of Julie Kuehndorf)*

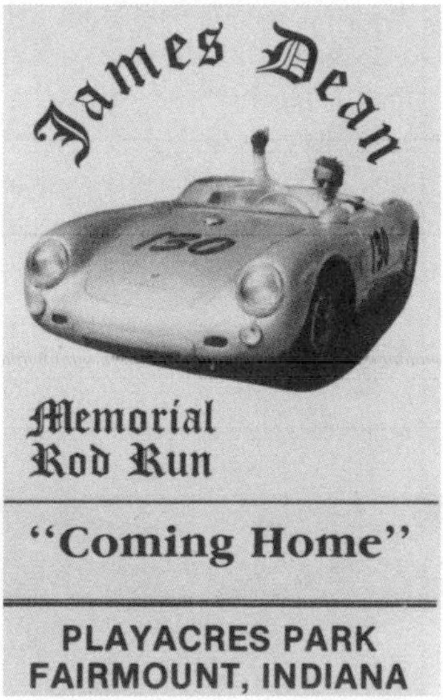

James Dean Memorial Rod Run brochure.

Since 1975, on every anniversary of Dean's death (September 30, 1955), fans have gathered for a three-day celebration: Fairmount Museum Days Remembering James Dean, consisting of a street fair, an antique car parade (the Rod Run), a wrestling match, and a lookalike contest. In recent years, more than 20,000 people have attended.

The Fairmount Historical Museum's Dean Room has his first motorcycle, his boots from *Giant*, a replica of his crushed Porsche, his baseball and basketball letter sweaters, his favorite shirt, his conga drum, and his grammar school art (signed Jimmie Dean). His 1949 high school class photo (townfolk are trying to save the school building as a memorial, but renovation will cost $1 million) is on display: replicas are for sale, for $6. You can also buy souvenir dishes and rock lassos (like what he twirled nervously in *Giant*). 203 East Washington.

The James Dean Gallery, a 12-room Victorian house, displays David Loehr's collection of Dean artifacts—the "largest in the world." 425 North Main Street, or call 317/948-DEAN.

Fort Wayne: Carole Lombard's birthplace. A small plaque on the house was installed in 1938 to commemorate her appearance in the screwball classic *Nothing Sacred.* 704 Rockhill Street.

Jonesboro: The Winslow farm, where James Dean grew up with his relatives, is at 7184 South 150th Road East. Near Fairmount.

Marion: James Dean's birth site, at the southwest corner of South McClure and East Fourth streets, is now a parking lot.

MICHIGAN

MADE IN MICHIGAN

AUTO WORLD

***The Betsy* (1978), *Blue Collar* (1978), and *Roger & Me* (1989),** present three views of the auto industry: as a source of vast family fortunes, as an employer that grinds down its workers, and as a cold, impersonal business that refuses to acknowledge its power to make or destroy whole towns.

MURDER CITY: DETROIT

***Action Jackson* (1987), *Beverly Hills Cop* (1984), *Beverly Hills Cop 2* (1987):** The violent *Robocop* is also set in Murtown, but the film was shot in Dallas.

SEE YOU IN COURT

***Anatomy of a Murder* (Ishpeming, Marquette, 1952):** The Ishpeming home of Robert Traver, the author of the book upon which the film is based, was used as James Stewart's law office. In Marquette, shooting was at the Marquette County Courthouse, where Traver served as prosecutor for 14 years.

***Presumed Innocent* (Detroit, 1990):** This investigative drama is set in a nondescript Anywhereville in the Scott Turow book, and so in the movie, too.

THE SCENIC NORTHLAND

***This Time for Keeps* (Mackinac Island, 1946):** This Esther Williams vehicle was shot at the fabulous Grand Hotel on this no-cars resort island in Lake Huron. Reservations: 906/847-3331.

MICHIGAN'S GIFTS TO HOLLYWOOD

★ ★ ★ ★ ★ ★ ★ ★ ★ ★ ★ ★ ★ ★ ★ ★

Ellen Burstyn (b. Edna Rae Gillooly, Detroit): Actress best known for playing Linda Blair's mom in *The Exorcist.* She also starred in *Alice Doesn't Live Here Anymore* and *The Last Picture Show.*

Francis Ford Coppola (Detroit): An extremely gifted director (*The Godfathers*, *The Conversation*) who has trouble getting it up without his entire career and fortune on the line. He gambled the farm (actually a winery) and won with *Apocalypse Now,* then crapped out and lost his Zoetrope Studio with the wretched *One from the Heart.*

Jeff Daniels (Chelsea): The slightly goofy-looking Daniels continually gets cast in interesting films, such as

Terms of Endearment, The Purple Rose of Cairo, and *Something Wild.*

Julie Harris (Grosse Pointe Park): The Amanda Plummer of the fifties and sixties (so unattractive you *know* she can act), her films include *The Member of the Wedding, East of Eden,* and *Requiem for a Heavyweight.*

Charlton Heston (Essexville): Star of countless overblown, overacted epics, including *The Ten Commandments, The Buccaneer, Ben Hur,* and *Planet of the Apes.* See What's There: St. Helen.

Thomas Hulce (Pontiac): Definitely goofy star of *Animal House* and *Amadeus.*

James Earl Jones (Manistee): This actor of commanding voice and presence was born in Mississippi but raised here. Best known as the voice of Darth Vader in the *Star Wars* trilogy, Jones has played a wide variety of roles in such films as *Dr. Strangelove, The Great White Hope, The Bingo Long Traveling All-Stars and Motor Kings,* and *Matewan.*

Buster Keaton (Muskegon): The great comedian was born on the road but had a childhood home in Bluffton, on Lake Muskegon, where he enjoyed the happiest summers of his life.

Madonna (Bay City): A modestly talented singer whose massive success and movie career prove there's no accounting for taste. She upset locals when she described Bay City on the "Today" show as "a smelly little town." She also complained "they wouldn't even give me a key to the city." Wags refer to her in *Dick Tracy* (1990) as "Beatty and the Beast." See What's There.

Tom Selleck (Detroit): Hunky "Magnum, P.I." star who struck gold in *Three Men and a Baby* and may or may not persist as a film star.

Lily Tomlin (Detroit): Broke in with "Laugh-In," then spun off into a one-woman show and a moderately successful film career, with films including *Nashville,*

Nine to Five, and *All of Me.* See What's There: Paducah, Kentucky.

Robin Williams: Zanily inventive "improv" comedian with a reputed penchant for stealing material. His interesting film career has included *The World According to Garp, Good Morning, Vietnam,* and *Dead Poets Society.*

WHAT'S THERE

Bay City: Madonna was born at Mercy Hospital, which is now the Bradley House retirement home, at 100 15th Street.

Dearborn: Greenfield Village has the plane flown by Jimmy Stewart as Charles Lindbergh in *The Spirit of St. Louis.* Also at Greenfield Village, in a tube, is the last breath of the man who invented motion pictures—Thomas Edison. Village Road and Oakwood Boulevard.

Detroit: The Fox Theater, the largest in the world, is done in Siamese-Byzantine style and has 5,041 seats. It opened in 1928, and has swung with the times: it hosted Motown revues in the 1960s, Kung Fu films in the 1970s, and rock in the 1980s. The Fox now features mostly live entertainment, but movies still play here on occasion. It was bought by Chuck Forbes in 1984 for $1 million; he's pumped in $8 million so far for restoration. 2211 Woodward Avenue.

Escanaba: In December the International Wizard of Oz Club hosts the Ozcanabans of Oz Convention. Contact: Fred M. Meyer, 220 North 11th Street, Escanaba, Michigan 49829.

Wiz-heads abound in Michigan. The town of Macatawa, near Holland, also hosts an Oz Festival. Contact the Holland Convention and Visitors Bureau, 800/822-2770.

St. Helen: Charlton Heston owns 1,400 acres in this tiny tourist town near his childhood home.

NEW JERSEY

MADE IN NEW JERSEY

With so much of New Jersey a part of the New York metropolitan area, this section will only cover films that have a true Jersey feel to them. Urban sophistication is not what New Jersey—no offense—is all about.

ATLANTIC CITY

Few films were shot in Atlantic City during its heyday, the era when horses dove off the steel pier and the town was a happy seaside resort for promenading working-class families. The first major production of the modern era is Bob Rafelson's *The King of Marvin Gardens* (1972), which stars Jack Nicholson, Bruce Dern, and Ellen Burstyn, has a European sensibility, and catches the city at the beginning of its transition from blighted urban area to blighted urban area with cheesy casinos along the beach.

James Toback's *The Gambler* (1974) uses Atlantic City purely as an eastern Vegas, a place for compulsive types to crap out. By the time of *Atlantic City* (1980), the place had already become renowned as a seedy magnet for losers of all persuasions, and director Louis Malle brings *his* European sensibility to bear in creating sympathy for a pair of them, Susan Sarandon (an aspiring blackjack dealer who boosts the lemon-growing industry in a memorable scene) and Burt Lancaster.

More recent films toe the Trump line, and celebrate the second-rate glitz of the casinos: Toback's *The Pick-Up Artist* (1987), Martin Scorsese's *The Color of Money* (1986), *Penn and Teller Get Killed* (1989), and *The Lemon Sisters* (1990). None offers the insight into the denizens of this sleaze capital that *The King of Marvin Gardens* or *Atlantic City* do.

DAFFY MOBSTERS r US

New Jersey's movie gangsters lack the menacing quality of Chicago or New York mob toughs. In fact, they're downright nutty! Maybe being top dog in a junkyard gives you a sense of humor. Addled Garden State baddies include those in *Prizzi's Honor* (Alpine, Palisades Parkway, 1985), *Married to the Mob* (South Hackensack, 1988), and *Cookie* (Atlantic City, Absecon, Secaucus, 1989).

WOODY'S NEW JERSEY, A PLACE WHERE MUTANTS DWELL

Woody Allen doesn't like to leave Manhattan, so you know things are gonna get pretty hairy when he ventures across the Hudson. He gets shot at in a float factory in *Broadway Danny Rose* (1984), which filmed in Guttenberg, Weehawken, North Bergen, Englewood, and Jersey City. He attends a seminar honoring his films in *Stardust Memories* (1980) and encounters a menagerie of subhumans. Locations included Ocean Grove, Asbury Park, Neptune, Belmar, Hoboken, and Deal.

Other Woody films and their New Jersey locations: *Manhattan* (Englewood, 1979), *Zelig* (Englewood, Alpine, Paramus, Weehawken, Saddle River, Jersey City, Union City, 1983), *The Purple Rose of Cairo* (Bertrand's Island Amusement Park in Mount Arlington, South Amboy, Paterson, 1985), and *Another Woman* (Alpine, Demarest, 1988).

HOBOKEN: GENIUS AT WORK

John Sayles: novelist, screenwriter, director, certified genius. His first and best film, *Return of the Secaucus Seven* (1980), became a hit when it was remade as *The Big Chill.* His follow-up work was shot whenever possible in his native Hoboken, where the previous claim to fame was as Frank Sinatra's hometown and as the location for *On the Waterfront.*

Hoboken productions include *Baby It's You* (also Newark, Jersey City, Cliffside Park, Fort Lee, Lawrenceville, Trenton, Belleville, Asbury Park, Spring Lake,

1983), *Lianna* (1983), and *The Brother from Another Planet* (also Jersey City, Harlem, 1984).

THE WIDE WORLD OF NEW JERSEY

***Friday the 13th* (Blairstown, 1980):** This first installment of an inexplicable series, a megahit shot on a shoestring, includes young Kevin Bacon in its cast.

***Annie* (Monmouth College, West Long Branch, Passaic River, East Newark, 1982):** Shadow Lawn (Woodrow Wilson Hall) was Daddy Warbucks's manor. The lawn of the Monmouth College library, formerly the Murry Guggenheim mansion, subbed for the White House lawn.

***The World According to Garp* (Lincoln Park, Denville, Madison, New Brunswick, 1982):** Entertaining adaptation of John Irving's hit novel.

***Desperately Seeking Susan* (Tenafly, Edgewater, Lakehurst, Atlantic City, 1985):** Rosanna Arquette and hubby live in one of those New Jersey condos that have a better view of Manhattan than Manhattanites get, but she wants something more. Directed by New Jersey's Susan Seidelman.

***Something Wild* (Rahway, Paramus, Ringwood, New Jersey Turnpike, Jersey City, 1986):** Melanie Griffith takes Jeff Daniels on a wild ride through beautiful Jersey.

***Lean on Me* (Paterson, 1989):** Real-life story of bat-wielding principal Joe Clark shot at his old stomping grounds, Eastside High School, 150 Park Avenue. Clark, who promoted the film for free, got upset when Mike Tyson was paid a large sum to do the same.

NEW JERSEY'S GIFTS TO HOLLYWOOD

★ ★ ★ ★ ★ ★ ★ ★ ★ ★ ★ ★ ★ ★ ★ ★

Bud Abbott (Asbury Park) and Lou Costello (Paterson): They teamed up one night in vaudeville—Lou's partner called in sick—and went on to become the second most successful duo in movie history, after Hope and Crosby.

Danny DeVito (Asbury Park): Gnomish character actor whose career—now as a director—grows and grows. He was raised here, but was born in Neptune. Films include: *One Flew Over the Cuckoo's Nest, Tin Men, Throw Momma from the Train, War of the Roses,* the last two of which he also directed.

Michael Douglas (New Brunswick): Son of Kirk who has made all the right career moves, from "The Streets of San Francisco" to producing *Cuckoo's Nest* and *The China Syndrome* to starring in films like *Romancing the Stone, Wall Street,* and *Fatal Attraction.* One of Jann Wenner's best pals, so he gets on the cover of *Rolling Stone* whenever he so much as gets a haircut.

Sterling Hayden (Montclair): Commanding presence on and offscreen who's made great films in several eras, including *The Asphalt Jungle, Johnny Guitar, Suddenly, Dr. Strangelove,* and *The Godfather,* in which he plays the cop killed by Al Pacino.

Jerry Lewis (Newark): Mr. Funny Entertainment himself.

Jack Nicholson (Neptune): Most sought-after actor of the 1980s, he broke into the biz with Roger Corman's American International Pictures. His big break came when Rip Torn bagged out of *Easy Rider.*

Meryl Streep (Basking Ridge and Summit): The female Paul Muni—her career is about giving performances. Films include: *The Deer Hunter, The French Lieutenant's Woman, Sophie's Choice, Silkwood, Out of Africa, Ironweed.*

Bruce Willis (Penns Grove): Fox pays him $5 million for *Die Hard,* then decides he isn't a promotable star, so the ads feature not him but the building. And it works. Then, he doesn't even *appear* in *Look Who's Talking,* but the ads promote him, and *this works too!* Smarm equals charm.

WHAT'S THERE

Alpine: Enclave of rich celebrities, including Eddie Murphy. Homes are not numbered here, it's so cool.

Asbury Park: In 1948, the Fly-In Theater opened here, with space for 500 cars and 50 aeroplanes. It is now defunct.

Camden: The Camden Drive-in movie theater, the world's first, opened here June 6, 1933, on Admiral Wilson Boulevard. The lot could accommodate 400–500 cars; sound came from speakers mounted atop the screen. The first film shown was *Wife Beware*, starring Adolphe Menjou. The theater closed in 1937, giving way to an A&P. Now it's just an abandoned lot alongside the highway.

Fort Lee: The town across the George Washington Bridge from Manhattan was a movie production center from 1907–1916. What is this, What's *Not* There?

Wayne: The gatehouse to Cecil B. DeMille's boyhood spread remains, with a tablet marking the spot, at 266 Terhune Drive.

West Orange: The Edison National Historic Site is the site of Thomas Edison's Black Maria movie studio, the world's first. A full-size replica is displayed here. West Main Street and Lakeside Avenue. Tours: 201/736-0550.

OHIO

MADE IN OHIO

CINCINNATI

***Eight Men Out* (1988):** Older parts of town, specifically Over-the-Rhine, stood in for 1919 Chicago. In Queensgate, the rowhouse of Buck Weaver (John Cusack) is on Elizabeth Street, near Central Avenue; here he explains the scandal to a pack of moppets. A room in Pendleton House, the oldest in town, was where Eddie Cicotte's wife rubs his arm with linament. At the Covington Railway Exhibition, antique train interiors were employed for travel scenes, like when John Sayles sings an ultraembarrassing rendition of "I'm Forever Blowing Ballgames."

***Rain Man* (1988):** The film's trek began in greater Cincinnati. Cruise and Hoffman's father's mansion was in East Walnut Hills; he was buried in Evergreen Cemetery. The Dixie Terminal lobby stands in for the bank where Cruise learns his father's money is in a trust fund. The Vernon Manor Hotel, 400 Oak Street, is where they spend their first night. Hoffman has a panic attack and plugs Qantas Airlines at the Greater Cincinnati International Airport.

CLEVELAND

***The Fortune Cookie* (1966):** This acerbic Billy Wilder comedy shot its football scenes at Memorial Stadium, employing more than 10,000 extras. Other setups included outside Public Square and at St. Vincent Charity Hospital, called St. Mark's in the movie.

***The Deer Hunter* (1978):** Unable to find the *perfect* locale in Pennsylvania, persnickety director Michael Cimino brought the production here, to St. Theodosius Russian Orthodox Church and Lemko Hall, which were used for wedding and reception scenes. He also filmed in U.S. Steel Corporation facilities and in near West Side neighborhoods. Other Ohio locations were Mingo Junction and Struthers.

***One Trick Pony* (1980):** Paul Simon wanted his fizzled film debut shot in "America's rock & roll capital." Some filming was done at Baldwin-Wallace College; auditions and other sequences were held at The Agora, a legendary rock venue.

***Stranger than Paradise* (1984):** Ohio native Jim Jarmusch shot scenes for his outstanding, loopy comedy here at the East Ninth Street pier (behind Captain Frank's Seafood House), on the west side, and on I-71.

***Light of Day* (1987):** This almost-believable rock & roll family drama starring Michael J. Fox and Joan Jett shot at a Cleveland Heights playground near Euclid Heights Boulevard and Hampshire Road; at the Euclid Tavern, Euclid near East 116th Street; and at Marshallan Industries, West 85th Street.

***Major League* (1989):** The film was supposedly set in Cleveland, and even uses the Randy Newman song "Burn On, Big River" to poke fun at this much-besmirched old metropolis. Establishing shots were filmed here at Memorial Stadium, but most of the shooting was done in Milwaukee.

AND . . .

***Brubaker* (Junction City, 1980):** Robert Redford plays a cool warden in this jailhouse drama shot at the Junction City Prison Farm, which is now a cheese factory.

***Gung Ho* (Shadyside, 1986):** The 1943 *Gung Ho!* was a xenophobic war story; in this one, the Japs come to the rescue. The auto factory scenes were shot at the General Motors Stamping Plant.

OHIO'S GIFTS TO HOLLYWOOD

★ ★ ★ ★ ★ ★ ★ ★ ★ ★ ★ ★ ★ ★ ★ ★

Theda Bara (b. Theodosia Goodman, Cincinnati): An exotic background was concocted for Bara, the original vamp of the silent era famous for propagating the phrase, "Kiss me, you fool!"

W. R. Burnett (Springfield): Crime novelist who became top gangster-movie screenwriter. Films include: *Scarface, High Sierra,* and the novel basis for *The Asphalt Jungle.*

Dorothy Dandridge (Cleveland): This singer became one of the first black female romantic stars. Films include: *A Day at the Races, Carmen Jones, Porgy and Bess.*

Beverly D'Angelo (Columbus): Attractive supporting actress who is effective in comedy. Films include: *Na-*

tional Lampoon's Vacation series, *Coal Miner's Daughter* (as Patsy Cline).

Doris Day (b. Doris von Kappelhoff, Cincinnati): Singer who became America's Virgin in such Technicolor romps as *Pillow Talk, Lover Come Back,* and *Do Not Disturb.* Be kind to animals or she'll kill you.

Ruby Dee (Cleveland): Classy actress who's appeared in several "message" films, including *Imitation of Life, A Raisin in the Sun,* and *Do the Right Thing.*

Thomas Edison (Milan): More than anybody else, the inventor of the motion picture. His life is portrayed in *Young Tom Edison* and *Edison the Man.*

Clark Gable (Cadiz): Top romantic star of the 1930s whose performance in *Gone with the Wind* is only one reason why he's so important. He had a headline marriage—to the thirties' best comedienne, Carole Lombard—and appeared in dozens of big films, including *It Happened One Night, Manhattan Melodrama* (John Dillinger's last movie), *Mutiny on the Bounty,* and *The Misfits.* See What's There.

Teri Garr (Lakewood): Likable lightweight film comedienne who's achieved more fame as a "fabulous babe" on "Late Night with David Letterman." Films include: *Young Frankenstein, Tootsie.*

Lillian Gish (Springfield): An enduring figure in American cinema, she was D. W. Griffith's chief actress: their collaborations include *The Birth of a Nation, Intolerance,* and *Way Down East.* She also starred through the years in *The Scarlet Letter, The Night of the Hunter,* and *The Whales of August.*

Arsenio Hall (Cleveland): Eddie Murphy's pal seems like he'll be around for a long ride. He and Murphy played multiple roles in *Coming to America.*

Dean Martin (b. Dino Paul Crocetti, Steubenville): Singer who teamed with Jerry Lewis for top box office honors in the 1950s. After they split, he smirked through a variety of Rat Pack farces and starred as a swingin'

James Bond ripoff, Matt Helm. Films include: *My Friend Irma, Hollywood or Bust, Robin and the Seven Hoods, The Silencers.* See What's There.

Burgess Meredith (Cleveland): The Penguin, Rocky's manager, and a voiceover in commercials to those under 40, Meredith stole earlier films in character roles, including *Second Chorus, That Uncertain Feeling,* and *The Day of the Locust.*

Paul Newman (Cleveland): Newman, with the most famous blue eyes in history, has selected roles well in his career. Films include: *The Hustler, Hud, Cool Hand Luke, Butch Cassidy and the Sundance Kid, The Sting, The Color of Money.* He has been married for many years to actress Joanne Woodward. See What's There: Shaker Heights.

Dudley Nichols (Wapakoneta): Top-drawer screenwriter of the thirties and forties who worked with great directors on comedies and manly dramas. Films include: *The Informer, Bringing Up Baby, Stagecoach, Scarlet Street, For Whom the Bell Tolls.*

Tyrone Power, Jr. (Cincinnati): Middle and most successful of three generations of handsome actors named Tyrone Power, he starred in A-minus films of the thirties through the fifties, including *Jesse James, The Mark of Zorro, Nightmare Alley,* and *The Sun Also Rises.*

Roy Rogers (b. Leonard Slye, Cincinnati): Singing horse-opera-hero-turned-burger-magnate, he made a string of popular, forgettable westerns astride his horse Trigger and aside his wife, Dale Evans. See What's There: Victorville, California.

Martin Sheen (b. Ramon Estevez, Dayton): Intense, rich-voiced actor who begat a brood of smug acting punks. Films include *Apocalypse Now, Badlands, Wall Street* (as the father of real-life son Charlie).

Steven Spielberg (Cincinnati): The most powerful director in Hollywood, his ultrasuccessful oeuvre includes *Jaws, Close Encounters of the Third Kind, E.T.: The Extraterrestrial,* and *Raiders of the Lost Ark.*

CLARK GABLE

Akron: Clark Gable roomed at 1163 Getz Street while working in a factory.

Cadiz: A sign outside town heralds HOME OF JOHN A. BINGHAM, PROSECUTOR OF LINCOLN'S ASSASSINS, but nowadays the draw in Cadiz is Clark Gable. There's a monument at the site of Gable's razed birthplace, 138 Charleston Street. Across from the monument, at 151 Charleston, Christine's Nostalgia Shop features Gable memorabilia, including certified copies of his birth record ($2.25) and Army discharge (signed by his commander, Ronald Reagan, also $2.25). There are also T-shirts, plates, postcards, books, mugs, etc.

An annual Clark Gable birthday bash is held the Saturday closest to his birth date, February 1. Past highlights have been lookalikes of Gable, Vivien Leigh, and Marilyn Monroe; screening of a Gable movie with an appropriate costume dinner; and a collectors meet. For information, call 614/942-8861.

Clark Gable's boyhood home (Hopedale).

Freeport: Clark Gable's Cadillac, a 1954 Coupe de Ville, is part of a unique collection, Cars of Yesteryear, that includes a Cy Young Olds and a Tammy Bakker Caddy. This is not a dull museum, but rather the personal collection of a man named Jim McCartney. Drive up Philadelphia Street past the grade school, veer right at the fork and you're there—it's in a big garage.

Hopedale: Clark Gable's attractive boyhood home, painted blue and white, used to be marked until the sign was stolen one Halloween. It's on Mill Street, across from the Mountain Dew sign. A sign outside says The Agostini Palace.

ALSO . . .

Lucas: Louis Bromfield's Malabar Farm. Bromfield was a Pulitzer Prize–winning author who wrote several screenplays and cultivated an array of Hollywood chums who would spend time here on this picturesque Ohio farm, now a state park.

Tours of the main house go into its star-studded history. It was visited by Mary Astor, James Cagney, Alice Faye, Errol Flynn, Kay Francis, Hedy Lamarr, Dorothy Lamour, Carole Lombard, William Powell, Tyrone Power, and Shirley Temple. A wall of photos upstairs attests to this.

But the highlight of the tour concerns the fact that Humphrey Bogart, 45, and Lauren Bacall, 19, were wed here in 1945. Their honeymoon suite has *two beds.* Everybody asks, but nobody knows how they reconfigured them for the wedding night.

From Mansfield take Route 603 to Pleasant Valley Road. Turn right and go to Bromfield Road, then turn left.

Marion: The Wyandot Popcorn Museum honors the moviegoer's Number One food staple. Vintage movie-palace poppers of the late 1920s are here, along with drive-in poppers from the late 1930s. The museum also hosts an annual Popcorn Festival. 343 South State Street.

Vintage popcorn popper at the Popcorn Museum in Marion. *(Courtesy of Julie Kuehndorf)*

Shaker Heights: Paul Newman attended Shaker Heights High School in this wealthy Cleveland suburb. 15911 Aldersyde Road.

Steubenville: The main thoroughfare in town is Dean Martin Boulevard.

PENNSYLVANIA

MADE IN PENNSYLVANIA

BLUE COLLAR/BLACK LUNG

***The Molly Maguires* (Eckley, 1970):** Coal-mining saga starring Sean Connery and directed by Martin "Look For The Union Label" Ritt, set in a restored miner's village. Eckley tries to pass itself off as an authentic historical attraction, but they did too good a job preserving the past—it's drab and depressing.

***Slap Shot* (Johnstown, 1977):** Rowdy high jinks of a minor-league hockey team, starring Paul Newman and set in dark, depressing, working-class Johnstown.

***The Deer Hunter* (Clairton, McKeesport, Pittsburgh, 1978):** Although the film was shot all over the country, the old industrial town of Clairton was precisely the sort of place the characters would have lived.

THE PHILADELPHIA STORY

An excellent driving tour is available from the Philadelphia Film Office, 215/686-2668.

***Rocky* (1976):** The most popular tourist activity in town is not ringing the Liberty Bell but running up the steps of the Philadelphia Museum of Art, at 26th and the Benjamin Franklin Parkway, in emulation of Rocky. See What's There.

The famous *Rocky* steps of the Philadelphia Museum of Art. *(Courtesy of the Office of the City Representative and Director of Commerce, Philadelphia)*

***Rocky II* (1979):** Stallone and Talia Shire stroll in Rittenhouse Square. He trains for his match at the now-remade Bellevue-Stratford "Legionnaires' Disease" Hotel, at Broad and Locust. The Italian Market, on Ninth Street from Christian Street to Washington Avenue, was seen in both *Rocky II* and *III.*

***Dressed to Kill* (1980):** The Philadelphia Museum of Art doubled as New York's Metropolitan Museum, where Angie Dickinson is pursued by a stud.

***Blow Out* (1981):** John Travolta, Nancy Allen, and John Lithgow meet at 30th Street Station. Travolta drives a jeep through a narrow pedestrian passageway outside

Shooting *Blow Out* at Philadelphia City Hall. *(Courtesy of the Office of the City Representative and Director of Commerce, Philadelphia)*

City Hall. He crashes through a window at John Wanamaker's department store, at Market and Penn Square.

During production, a thief broke into a van parked in Manhattan that contained original footage from this Brian DePalma film. Reshooting the sequence cost about $1 million.

***Trading Places* (1983):** Dan Aykroyd's swanky house, before he gets bounced from it, is at 2014 Delancey. Eddie Murphy pretends to be legless and begs in Rittenhouse Square. The Duke and Duke Bank, run by Don Ameche and Ralph Bellamy, is the Fidelity Bank Building, 135 South Broad Street.

***Witness* (1985):** Before traipsing off to Amish Country (Lancaster County), Harrison Ford quizzes the little boy at 30th Street Station.

***Birdy* (1984):** Matthew Modine and Nicolas Cage chase pigeons by the elevated train at 46th and Market streets.

***Mannequin* (1987):** Dismal comedy that was heavily

Wanamaker's Department Store, done up for *Mannequin*, in Philadelphia. *(Courtesy of the Office of the City Representative and Director of Commerce, Philadelphia)*

advertised and did amazing box office in those desperate days of 1987. The film is set in a grand department store; the legendary John Wanamaker's, at 13th and Market streets, was used for exteriors. Boscov's Department Store, in Camp Hill, was the set for interiors.

***Clean and Sober* (1988):** In this first film effort from the producer of "Moonlighting," Michael Keaton meets M. Emmet Walsh to talk over milkshakes at the Snow White Coffee Shop, Market Street at Second. He meets Kathy Baker at the Colonial Theatre, 11th and Moyamensing.

PITTSBURGH

***The Fish that Saved Pittsburgh* (1979):** This 1970s relic didn't actually use much in the way of Pittsburgh locations, but it's so nutty I just had to include it.

***Flashdance* (1983):** Jennifer Beals, welder by day and superhot dancer by night, is snubbed at the Carnegie Institute, 4400 Forbes Avenue, in the Oakland section.

***Mrs. Soffel* (1984):** Diane Keaton, the warden's wife, falls for Mel Gibson and helps him break out of Allegheny County Prison, Forbes Avenue and Ross Street.

***The Silence of the Lambs* (1991):** This film is set all over the country; the producers chose the Pittsburgh area for the bulk of the shooting, praising its variety of landscape and architecture.

GEORGE ROMERO: THE ZOMBIES THAT SAVED PITTSBURGH

Romero attained instant success with the truly terrifying *Night of the Living Dead* (1968). The old farmhouse in the film is located near Evans City. Although he's only hit the mark once since, with the sequel *Dawn of the Dead* (1979), shot in a Pittsburgh area shopping mall, he's remained faithful to his fair city, continuing to work and film here. Other Pittsburgh productions include: *Creepshow, Day of the Dead, Monkey Shines,* and *Knightriders,* shot in Tarentum.

PENNSYLVANIA'S GIFTS TO HOLLYWOOD

★ ★ ★ ★ ★ ★ ★ ★ ★ ★ ★ ★ ★ ★ ★ ★

Frankie Avalon (Philadelphia): White-bread prince of the beach movie.

Carroll Baker (Johnstown): Fizzled as a Marilyn clone but found her way into some good films, such as *Giant, Baby Doll,* and *Ironweed,* in which she played Jack Nicholson's abandoned wife.

Ethel, John, and Lionel Barrymore (Philadelphia): Classy family included Ethel, a top stage actress who made several films, none too memorable; John, who excelled at playing suave but flawed charmers in such classics as *Grand Hotel, Dinner at Eight,* and *Twentieth Century;* and Lionel, who had the longest career and is best remembered as the evil Mr. Potter in *It's a Wonderful Life* and the doomed nebbish in *Grand Hotel.* See What's There.

Billy Barty (Millsboro): This omnipresent actor rivals Tom Thumb as history's most famous midget.

Charles Bronson (b. Charles Bunchinsky, Ehrenfeld): Ethnic tough guy who escaped the coal mines and became internationally famous for committing vengeful mayhem in such body-counters as *The Great Escape, The Dirty Dozen,* and the *Death Wish* series.

Bill Cosby (Philadelphia): Cos has never had a film success to match that in TV. An attempt to cash in at the height of his megastardom, *Leonard Part 6,* bombed on the order of *Howard the Duck* and *Heaven's Gate.*

Broderick Crawford (Philadelphia): Like Ernest Borgnine, a stereotyped TV role ("Highway Patrol") cost him lasting respect, despite fantastic starring work in *All the King's Men* and *Born Yesterday.*

Brian DePalma (Philadelphia): The hip-pocket Hitchcock, DePalma returned to Philly to make *Blow Out* and *Dressed to Kill.*

W. C. Fields (b. William Claude Dukenfield, Philadelphia): One of the most enduring comic presences, still imitated by everyone from Rich Little on down to Ed

McMahon. Fields, a vaudeville juggler, probably would have been even bigger if talkies had come in earlier. He wrote many of his best films, including *It's a Gift, You Can't Cheat an Honest Man,* and *The Bank Dick,* under wacky pseudonyms. His boyhood home, at 6320 Woodland Avenue, has been torn down.

Larry Fine (Philadelphia): The Three Stooges' "porcupine head," a vaudeville fiddler who hooked up with the Howard brothers to find eternal fame.

Janet Gaynor (Philadelphia): The first actress to cop an Oscar, she was a big star in the 1930s and appeared in several classics, including *Sunrise* and *A Star Is Born.*

Jeff Goldblum (Pittsburgh): Twitchy, neurotic stringbean who keeps on getting roles in decent films like *The Big Chill, The Fly,* and *Invasion of the Body Snatchers.*

Charles Grodin (Pittsburgh): Smart, sullen deadpan master who can take a good role and really run with it. His work includes *The Heartbreak Kid, Heaven Can Wait, Real Life, Midnight Run,* and *Taking Care of Business.*

Hedda Hopper (Hollidaysburg): Ultrapowerful hat-wearing actress-turned-gossip-columnist who dictated Tinseltown chatter in the forties and fifties.

Shirley Jones (Smithton): Cutie-pie of musical comedy, best known as Shirley Partridge. Films include: *Oklahoma!, Elmer Gantry, The Music Man.*

Michael Keaton (Pittsburgh): Uninspired stand-up comedian who found riches in the Likable Guy Decade. His best performance was in *Night Shift,* as a hyperactive wild man, but he'll be best remembered for the role that made us take him "seriously," *Batman.*

Gene Kelly (Pittsburgh): Kelly is to color what Astaire was to black & white. Kelly's greatest contribution might be his muscular approach to choreography, allowing men to feel like men even while dancing. His many hits include *On the Town, An American in Paris, Singin' in the Rain,* and *It's Always Fair Weather.* See What's There.

Grace Kelly (Philadelphia): A daughter of Philly's

posh Main Line, Kelly played in a handful of strong films—including *High Noon, Rear Window, Dial M for Murder,* and *The Country Girl*—before becoming the Princess of Monaco.

Joseph L. Mankiewicz (Wilkes-Barre): Younger brother of screenwriter Herman (who cowrote *Citizen Kane*), Joseph wrote and directed *A Letter to Three Wives, All About Eve, Guys and Dolls,* and *Cleopatra.*

Jayne Mansfield (Bryn Mawr): Likable blond bombshell who was decapitated in a car wreck. Films include: *The Girl Can't Help It, Will Success Spoil Rock Hunter, Las Vegas Hillbillies* (costarring with her successor, Mamie Van Doren). See What's There: Pen Argyl; New Orleans; St. Augustine, Florida.

Jeanette MacDonald (Philadelphia): Nelson Eddy's musical partner in successful 1930s teaming.

Adolphe Menjou (Pittsburgh): John Barrymore type with many, many credits, including *The Front Page, A Star Is Born,* and *Paths of Glory.*

Tom Mix (Driftwood and DuBois): Mix played a more romanticized and flamboyant western hero than the gritty William S. Hart, whom he succeeded at the top of the box office in the 1920s. His horse, Tony, remained with him throughout his career. See What's There: Drift-

Tom Mix's birthplace in Driftwood. *(Courtesy of the Tom Mix Birthplace Park)*

wood, DuBois; also Florence, Arizona, and Dewey, Oklahoma.

William Powell (Pittsburgh): Like Barrymore and Menjou, another Keystone State mustache guy who was big in the 1930s. His family moved to Kansas City when he was in his teens. Best known for the Thin Man series, he also appeared in *My Man Godfrey, The Great Ziegfeld* and *Ziegfeld Follies* (both times as Ziegfeld), and *Mister Roberts.*

George Romero: See Made in Pennsylvania.

David O. Selznick (Pittsburgh): Big-time Hollywood producer, a titan in the thirties and forties—and it didn't hurt being Louis B. Mayer's son-in-law. He produced, of course, *Gone with the Wind,* but his credits also include *King Kong, Anna Karenina, Nothing Sacred, Rebecca* (for which he brought Hitchcock to America), *The Third Man,* and *Duel in the Sun,* which starred his second wife, Jennifer Jones, whom he groomed for success.

James Stewart (Indiana): Beloved all-American actor. See What's There.

James Stewart's birthplace plaque in Indiana, Pennsylvania. *(Courtesy of the Indiana County Visitors and Convention Bureau)*

Andy Warhol (Pittsburgh): Remembered more for his art and lifestyle, Warhol, who was born in Cleveland but studied at Carnegie Tech, was a major influence on film's avant-garde in the sixties and seventies. *Sleep,* his eight-hour study of a man sleeping, has probably been heard-about-but-not-seen by more people than any other movie (excepting perhaps Jerry Lewis's *The Day the Clown Cried*). Others: *Flesh, Trash,* and *Andy Warhol's Frankenstein, Dracula,* and *Bad.* See What's There: Castle Shannon.

Johnny Weissmuller (Windber): Olympic swimmer who played Tarzan in the thirties and forties.

WHAT'S THERE

Castle Shannon: Andy Warhol's grave is at the St. John the Baptist Byzantine Catholic Church Cemetery, about 15–20 minutes south of Pittsburgh, where he grew up. Mourners have been known to leave flowers in Campbell Soup cans. Off Route 88 (Library Road).

Clark: Tara, a tony inn, is a nineteenth-century mansion remodeled to resemble the *GWTW* pad and opened as a romantic getaway. Many rooms are themed to the film: Melanie's Room, "gentle and luxurious," has a Jacuzzi. Rhett's Room is "slightly scandalous, as you would expect." Belle's Boudoir is a tad naughty. The staff wears period costumes, and tours are available. Ashley's Restaurant has murals of scenes from *GWTW.* Highway 18, 10 minutes north of I-80 exit 1N. Reservations: 412/962-3535.

Downington: Mickey Rooney's Five Star Tabas Hotel, a little slice of Poconos heaven, is off Route 30, exit 23. Reservations: 800/345-8220.

Driftwood: Tom Mix Birthplace Park. Tom Mix's 1880 birthplace, in a section known as Mix Run, is remembered with a museum, a state historical marker, the original barn and flagstone walkway, the old well, and another preserved structure labeled the TOM MIX OUT-

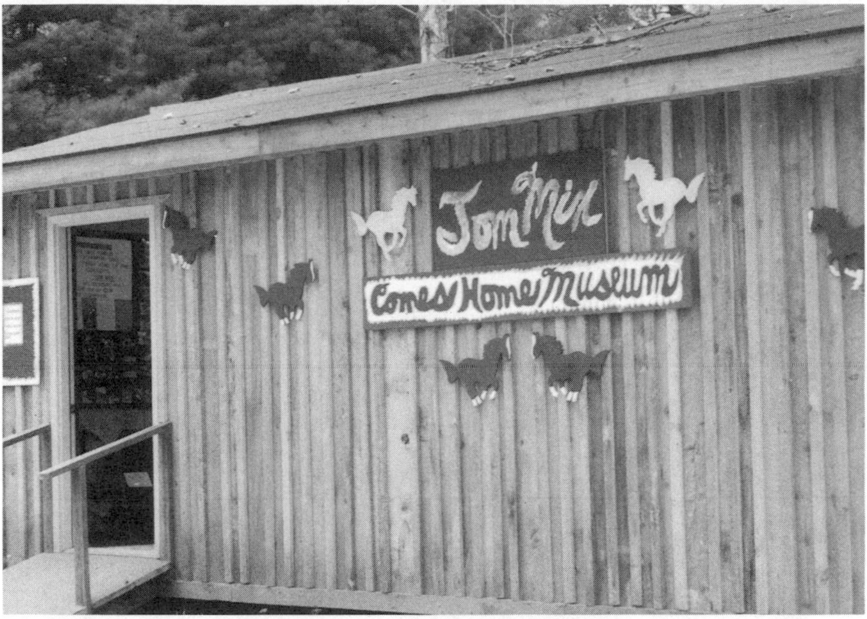

The Tom Mix Museum in Driftwood. *(Courtesy of the Tom Mix Birthplace Park)*

HOUSE. Souvenirs include Tom Mix toy six-shooters and Tom Mix soap. You can buy one square inch of the Mix homestead for $12 plus postage. July brings the Tom Mix Roundup, which includes a wagon train and other Western events. The park is on Mix Run Road, one mile west of town on Highway 555.

DuBois: Tom Mix's childhood home from age nine (it was on Front Street) is the site of an annual mid-September Tom Mix Festival. Check in at headquarters, the Paradise Gulch Saloon. His films are shown at the Playhouse Theater.

Serge Derrigrand, the festival's official Tom Mix lookalike, rides his horse, Dynamite, and does trick shooting. Allen "Slim" Binkley, of Annville, Mix's valet during his circus days of the thirties and forties, performs as Happi the Clown. There's a parade, pizza- and ice-cream-eating contests, memorabilia displays, and public shoot-outs. The town has a Tom Mix Drive. (A portion of the DuBois Mixabilia collection is being transferred to Las Vegas for a separate attraction there.)

Indiana: A bronze statue of Jimmy Stewart beckons from the courthouse lawn; it was dedicated in 1983, when he returned to his hometown for his 75th birthday. (That magical day also featured a parade, an air show, and a reenactment of the French and Indian War.)

James Stewart's boyhood home in Indiana, Pennsylvania. *(Courtesy of the Indiana County Visitors and Convention Bureau)*

There's an annual festival here at the "Hometown of Jimmy Stewart and Christmas Tree Capital of the World!" His boyhood home still stands at 104 North Seventh Street, on Vinegar Hill. There's also a plaque on a stone at the site of his birthplace, 965 Philadelphia Street; the lot now hosts a funeral home. The area proudly boasts a Jimmy Stewart Airport and a James Stewart Avenue. A James Stewart Visitors Center, which will house memorabilia, is "in the planning stages."

Kennett Square: Linda Darnell, who died in a fire

while watching one of her old films on TV, is buried at Union Hill Cemetery, on Route 82, just outside town.

Orefield: Shankweiler's Drive-in Movie Theater is the United States' oldest remaining drive-in. It's west of Allentown on Route 309, four miles north of Route 22. Info: 215/398-1652.

Pen Argyl: Jayne Mansfield's grave is heart-shaped, like the pool in her Hollywood mansion. Fairview Cemetery, near the exit. Route 22.

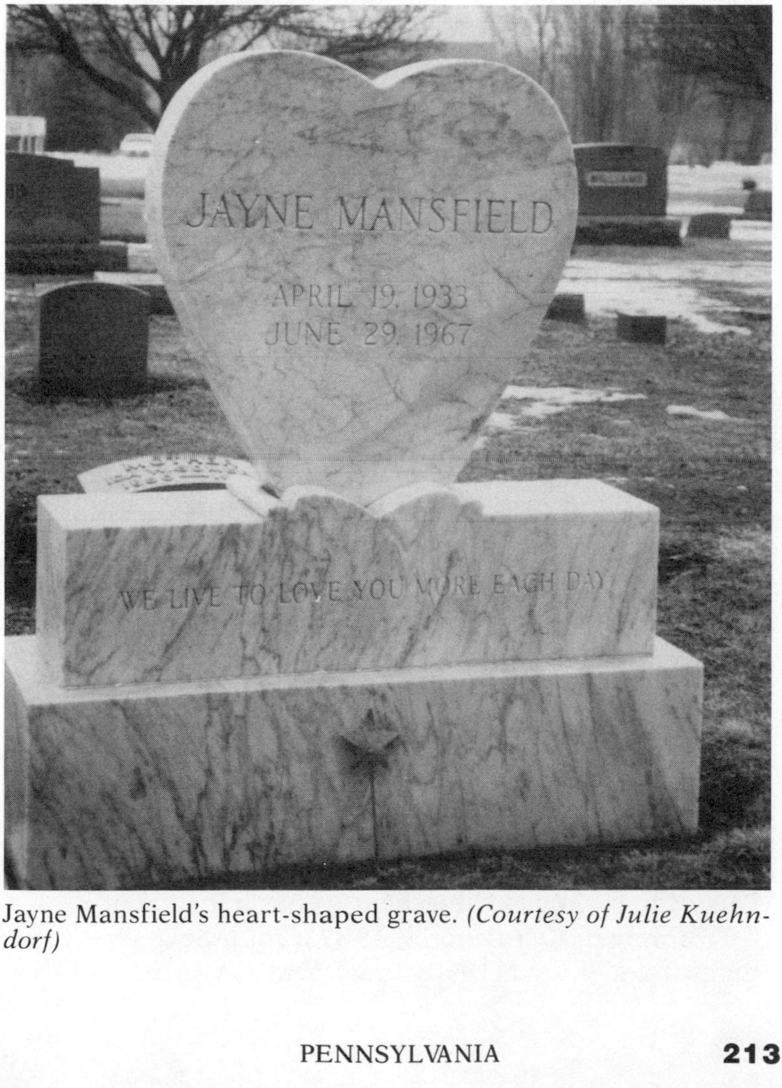

Jayne Mansfield's heart-shaped grave. *(Courtesy of Julie Kuehndorf)*

Philadelphia: John Barrymore's 1882 birth site is now a vacant lot, at 2008 West Columbia Avenue. Lionel and Ethel's birth site, 119 North Ninth Street, is no longer there either.

There's a Mario Lanza Museum (he made 10 films, including *The Great Caruso*) inside the Settlement Music School, 416 Queen Street.

The Rocky statue is in front of the Spectrum sports arena, Broad and Pattison streets. Stallone wanted it placed in front of the Philadelphia Museum of Art, the way it is in his movies, for gosh sakes; appalled museum directors told him to forget it. It cost $12,000 for the museum to move it to the Spectrum after *Rocky 2.* Sly moved it back for *Rocky 5.* "Why don't you leave it there this time?" he grunted. "Why don't you go away?" they replied.

Pittsburgh: There's a Gene Kelly Square in the East Liberty neighborhood, where he grew up. It's a street, despite the name.

WEST VIRGINIA

MADE IN WEST VIRGINIA

***Pudd'n'head Wilson* (Harpers Ferry, 1984):** An American Playhouse adaptation of Mark Twain's clever courtroom dramedy.

***Reckless* (Weirton, 1984):** The rusty red clouds that hover above this fragrant burg set the hopeless tone for our heroes. Industrial landscapes from *The Deer Hunter* were shot here as well.

***Sweet Dreams* (Martinsburg, 1985):** Scenes for the Patsy Cline bio were shot here in her hometown.

***Matewan* (Thurmond, 1987):** John Sayles searched high and low for a 1980s town that was preserved and dismal enough to look like a depressed 1920s West Virginia coal-mining town. Thurmondites can be proud he selected their town, sort of, not really.

WEST VIRGINIA'S GIFTS TO HOLLYWOOD

★ ★ ★ ★ ★ ★ ★ ★ ★ ★ ★ ★ ★ ★ ★ ★

MOMMY, WHAT'S A CHARACTER ACTOR?

Bernie Casey (Wyco): Former receiver with the L.A. Rams who has become the movies' quintessential "good cop."

Paul Dooley (Parkersburg): Character actor who gained acclaim as the father in *Breaking Away* and appeared in several Robert Altman films, including *Popeye,* in which he played Wimpy.

Brad Dourif (Huntington): Intense actor who plays weirdos like the preacher in *Wise Blood,* the bomber brother in *Ragtime,* and Billy "You won't tell my m-m-m-m-m-m-mother" Bibbitt in *One Flew Over the Cuckoo's Nest.*

Don Knotts (Morgantown): An outstanding actor, Barney Fife of "The Andy Griffith Show" found a career as a lovable weakling in entertaining kid flicks like *The Incredible Mr. Limpet, The Ghost and Mr. Chicken,* and *How to Frame a Figg.*

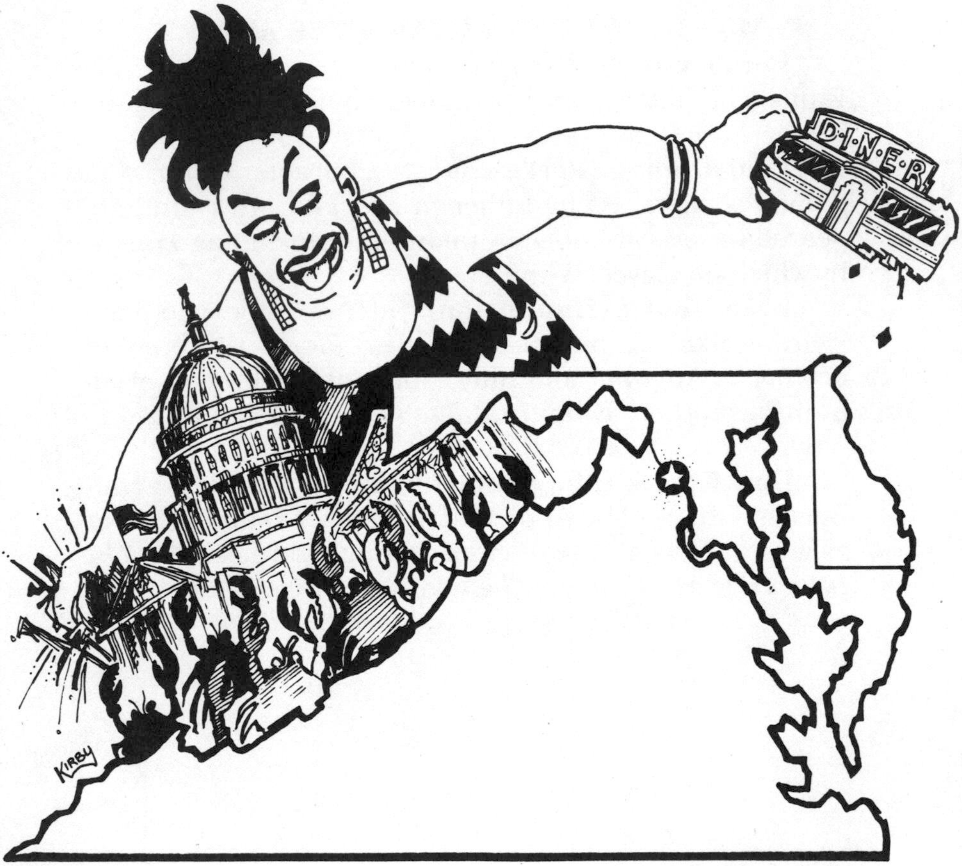
D·I·N·E·R
KIRBY

Chapter 9

CRABLAND

Delaware •
Washington, D.C. •
Maryland •
Virginia •

DELAWARE

A small state. Lots of nice corporate headquarters. Tax reasons.

MADE IN DELAWARE

***Dead Poets Society* (1989):** The Robin Williams hit, which won a surprising Oscar for best screenplay—beating out *Do the Right Thing* and *sex, lies and videotape*—was the first feature shot in the state.

DELAWARE'S GIFT TO HOLLYWOOD

★ ★ ★ ★ ★ ★ ★ ★ ★ ★ ★ ★ ★ ★ ★ ★

Valerie Bertinelli (Wilmington): The small-screen version of Diane Lane, Bertinelli is trying to carve out a career in made-for-TV movies. She is married to guitar hero Eddie Van Halen.

WASHINGTON, D.C.

MADE IN D.C.

***Mr. Smith Goes to Washington* (1939):** This Frank Capra fable created a furor when screened for a group of politicos because of its healthy skepticism in such dangerous times, but was well received by the general public. James Stewart at the Lincoln Monument is an indelible movie moment. Second-unit background shots only.

***The More the Merrier* (1943):** Jean Arthur bunks with Joel McCrea and avuncular Charles Coburn in wartime, housing-shy D.C. Second unit only.

***Born Yesterday* (1950):** A dumb blond, played by Judy Holliday, goes to Washington and figures it out. Misinterpreted as froth, the film is actually so knowing as to be downright depressing.

***The Day the Earth Stood Still* (1951):** An alien robot tries to straighten us out. What do you think, did it work?

***Advise and Consent* (1962):** This 139-minute filibuster of a movie takes us into the sleazy back rooms of D.C. Henry Fonda plays a slimy power wielder.

***Seven Days in May* (1964):** A Rod Serling story, about a military plot to take over the government, with an all-star cast.

***The Exorcist* (1973):** One of the first "blockbuster" movies of the 1970s, it was shot on location at Georgetown University, the alma mater of the book's author, William Peter Blatty.

***All the President's Men* (1976):** The toppling of King Nixon plays like a gripping mystery. Locations include, naturally, the Watergate Building. Security guard Frank Wills re-created his detection of the intruders for the movie cameras. The newsroom of the *Washington Post* was meticulously duped in a studio, including the use of authentic *Post* garbage.

***Billy Jack Goes to Washington* (1977):** Mr. Smith couldn't throw a side-kick like our Billy.

***Being There* (1979):** Peter Sellers's great swan song shows his rise in government through sheer ignorance.

***The Seduction of Joe Tynan* (1979):** Alan Alda as a sensitive senator experiencing life, and an affair with Meryl Streep, in the political limelight.

***D.C. Cab* (1983):** The film that cashed in on the phenomenon that is Mr. T.

***Broadcast News* (1987):** Frolics in an authentic-looking TV newsroom in D.C. Shot almost entirely on location.

***No Way Out* (1987):** A tour of D.C. by limo is spiced by hot sex between Kevin Costner and Sean Young in the back seat.

***Suspect* (1987):** Cher's stomach versus Dennis Quaid's. There's also a D.C. murder trial.

***The Silence of the Lambs* (1991):** This Jonathan Demme movie shot in the office of the Secretary of Labor, Elizabeth Dole; it was supposed to be that of the F.B.I. director.

D.C.'S GIFTS TO HOLLYWOOD

★ ★ ★ ★ ★ ★ ★ ★ ★ ★ ★ ★ ★ ★ ★ ★

Blair Brown: Intelligent, red-haired star of *Altered States, Continental Divide, A Flash of Green,* and TV's "Days and Nights of Molly Dodd."

Billie Burke: Able comedienne who excelled as a bubble-headed society wife with a high pitched voice. Best known as Good Fairy Glinda in *The Wizard of Oz.* Other films: *Dinner at Eight, Topper, The Man Who Came to Dinner.*

Alan Hale: Have ever a father and son looked so alike as Hale and Alan, Junior (the skipper from "Gilligan's Island")? Husky Hale played hundreds of character roles and invented folding seats for movie theaters. Films include: *It Happened One Night, Babbitt, The Inspector General.*

Goldie Hawn: "Laugh-In" starlet who was merely appealing in the movies until the success of *Private Benjamin,* which gave her a surprising amount of power that she has since totally wasted.

Helen Hayes: Primarily a theater actress, Hayes had a limited movie career. Highlights were *The Sin of Madelon Claudet* (Oscar for Best Actress), *Anastasia,* and *Airport.*

WHAT'S THERE

The Smithsonian Museum of American History has some movie memorabilia on display, although overall it's seriously remiss in recognizing the importance of this stuff. On the Mall.

The Smithsonian Air and Space Museum has on display the flying-wing bomber that dropped the A-bomb on the Martians in *War of the Worlds* (1953). On the Mall.

MARYLAND

MADE IN MARYLAND

Maryland has hosted a modicum of film production, but no other state can boast a town with two major filmmakers concurrently plying their trade, capturing the distinct flavor of the region, and achieving consistent success. Herewith a guide to the work of these Baltim-*auteurs.*

BARRY LEVINSON'S BALTIMORE

Barry Levinson shoots in Baltimore not because he thinks his stories or characters are particular to that city, not because a Baltimore setting adds another dimension to his work; he just happens to come from there. "My films are about the people I know in Baltimore," he says. "Those characters and those neighborhoods. Everything else, in my mind, would be a cheat."

***Diner* (1982):** The Fell's Point Diner in the film was originally the Oakland Diner, in Oakland, New Jersey. It was towed here for filming to an empty lot at Boston and Montford Streets, a site that now boasts a homely cluster of condos. The climactic wedding of Steve Guttenberg takes place in the basement of the 150-year-old Engineers Society, at 11 West Mt. Vernon Place.

***Tin Men* (1987):** The Caddy showroom belongs to an actual Cadillac dealer, at 242 West 29th Street (at Remington, near Johns Hopkins). After smacking into Richard Dreyfuss's one-sixteenth-of-a-mile finny beauty, Danny DeVito repairs to his home at 3107 Cliftmount, one of a mind-boggling two-block stretch of identical home-sweet-row houses. The house in the Forest Park section where a housewife is duped by The Old *Life* Magazine Photographer Gag was formerly the home of the Levinsons.

Avalon **(1990):** The late 1940s street scenes were filmed along Appleton Street, in the southwest section of town. Interiors were shot at Baltimore's Flite Three studio (1130 East Coldspring Lane).

JOHN WATERS'S CHARM CITY

"Think of it as Trashtown, USA, the Sleaziest City on Earth, the Hairdo Capital of the World," writes John Waters in his distinguished sleaze primer, *Shock Value*. Visually, Waters's oeuvre does not look all that Baltimorey: no crabcakes, no Orioles, no well-scrubbed old white-granite-stoop, painted-screen, blue-collar row houses, no million-dollar harbor condos, no diners. Until his last few films, his location requirements seemed, for the most part, "Can I shoot there for free, without a permit, without nosy bystanders?" (Because of this, some locations must remain secret.) Still, a cumulative ambience is evoked by his work, one that clearly defines a unique and prevalent aspect of the city's makeup, a state of mind that can't be captured in a tourist brochure—and wouldn't be if it could.

Mondo Trasho **(1969):** This one comprised nondescript anywhere/nowhere locations: empty lots, scraggly woods, landscapes of brick and asphalt. The exterior of the laundromat where the Virgin Mary appears is on St. Paul Street, one block south of 25th. Mary Vivian Pearce feeds roaches hamburger meat in Wyman Park.

Multiple Maniacs **(1970):** The name of the church where Divine ecstatically receives a "rosary job" is a secret. The giant lobster that molests Divine has returned to the briny depths; it got all decrepit, so Waters and art director Vincent Perenio buried it at sea, at Fell's Point Harbor. Waters's parents' suburban front lawn (313 Morris Avenue in Lutherville), which he refers to as "the

Dreamland lot," was used for the Cavalcade of Perversion.

***Pink Flamingos* (1972):** The filthy family's trailer was on the grounds of a now-disbanded commune. Its burnt-out hulk remained for several years as a tourist attraction for die-hard fans, but it was finally carted away. Connie and Raymond Marble's house (3900 Greenmount Avenue), where they stored teenage girls in the

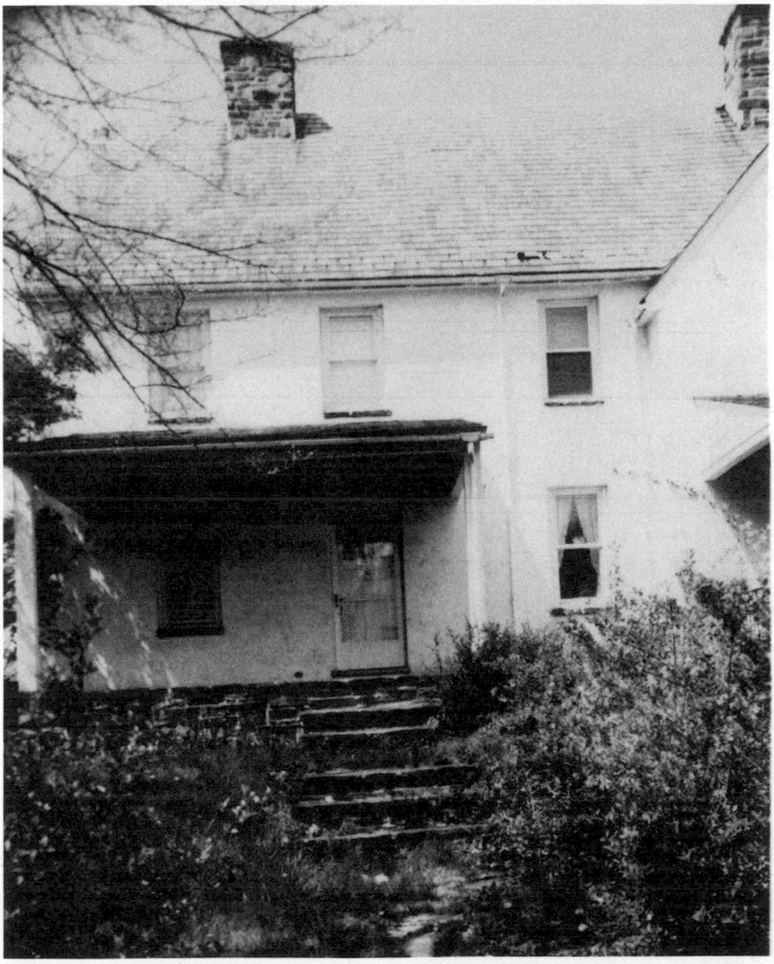

The Marble House from *Pink Flamingos*.

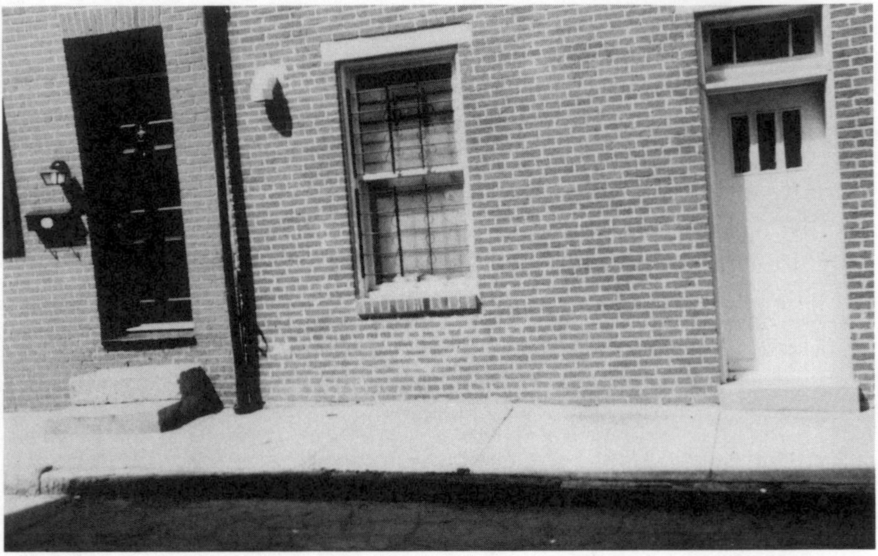

The stoop where Divine scooped poop.

basement, was owned by Waters at the time of filming, and looks much the same today. The spot where Divine made cinematic history by gobbling poodle poop is in front of 894 Tyson Street, just off Reed, which at the time was the home of Pat Moran, Waters's casting director; it was her dog, too.

***Female Trouble* (1974):** Dawn's childhood home ("I hate Christmas!" shrieks Divine, overturning the tree and trimmings onto Mom) is in Orchard Hills. The bridal shop where she buys her sheer wedding dress is at Broadway and Fell's Point, near the Pink Flamingos store.

***Desperate Living* (1977):** The stately Gravel house, where Connie Gravel goes violently mad ("Our children are having sex!"), at 313 Morris Avenue, in Lutherville, was Waters's parents' house at the time. The deviate-ridden hamlet of Mortville was erected on private property, with Queen Edith Massey's castle constructed by Vincent Perenio.

Kampus Kut-Ups: Johns Hopkins Hospital, where

Mole has her sex-change-in-a-jiffy, at one time actually performed those operations. Waters had been arrested on Hopkins soil years earlier while shooting *Mondo Trasho*'s nude-hitchhiker scene.

***Polyester* (1981):** The Edmondson Drive-In, where Tab Hunter screened Marguerite Duras classics, is still there, on Route 40. It is no longer an art house. The Fishpaw residence is at 528 Heavi Tree Hill, in the Chartwell section of Severna Park. According to Perenio, the house was rented for the filming by him and an assistant, posing as normal people.

***Hairspray* (1988):** The Turnblad apartment was in Highlandtown, a solid blue-collar area. The Hefty Hideaway, where Tracy and Divine get outfitted, is actually Pacey's, a magnificently streamlined shop at 3311 Eastern Avenue, next to a beauty academy. Tracy's high school is Mergenthaler Vocational Tech (known as Mervo). Tilted Acres, site of the race riot that finally integrates the *Corny Collins Show*, was an amusement park in Allentown, Pennsylvania.

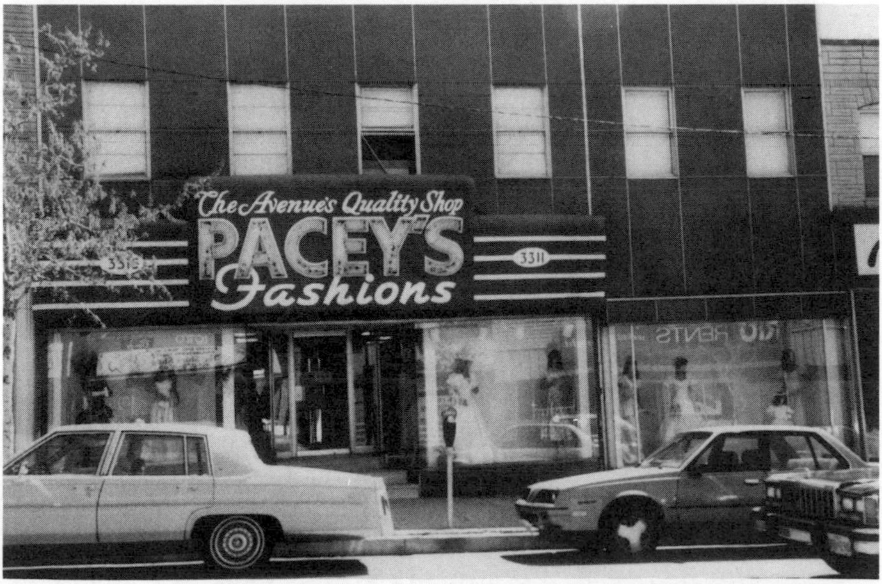

Pacey's, *Hairspray*'s Hefty Hideaway

***Cry-Baby* (1990):** The Milford Mill Swim Club was the Turkey Point Swim Club, the location for the "King Cry-Baby" musical number. It's at 3900 Milford Mill Road.

OTHER BALTIMORE

The al Pacino Cafe in Baltimore. No relation.

***. . . And Justice for All* (1979):** Exteriors were shot at the Clarence Mitchell Courthouse, which has photogenic animal statues at its Calvert and Fayette streets entrance. Written by Barry Levinson and Valerie Curtin.

***Violets Are Blue . . .* (1986):** Sissy Spacek plays an intrepid photographer who in one perilous scene is seen risking her neck in strife-torn Northern Ireland; the grim spectacle was actually shot in calm Fell's Point, at the corner of West Baltimore and Poppleton streets, near a great Irish bar, Gandy Dancer (McHenry and Carey streets). The film was primarily set, however, in Ocean City, an overdeveloped resort.

***The Bedroom Window* (1987):** Despite its comical attempts to give this a real "Baltimore" flavor—the titular window is located at 12 East Mt. Vernon Place, near the Washington Monument, in a photogenic historic district; Steve Guttenberg and Isabelle Huppert decide to meet at the aquarium, at the touristy harbor; Elizabeth McGovern works in a nonexistent bar with a big neon Poe head and a bright BALTIMORE! sign on the wall—the town looks sparkly clean and sterile, like Toronto. John Waters's Baltimore, even in washed-out black and white, looks better.

***The Accidental Tourist* (1988):** The Learys live in the leafy Roland Park area: Macon's sister and brothers live at the southwest corner of Woodlawn and Windhurst; his house is nearby, at 324 Hawthorne. Muriel's shabby neighborhood is supposed to be South Baltimore, but Geena Davis actually trod on North Greenmount, on the real-life rundown block between 20th and 21st streets. Anne Tyler, the book's author, lives not far from the Leary home.

The Learys' house from *The Accidental Tourist.*

***Clara's Heart* (1988):** In addition to the eastern shore mansion location, the film used a slew of Baltimore settings, including the Congress Hotel (300 West Franklin), the Rusty Scupper restaurant (402 Key Highway), the Engineers Club (a site reaching critical exposure mass; it also served as the Romanian Embassy in *Her Alibi*), Children's Hospital (3825 Green Spring Avenue), Roland Park Shopping Center (4800 Roland Avenue), St. Anne's Church (22nd and Greenmount—near Muriel's house in *The Accidental Tourist*), and Friend's School (5114 West Charles).

***Men Don't Leave* (1989):** Scenes for this Jessica Lange vehicle were shot at the stunning Peabody Library (17 Mt. Vernon Square, with exteriors in the square), the B&O Railroad Museum (West Pratt Street at Poppleton), and Keepers Inc., an antique shop that doubled as a cheese shop (northeast corner of Reed and Tyson streets, across the street from where Divine made canine history).

MARYLAND'S GIFTS TO HOLLYWOOD

★ ★ ★ ★ ★ ★ ★ ★ ★ ★ ★ ★ ★ ★ ★ ★

Karen Allen: This perky, big-eyed girl next door was the original Indiana Jones love interest.

Charlie Chase (b. Charles Parrott, Baltimore): A solid second-tier comic performer and director who made a smooth transition from silents to the sound era but died young. Chase worked with the likes of Chaplin, the Three Stooges, Fatty Arbuckle, Hal Roach, and Mack Sennett.

Barry Levinson (Baltimore): The director of *Rain Man* and *Good Morning, Vietnam* and writer-director of a Baltimore trilogy, Levinson attended Forest Park High School, where he met the characters who populate *Diner*. In real life, they hung out at Brice's Hilltop Diner—now a package store—in northwest Baltimore.

John Waters (Baltimore): Waters began on a shoestring, made a series of culty low-budget features, and now makes genial, moderately budgeted features. Despite his manufactured reputation for sleaze, the amiable Waters is one of the most consistently entertaining directors around, an adept magazine writer, and an engaging speaker.

WHAT'S THERE

Baltimore: The diner from *Diner* has recently found new life at breakfast and lunchtime as the Kids Diner; here, a staff of urban high-schoolers learns the food industry while serving fries and gravy to *Diner* aficionados. The diner looks like it did in the film, minus the neon sign, and has been relocated to an isolated plot at the corner of East Saratoga and Holliday streets like a historical artifact—which, of course, it is.

The diner from *Diner*.

Movies past have left their mark on this town. In front of the fabulous old Senator Theater, on Yale Road and Belvedere, is a Baltimore Walk of Fame, commemorations in cement of recent films that were shot here and premiered at the Senator. There's Anne Tyler's signature from the opening of *The Accidental Tourist,* Levinson's for *Diner* and *Tin Men,* and *Hairspray*'s Waters and Divine.

At the historic Belvedere Hotel (1 East Chase Street), where, in the John Eager Howard Room, Danny DeVito and his pitchmen pals compare notes at day's end in *Tin Men,* a photographic Wall of Fame recalls the many stars who have bivouacked here over the years: Fred Astaire, Claudette Colbert, Cecil B. DeMille, Divine, Marie Dressler, Richard Dreyfuss, Henry Fonda, Clark Gable, Jean Harlow, Tab Hunter, Al Jolson, Carole Lombard, the Marx Brothers, Tom Mix, Mary Pickford, Tyrone Power, Ginger Rogers, Roy Rogers, Barbara Stanwyck, and Rudolph Valentino. (The hotel has hit hard times, and may not be open much longer.)

The most popular landmark of all is the former Edith's Shopping Bag thrift store, now called Pink Flamingos, at 728 South Broadway in the Fell's Point dis-

Pink Flamingos, formerly Edith's Shopping Bag thrift store.

trict. The shop, formerly the domain of the beloved Edith Massey, ever-sunny star of many a Waters saga, is now owned by Bob Adams, a member of the Waters production team. Massey, who died in 1983 (her ashes were scattered at Marilyn Monroe's grave site, in Los Angeles' Westwood Memorial Park), still receives fan mail from around the world. Pilgrims are constantly pilfering the store's vivid, hand-painted signs.

Here you can buy, along with posters, soundtrack albums, and a varying line of memorabilia, cans of Aqua Net hairspray autographed by Waters. (They're $5, with profits going to AIDS relief.) Even more enticing is the prospect of encountering the shop's cast of habitués, which on my visit included the affable Egg Man from *Pink Flamingos,* who greets customers with a snaggle-toothed grin and says, "You recognize me? The *Egg Man.*" Across the street, at 721 South Broadway, is Dionysos, a Greek disco, which was once Pete's Hotel, a seedy dive where Massey was discovered by Waters tending bar and charming her sordid clientele.

Chestertown: Tallulah "I can say shit, darling, I'm a lady" Bankhead's grave is in St. Paul's Churchyard. Go seven miles west of town on Route 20, turn left at the Sandy Bottom Road sign, and drive on one mile.

Eldersburg: Blaze Starr's Handmade Jewelry, Carrolltowne Mall. The legendary stripper, whose relationship with the former governor of Louisiana was the subject of *Blaze,* is waiting to chat and sell you things.

Lilypons: The post office of this nontown (it's a cluster of ponds where water lilies and goldfish are raised) was named in 1932 after Lily Pons, a French opera singer. Out of gratitude, she visited here (with an amorous Andre Kostelanetz) on June 21, 1936, when her film, *I Dream Too Much* (costarring Henry Fonda and Lucille Ball), was released. The post office has been eliminated, but a bronze plaque commemorates its unfathomable onetime existence.

Mount Rainier: The home where the real-life basis of *The Exorcist* occurred was at 3210 Bunker Hill Road; it's been torn down. In 1949, a 14-year-old boy was seemingly possessed by Lucifer. A four-month exorcism—including, perhaps, the playing of Frank Sinatra albums backwards at 16 rpm—was a failure; eventually, the boy was sent to St. Louis for successful treatment.

Silver Springs: Petey, the Little Rascals' dog, is entombed at the Aspen Hill Pet Cemetery, 13630 Georgia Avenue.

Towson: Mourners bring strange gifts, like Christmas trees and donuts, to the grave of Divine (Harris Glenn Milstead). Prospect Hill Cemetery, York Road.

VIRGINIA

MADE IN VIRGINIA

***Brother Rat* (Lexington, Virginia Military Institute, 1938):** Ronald Reagan and Jane Wyman appear in this comedy about three zanies at VMI; the film is based on a story by two VMI grads.

***Dirty Dancing* (Mountain Lake, 1987):** Jennifer Gray and Patrick Swayze in a hit that kept Vestron Pictures in business for years. See What's There.

***Gardens of Stone* (Arlington, 1987):** Francis Coppola's bummer included extensive filming at Arlington National Cemetery, which houses many film notables alongside presidents and the Unknown Soldier.

VIRGINIA'S GIFTS TO HOLLYWOOD

★ ★ ★ ★ ★ ★ ★ ★ ★ ★ ★ ★ ★ ★ ★ ★

Richard Arlen (Charlottesville): Big Rich starred in *Wings* (1927), the winner of the first best picture Oscar, and continued to find work for almost 50 years.

Joseph Cotten (Petersburg): A member of Orson Welles's Mercury Theater, Cotten participated in the 1938 "War of the Worlds" broadcast as well as *Citizen Kane* and *The Magnificent Ambersons.* His thoughtful presence also clicked in *The Third Man, Duel in the Sun,* and Hitchcock's *Shadow of a Doubt.* See What's There.

Kathryn Harrold (Tazewell): This smart, good-looking actress was memorable as Albert Brooks's on-again-off-again girlfriend in *Modern Romance,* but is of historical interest for starring in "Magruder and Loud," billed as "television's first married cops," and *Yes, Georgio,* the mind-numbing dramatic debut of Luciano Pavarotti, a singer.

Henry King (Christiansburg): Ultraprolific director with an unobtrusive, straightforward technique who grew up on his family's Virginia plantation. His career spanned from the early silent days to the 1960s. Films include: *In Old Chicago, Twelve O'Clock High, Alexander's Ragtime Band, The Gunfighter.*

Rob Lowe (Charlottesville): The jury's still out on this guy, one of filmdom's few males who is forced, like a "dumb blond," to prove that his talent is not merely his looks. He's not bad as a demonic bimbo in *Bad Influence.*

Bill "Bojangles" Robinson (Richmond): Shirley Temple's tap-dancing sidekick. In his last feature, *Stormy Weather,* he finally got to play a romantic lead to a black grownup—Lena Horne.

George C. Scott (Wise): This Oscar decliner was born in Virginia but raised in Detroit.

Randolph Scott (Orange County): Classic western hero whose films include *The Last of the Mohicans, Western Union,* and *Comanche Station.*

Margaret Sullavan (Norfolk): The sassy star of *Shop Around the Corner* married Henry Fonda, William Wyler, and Leland Hayward. Her daughter Brooke Hayward's book *Haywire* relates the story of her untimely death. See What's There: Lancaster.

WHAT'S THERE

Arlington: Buried in the Arlington National Cemetery are actress Constance Bennett, writer Dashiell Hammett, and palimony defendant Lee Marvin, whose grave is near those of Watergate defendant John Mitchell and boxer Joe Louis.

Lancaster: Margaret Sullavan's grave is at St. Mary's Whitechapel Trinity Episcopal Churchyard, at the intersection of Routes 201 and 354. The grave is located just after the curve in the path.

Mountain Lake: Mountain Lake Hotel was the location for *Dirty Dancing.* The main building of this Appalachian resort, with its recognizable stone facade, was built in 1936. It substituted in the film for an early-1960s Catskills getaway. About 30 miles west of Roanoke. Reservations: 800/346-3334.

Petersburg: While there's no commemoration for Joseph Cotten, you can see a film he made about Petersburg's role in the Civil War, *The Echo Still Remains,* at the Siege Museum, at 15 West Bank Street.

Richmond: The stairway from *Gone with the Wind*'s Tara was based on that of Richmond's Jefferson Sheraton Hotel, an 1895 Beaux Arts–Renaissance Revival hotel that once housed fish and alligator ponds. The well-regarded talkfest *My Dinner with Andre* (1982) was filmed here. Franklin and Adams streets. Reservations: 804/788-8000.

The childhood home of Shirley MacLaine and Warren Beatty (né Beaty) is at 3954 Fauquier Avenue. The director of the Virginia Film Office now lives here.

Winchester: The grave of Patsy (*Sweet Dreams*) Cline (b. Virginia Hensley Dick) and a memorial bell tower are at Shenandoah Memorial Park, Route 522 South.

The finest movie mecca in the state has recently shut down. Madigan's Movie Museum was started by a movie fan, Bill Madigan, and presented an impressive collection of memorabilia: oversized baby blocks that appeared in Shirley Temple's *Captain January*; Patsy Cline's second wedding dress; Gary Cooper's shirt, makeup mirror, and handkerchief from *Cowboy and the Lady*; a brick from the Loews Grand Theater in Atlanta, where *Gone with the Wind* premiered; an oil painting from the set of Ashley's home in *GWTW*; Bing Crosby's hat, tobacco pouch, necktie, and sweater; Agnes Moorehead's sterling silver carafe bottle and troubadour harp; plaster column pieces from Andy Hardy's home; a cross given to Oscar Levant by Judy Garland; Vilma Banky's pocketbook; a scotch bottle from the set of Bogie's *Left Hand of God*; the costume worn by Luise Rainer in *The Good Earth* (the skirt was stolen from the museum); a Japanese airplane mechanic's uniform from *Tora! Tora! Tora!*; James Mason's toga from *Julius Caesar*; shields used by Robert Taylor and George Sanders in *Ivanhoe*; an oil painting of Maureen O'Hara seen in *Sentimental Journey*; and much, much more. It was at 16 South Loudoun Street, and here's hoping the collection resurfaces soon.

CUJO
Pet Sematary
Skeleton CREW
The STAND
Cat's Eye
TOMMY KNOCKERS
CARRIE
IT
STEPHEN KING
SALEM'S LOT
The SHINING
The STAND
DIFFERENT SEASONS
Stephen King

Chapter 10

QUAINT boring NEW ENGLAND

- Connecticut
- Maine
- Massachusetts
- New Hampshire
- New York
- Rhode Island
- Vermont

MADE IN CONNECTICUT

A Connecticut home indicates affluent suburban living in many a New York film, but rarely have productions actually ventured there. *The Swimmer*—based on a short story by commuter scribe John Cheever—might be the most famous example of a quintessential Connecticut film that wasn't shot there.

The most popular location in the state is Yale University, in New Haven. Films shot there include *All About Eve* (1950), *Volunteers* (1985), *Mystic Pizza* (1988), and *Chances Are* (1989).

***Gentleman's Agreement* (Darien, 1947):** Elia Kazan's "Jewish Like Me" starred Gregory Peck.

***Mystic Pizza* (Mystic, 1988):** *Diner* on estrogen, the film is ostensibly based in Mystic, a touristy seaport, where there actually is a Mystic Pizza parlor. It's not the one in the movie. Nonetheless, its owner contemplated franchising a national chain. It didn't happen.

***Everybody Wins* (Norwich, 1991):** Locations included City Hall and the former King Cooley Thermos Plant. Written by Roxbury's Arthur Miller (see What's There), his first screenplay since *The Misfits.*

CONNECTICUT'S GIFTS TO HOLLYWOOD

★ ★ ★ ★ ★ ★ ★ ★ ★ ★ ★ ★ ★ ★ ★ ★

Linda Blair (Westport): Forever branded by *The Exorcist,* Blair has also brought much joy in *Roller Boogie* and *Born Innocent.*

Ernest Borgnine (Hamden): Forever branded by "McHale's Navy," Borgnine has played roles of startling sensitivity and insensitivity, as in *Marty* and *The Wild Bunch,* respectively.

Brian Dennehy (Bridgeport): Vietnam vet character actor who projects integrity. Films include *First Blood, Best Seller,* and *F/X.*

Linda Evans (Hartford): Actress best known for being a former wife of John Derek, for being a star of "Dynasty," and for cashing in so handsomely on the fact that she has aged well.

Katharine Hepburn (Hartford): Semireclusive movie grande dame from a high-class family. Her illustrious body of work includes *Holiday, The Philadelphia Story, The African Queen,* and several films with her boyfriend, Milwaukeean Spencer Tracy.

Christopher Lloyd (Stamford): Prime-time's first drug burnout character has carved a movie career with weirdo roles in *Back to the Future, The Dream Team,* and *Who Framed Roger Rabbit.*

Robert Mitchum (Bridgeport): Supercool Mitchum brings a sense of out-of-control mayhem to his work. Memorable Mitchumesque films include *The Night of the Hunter, Thunder Road, Cape Fear,* and *The Friends of Eddie Coyle.*

Alfred Newman (New Haven): Nine-time Oscar-winning composer with distinguished career but a name unfortunately the same as that of the goofy mascot for *Mad* magazine. Films scored include: *Gunga Din, The Grapes of Wrath, All About Eve, The Seven Year Itch,* and *Airport.*

Paul Newman (Westport): European men around the middle of the millennium who were successful movie stars and race car drivers *and* could cook up a mean spaghetti sauce were hailed as Renaissance men. Paul Newman, who lives here, is truly a man out of time.

Meg Ryan (Fairfield): Perky Goldie Hawn clone who made a big splash in the late 1980s with *When Harry Met Sally, Innerspace,* and a relationship with Dennis Quaid.

Middletown: The Wesleyan University Cinema Archives owns piles of movie memorabilia and mounts a show about once a year. The Ingrid Bergman collection comprises the usual—correspondence, photos, diaries—and her costume from *Joan of Arc*. The John Waters collection features costumes from *Hairspray*; the Frank Capra has shooting scripts and the unabridged version of his autobiography. The Clint Eastwood collection includes a costume from *Joe Kidd* and an evaluation and pink slip from Universal Pictures.

The archives are not exactly a tourist attraction, but are open to researchers by appointment: 203/347-9411.

Oneco: Cattletown Movie Ranch, which opened in the mid-eighties, is the only movie studio/western-

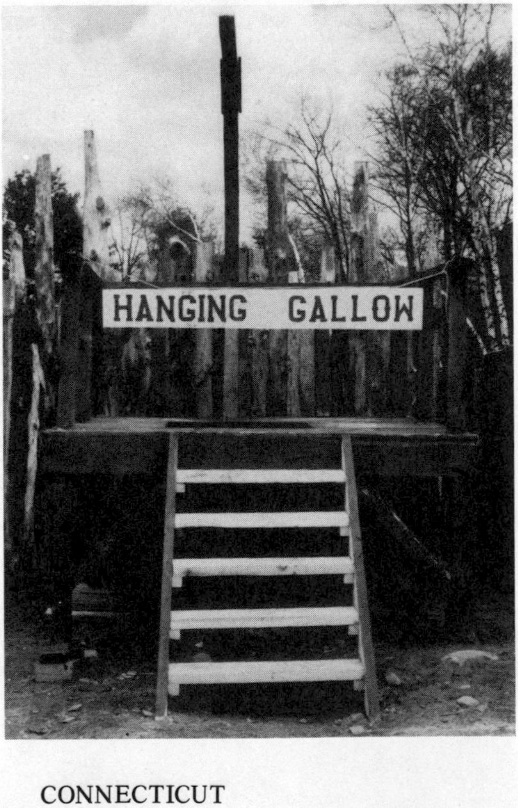

Cattletown Movie Ranch features an impressive Hanging Gallows.

A guy getting hanged at the Hanging Gallows.

themed tourist attraction this side of the Mississippi. It pales next to such longtime destinations as Texas's Alamo Village, Arizona's Old Tucson, and Colorado's Buckskin Joe, but it's a respectable effort. So far, there have been no features made here.

It's on Newport Road, off Route 14A.

Roxbury: The farm where Marilyn Monroe lived with Arthur Miller from 1957 to 1960 is on Tophet Road and is unnumbered. Miller is still a Roxbury resident.

MAINE

MADE IN MAINE

***Way Down East* (1920):** D. W. Griffith directs Lillian Gish. The film was famous for the scene, shot in Vermont, in which Gish drifts away on ice floes.

***Captains Courageous* (Camden, 1937):** Spencer Tracy fishes smack-'em brat Freddie Bartholomew out of the ocean. Tracy won an Oscar for his efforts.

***Leave Her to Heaven* (1945):** This Technicolor film noir has neurotic Gene Tierney tormenting Cornel Wilde in great Maine (and New Mexico) locations and splendid homes.

***Carousel* (Camden, 1957):** Gordon MacRae pitches musical, wide-screen woo at Shirley Jones in a rare location musical.

***Peyton Place* (Camden, 1957):** Soap opera set in New Hampshire and made into a synonym for Sinville by its TV adaptation, which starred the great, great Ryan O'Neal.

***Whales of August* (1986):** Shot on Cliff Island. Lillian Gish's filmmaking return to the Lobster State, 66 years after *Way Down East.* Costarring Bette Davis.

***Creepshow II* (Bangor, 1987):** Stephen King has a cameo as a truck driver in this adaptation of three of his short stories, shot in his hometown.

***Pet Sematary* (1989):** King scripted this adaptation of his bestseller and brought yet another production to his backyard.

MAINE'S GIFT TO HOLLYWOOD

Bette Davis: Davis lived with husband Gary Merrill (her *All About Eve* beau) in Cape Elizabeth during the

1950s. They had a nice place along Old Ocean House Road.

John Ford (b. Sean O'Feeney, Cape Elizabeth): The Babe Ruth of the western. Considered by Welles, Bergman, Kazan, Kurosawa, and Capra the greatest ever. His family is well remembered in the area.

Stephen King (Bangor): Richest novelist ever. Pretty much everything he does makes it to the big screen.

MASSACHUSETTS

MADE IN MASSACHUSETTS

WITCHES

Yes, Massachusetts means witches, and not just the warty, black-cone-hatted kind. *The Witches of Eastwick* (1987) features a yummy coven of Michelle Pfeiffer, Susan Sarandon, and Cher. It was slated for filming in Little Compton, Rhode Island, America's Red Hen Capital, but when city fathers got wind of the vomitous church scene, the John Updike–based film was exiled to Massachusetts. *Who's Afraid of Virginia Woolf* (1966), which was shot at Northampton's Smith College, features the scariest witch ever—Elizabeth Taylor as an acid-tongued man-eater.

SCHOOL DAZE

And yes, Massachusetts means the ivy-walled colleges of Boston. *The Paper Chase* (1973) and *Soul Man* (1986) were shot at Harvard, as were the tragic Crimson romances *Love Story* (1970) and *Oliver's Story* (1978). The yellow frame house at 119 Oxford Street, in Cambridge, is where Ryan O'Neal and Ali McGraw lived in *Love Story*. (The students living in the house agreed to clear out if they could be there for the filming of the love scene.) O'Neal's filthy rich pa's manse is actually the headquarters of the U.S. Equestrian Team, in Hamilton. *Altered States* (1980) was filmed outside the Harvard Medical School, on Beacon Hill, and at Logan Airport.

LOTS OF HISTORY HERE

These colonial places sure do have a lot of historical stuff, don't they? The silent version of Louisa May Alcott's *Little Women* (1919) was shot in and around the Alcott home (Orchard House, Lexington Road) in Concord, as well as at the home of Ralph Waldo Emerson (Cambridge Turnpike and SR 2A). The 1934 adaptation of Nathaniel Hawthorne's *The Scarlet Letter* was shot in witch-trial-gaga Salem. James Michener's *Hawaii* (1966) contained scenes of early New England life that were shot at Old Sturbridge Village, a quaintly restored tourist attraction. And the Merchant-Ivory Company, purveyors of art-directed period dramas, came here to film *The Bostonians* (1984) and *The Europeans* (1979), which was filmed in Concord and in Salem, at the Garner Pingree House (128 Essex Street).

THERE ONCE WAS A FISH FROM NANTUCKET . . .

Cape Cod and its islands—Nantucket and Martha's Vineyard—are playgrounds for the east coast movie establishment. So, naturally, several folks have gotten the notion to do some shooting in their summer paradise. *Jaws* (1975), *Jaws 2* (1978), and *Jaws: The Revenge* (1987) used Martha's Vineyard as the fictional resort of Amity. *Jaws* shot in Edgartown and Menemsha. (*Jaws: The Revenge* takes place mostly in the Bahamas, and *Jaws 3-D* [1983], starring Dennis Quaid, is set in Florida's Sea World.)

Jaws tourists should check out the Quint Memorial Shark Tower, at the center of the Menemsha harbor. Also, an overpass at the eastern town line of Oak Bluffs, on Beach Road, is known as Jaws Bridge; the stream under the Bridge leads to a seemingly safe inlet where the shark went on a rampage.

Nantucket is the setting for *The Russians Are Coming*

(1966), the 1920 melodrama *Sinners,* and the Nantucket whaling classic, *Moby Dick* (1956). And Norman Mailer's bizarrely gothic *Tough Guys Don't Dance* (1987) was shot at the bizarrely arty tip of the Cape, Provincetown.

BOSTON

Thomas Edison made films here as far back as 1899, with titles like *Boston Horseless Fire Department, Admiral Dewey at Statehouse, Boston,* and *Railroad Smashup* (1904), a full-speed, head-on collision between two locomotives. His *Vanity Fair* (1915) used Louisburg Square on Beacon Hill to represent London. Two other major film pioneers, Louis Lumiere and his brother Auguste, did some shooting in Boston before the turn of the century.

Early productions include D. W. Griffith's *America* (1924), about the American Revolution, starring Lionel Barrymore. It was shot at historic sights like Lexington and the Old North Church in Boston. The Bunker Hill sequences, however, were shot in Somers, New York, and Paul Revere took his ride on the back roads of Mamaroneck, New York.

More recent Beantown lensing:

***Charly* (1968):** Cliff Robertson's biggest film shot all over South Boston, inside the Dorothy Quincy Suite at John Hancock Hall, and at Faneuil Hall. Kasanoff's Bakery, in Roxbury, where Charly worked in the film, is no more.

***The Thomas Crown Affair* (1968):** Considered by Boston film critic Michael Blowen to be the quintessential Beacon Hill film. A major location was the library of the posh townhouse at 14 Otis Place.

***Field of Dreams* (1989):** Kevin Costner shanghais James Earl Jones and takes him to a baseball game at Fenway Park.

Boston's trademark crime and courtroom dramas have a tendency to delve into the seedy side of law and order. *The Boston Strangler* (1968) and *The Friends of Eddie Coyle* (1973) convey a vivid sense of Boston-area lowlife. *Eddie Coyle* was filmed in Somerville, Quincy, and Sharon, including the Sharon Railroad Station. In *The Verdict* (1982), Paul Newman plays a broken-down lawyer who gets it up for one big win.

MASSACHUSETTS'S GIFTS TO HOLLYWOOD

★ ★ ★ ★ ★ ★ ★ ★ ★ ★ ★ ★ ★ ★ ★ ★

Robert Benchley (Worcester): Witty cornerstone of the Algonquin Round Table who went Hollywood in the 1930s to create and star in a clever series of one-reel shorts and appear as an urbane character in such films as *Foreign Correspondent* and *The Major and the Minor.* His birthplace, 2 Shepard Street, is no longer there.

Walter Brennan (Swampscott): Three-time Oscar winner with a hunched-over walk who played sidekicks. His voice sounds like a bad Henry Fonda imitation.

Bette Davis (Lowell): One of the biggies, a genuine actress. Many solid performances include work in *Of Human Bondage, Jezebel, The Letter, Mr. Skeffington, All About Eve.* See What's There: Boston; Lowell.

Geena Davis (Ware): Kinda kooky Oscar copper for *The Accidental Tourist,* Davis appears headed for a career as the new Teri Garr, her costar in *Tootsie.*

Cecil B. DeMille (Ashfield): The master of the big-screen epic, a name synonymous with Hollywood. Films include: *The Ten Commandments* (1923 and 1956), *Samson and Delilah, The Greatest Show on Earth.* See What's There.

Samuel Fuller (Worcester): The cult version of John Huston, admired by the European New Wave. Films include: *Pickup on South Street, Shock Corridor, The Big Red One.*

Ruth Gordon (Wollaston): She hit it big in acting as a spunky old lady. Films include: *Rosemary's Baby, Harold and Maude, Every Which Way but Loose.*

Peter Guber (Boston): Hollywood powermeister whose production company was bought by Sony for an astronomical sum so that he and his partner might take the reins of Sony's Columbia Pictures. Films include: *Batman, Rain Man, The Color Purple.*

Madeline Kahn (Boston): Mildly funny comedienne who was plugged into the right people—Mel Brooks and Peter Bogdanovich—in the early 1970s. Films include: *Paper Moon, Blazing Saddles, Young Frankenstein.*

Joseph Kennedy (Boston): Political patriarch who used his money to dabble in Hollywood: he produced 80 films, formed RKO Pictures, and dabbled with Gloria Swanson.

Jack Lemmon (Boston): Scenery gobbler who you gotta either love or hate. Billy Wilder and Neil Simon love him. Not me. Films include: *Some Like It Hot, The Apartment, The Odd Couple, Macaroni.*

Joseph E. Levine (Boston): Producer and distributor who got rich on Italian exploitation flicks, then delivered *The Graduate, The Producers,* and *Carnal Knowledge.*

Louis B. Mayer (Boston): A scrap dealer from Russia and New Brunswick who arrived in Boston in 1903 and lived at 17 Rochester Street in the South End. Next thing you know, he's the second M in MGM.

Leonard Nimoy (Boston): Mr. Spock, who fancies himself a singer and poet, found surprising success directing *Three Men and a Baby* (1987).

Kurt Russell (Springfield): Disney child star who grew into self-deprecating tough-guy roles. Films include: *The Computer Wore Tennis Shoes, Escape from New York, Tequila Sunrise.*

WHAT'S THERE

Ashfield: Cecil B. DeMille's birthplace is just east of the post office, on Main Street.

Boston: 169 Tremont Street is the site of the first kinetoscope parlor, opened in 1894.

The Mugar Library, at Boston University, has over 9,000 items of Bette Davis memorabilia: 80–100 scrapbooks, correspondence, Oscar nomination cards, report cards, a mirror of Sarah Bernhardt's that was given to Davis, and much, much more. There should eventually be a permanent Bette Davis display here. Archivists have been promised many pieces from the estate, including an Oscar. The collection is open to the public with reservations: 617/353-3696. 771 Commonwealth Avenue.

Chilmark: John Belushi is buried here in Abel's Hill Cemetery. His gravesite, a beautiful stone in a private corral at the boneyard's entrance, is embellished with a fan's grease-pencil tribute. It's on the north side of South Road, about two miles east of the center of town. Belushi owned property on the Vineyard, where he cavorted like a wild man. According to *Wired*, he once jumped Vineyard doyenne Carly Simon and dry-humped her on a lawn as a joke.

Lowell: Bette Davis's childhood home is on Chestnut Street, off Stevens Street, in the Highlands area. Her parents were not married long, and she was shipped off as a child to the Cushing Academy, in Ashburnham, Massachusetts. No statue is planned by the city, probably just a memorial scholarship to the Merramac Repertory Theater. The Lowell Heritage State Park offers a free festival of Bette Davis films in August. Information: 508/459-1000.

Lynn: The Loew's Open Air Theater claims to be the world's largest drive-in: it has spaces for 5,000 autos.

NEW HAMPSHIRE

MADE IN NEW HAMPSHIRE

***Little Women* (Concord, 1933):** A provocative title, but it's just an adaptation of Louisa May Alcott's book, which was one of the first examples in our culture of a project being so successful it forces a sequel (*Little Men*). Starring Katharine Hepburn, who was to return to Concord (this time in color) 48 years later for *On Golden Pond*.

***Winter Carnival* (Hanover, 1939):** Budd Schulberg wrote the screenplay. Ten years later, he wrote a depressing novel called *The Disenchanted* about a young screenwriter who accompanies a debilitated, alcoholic ex-genius writer (read F. Scott Fitzgerald) to the Dartmouth winter carnival as research for a screenplay. The movie has been forgotten, but the book is a masterful chronicle of burning and selling out.

***On Golden Pond* (Squam Lake, near Laconia, 1981):** "You're my knight in shining armor," says Katharine Hepburn, back in the Other Maple Syrup State, and Henry Fonda as her befuddled hubby bites hook, line, and sinker.

WHAT'S THERE

Moultonborough: Claude Rains's grave is in Red Hill Cemetery. Rains is most famous for his rounding up the usual suspects and beginning a beautiful friendship with Bogie in *Casablanca,* and as *The Invisible Man.*

Red Hill Cemetery is 20 miles northeast of Laconia. Take Bean Road from Route 25 at the Center Harbor–Moultonborough town line for 1½ miles to the second cemetery on your right. The headstone is made of fashionable black marble.

NEW YORK

MADE IN NEW YORK

MOB CONNECTIONS

***The Godfather* (1972):** The Godfather's mansion is Fieldston, in Riverdale. Falaise, at Sands Point Preserve, is the estate where the horse's-head scene was filmed.

Sonny (James Caan) is murdered at an abandoned runway, Mitchel Field.

***Married to the Mob* (1988):** Michelle Pfeiffer is attacked with shopping carts at the Massapequa Food Town. Other Long Island locations were Farahs Cafe and the Travelers Building, in East Meadow.

PERIOD PIECES

***Hello, Dolly!* (Garrison, Poughkeepsie, Cold Springs, 1969):** Buildings in Garrison were made to resemble 1890 Yonkers, not by re-creating the past, but by *modernizing!* Victorian gingerbread was added to structures that date from the 1840s. La Streisand inflicted herself again on upstate New York four years later for *The Way We Were* (1973); Union College, in Schenectady, was the weeper's collegiate setting.

***The Natural* (Buffalo, 1984):** Bernard Malamud's dark baseball fable is desecrated by Robert Redford and Barry Levinson with an ending exactly opposite the book's. It was shot at one of the few remaining vintage ballparks, War Memorial Park, which is now being torn down as Buffalo spruces up for a major-league franchise.

OOZING WEALTH

The north shore of Long Island has long been the domain of the too-well-off. Oscar Hammerstein's Beechhurst estate, Wildflower, was a virtual clubhouse for the celebrated. W. C. Fields, Mary Pickford, Gloria Swanson, Will Rogers, and the Marx Brothers all lived or worked on the north shore of Queens, which was considered the Beverly Hills of the East in the early 1920s. Buster Keaton married Natalie Talmadge at the Bayside estate of his producer, Joe Schenck, and Schenck's wife, Natalie's sister Norma. It's off 222nd Street, between Corbett Road and Second Place.

Cary Grant becomes mixed up with bad guys in *North by Northwest* (1959) at the Pratt Estate, on Welwyn Preserve in Glen Cove. The film also shot in Old Westbury, at the Phipps Estate. *Sabrina* (1954), with Audrey

Hepburn, William Holden, and Humphrey Bogart, also shot at the Pratt Estate. *Arthur* (1981), John Gielgud's breakthrough movie, filmed at mansions in Glen Cove and Manhasset. The 23-room fixer-upper that seems too good to be true—and is—in *The Money Pit* (1986) dates from 1900, is known as Northway, and is located in Long Island's Lattingtown. It has since been renovated in real life and was offered for sale recently at $2.45 million.

NEW YORK'S GIFTS TO HOLLYWOOD

★ ★ ★ ★ ★ ★ ★ ★ ★ ★ ★ ★ ★ ★ ★ ★

Alec Baldwin (Amityville): A hot, ubiquitous young actor with nary a hair out of place. Films include: *Beetlejuice, Married to the Mob, The Hunt for Red October.*

Lucille Ball (Jamestown): The top movie comedienne of the late thirties and forties. She married Desi Arnaz in 1941 and went on to become the most successful TV star ever. See What's There.

Peter Bogdanovich (Kingston): A film-critic-turned-director whose career has hit dramatic peaks and valleys. Peaks: *The Last Picture Show, Paper Moon, Mask.* Valleys: *At Long Last Love,* the murder of his girlfriend, Dorothy Stratten, and his marriage to Dorothy's baby sister.

Kirk Douglas (b. Issur Danielovitch, Demsky, Amsterdam): An enduring, pugnacious leading man, his motto is: "I've made a career out of playing sons of bitches." (His son Michael has made a career out of playing wimpier sons of bitches.) Films include: *Out of the Past, Ace in the Hole, Lust for Life, Paths of Glory, Spartacus, The Bad and the Beautiful.* See What's There.

Charles Durning (Highland Falls): Chunky, slobby character actor who is not to be confused with Kenneth McMillan or Vincent Gardenia. Films include: *Dog Day Afternoon, The Sting, North Dallas Forty, Tootsie.*

Annette Funicello (Utica): Former Mouseketeer who became princess of the beach movie; her prince was

Frankie Avalon. Films include: *Beach Party, Beach Blanket Bingo, How to Stuff a Wild Bikini.*

Richard Gere (Syracuse): Prissy leading man who can be pretty darn unconvincing. Films include: *Looking for Mr. Goodbar, Days of Heaven, American Gigolo, An Officer and a Gentleman, Pretty Woman.*

William S. Hart (Newburgh): The first great cowboy star, his gritty, highly influential style of westerns gave way to the flamboyance of Tom Mix and the singing cowboys. Never made a sound film.

Robert Montgomery (Beacon): Leading man, union leader, war hero, director of *Lady in the Lake* (a Raymond Chandler adaptation filmed *in the first person!*), McCarthy-era stoolie, and, most important, father of "Bewitched" star Elizabeth Montgomery. Films include: *Here Comes Mr. Jordan, They Were Expendable.*

Eddie Murphy (Roosevelt): "Saturday Night Live" alum who swiftly became top box-office star. Films include: *48 HRS., Beverly Hills Cops, Coming to America,* and *Harlem Nights,* which he also directed. He lives in Alpine, New Jersey.

Hal Roach (Elmira): One of the two great comedy producers of the golden age. (The other, Mack Sennett, was more into slapstick than Roach.) Roach made landmark films with Harold Lloyd, Will Rogers, Charlie Chase, Our Gang, and Laurel & Hardy. His company, which still exists, colorizes old films.

Eva Marie Saint (Albany): Method actress who played a cool Hitchcock blond in *North by Northwest,* Brando's girlfriend in *On the Waterfront.* Saint's work—including *Exodus* and *The Sandpiper*—has been sporadic since the mid-fifties.

Denzel Washington (Mt. Vernon): Star of TV's "St. Elsewhere" has become top black leading man of today, comfortable with both heavy emoting and light comedy. Films include: *The Mighty Quinn, Glory, Mo' Better Blues.*

WHAT'S THERE

Amsterdam: Kirk Douglas's childhood home. His youth is described in his autobiography, *The Ragman's Son.* A small park on High Street commemorates his roots; a plaque on a huge rock there bears his likeness.

Binghamton: A display in the lobby of the Forum Theater and a historical marker in front of Binghamton High School note that this was Rod Serling's boyhood home. The Rod Serling Memorial Foundation sells a touching button that says, "Everyone has to have a home town, Binghamton's mine. —Rod Serling."

Chittenango: The hometown of L. Frank Baum, who wrote the Wizard of Oz books, boasts a yellow-brick sidewalk, one of three in America. The others are in Grand Rapids, Minnesota (the home of Judy Garland), and in Liberal, Kansas (site of Dorothy's House). On Falls Boulevard, Highway 13, at the south edge of town. A historical marker is planned.

Fonda: This small upstate town was founded by a distant ancestor of America's royal film family: Douw

Jane Fonda visits a namesake at the Fonda Village Cemetery. *(Courtesy of Anita A. Smith, Montgomery County Historian, 1977–1983)*

Fonda, Henry's sixth great-grandfather, who was scalped by Indians. Peter popped in a few years ago to research his memoirs and take a photo beside a namesake's grave at the Fonda Village Cemetery. Jane has also visited to pose for grave photos.

Hartsdale: Ferncliff Cemetery: Final Home of the Stars. A glittering array of Hollywood biggies "takes five" eternally here. Stars in the mausoleum section include Joan Crawford, Judy Garland, and Basil Rathbone. Bur-

Judy Garland's tomb at Ferncliff Cemetery. *(Courtesy of Julie Kuehndorf)*

ied underground are Paul Robeson, Conrad Veidt, and Adolph Caesar. Secor Road. Map available.

Hastings-on-Hudson: John Garfield, Judy Holliday, and Lee Strasberg are all buried at Westchester Hills Cemetery. Route 9A.

Hawthorne: Jimmy Cagney and Sal Mineo are laid to rest with Babe Ruth at Gate of Heaven Cemetery, Stevens Avenue. Map Available.

Jamestown: The Fenton Historical Center, 67 Washington Street, plans a small display honoring favorite daughter Lucille Ball. She is also enshrined in the town's Hall of Fame. Lucy's childhood home, in Celoron, is at 59 Lucy Lane. She was born at 92 Stewart Street and attended Celoron High School.

Mamaroneck: The Ethel Barrymore home, on the tip of Taylor's Lane, overlooking Long Island Sound, is now the Barrymore Estates development. Only a caretaker's cottage remains of the original dwelling.

Rochester: The George Eastman House displays many authentic artifacts from the first days of film, including an Edison kinetoscope, which was the first commercial movie machine (1893), and the Arnet Magniscope, the first 35-millimeter projector (1894). The museum also owns a collection of 10,000 films, ranging from the entire Cecil B. DeMille collection to the original negative of *Gone with the Wind* to films of Garbo and Kubrick. 900 East Avenue. Open Tuesday through Sunday.

The home of Louise Brooks in her later years was at 7 North Goodman Street.

Saratoga Springs: The grave of Edgar M. "Monty" Wooley, the memorable star of *The Man Who Came to Dinner* (1941), is in Greenridge Cemetery, 17 Greenridge Place, in the southwest part of town. He did a biting portrayal in the film of Algonquin wit Alexander Woolcott.

Southampton: Gary Cooper's remains were dug up in 1974, after 13 years in Los Angeles, and transported here by his widow. He can now be found under a three-ton rose-colored boulder. Sacred Heart Cemetery, Route 27.

Syracuse: The Landmark Theater, a 1928 Indo-Persian vision, shows the occasional classic film. It's at 362 South Salina Street. Program: 315/475-7979.

The Theatre Motel, before the movies died.

Westfield: The drive-in-movie portion of the Theatre Motel, one of two combination drive-in/motels in America, began in the early fifties and became wildly popular with locals—until it bit the dust in the late seventies. It will be missed. The only remaining example of the species is in Monte Vista, Colorado. The motel remains open, however, and the decaying screen looms over the premises on U.S. Route 20, one mile east of town. Reservations: 716/326-2161.

RHODE ISLAND

MADE IN RHODE ISLAND

***The Great Gatsby* (Newport, 1974):** Hammersmith Farm, JFK's summer white house, was Redford's West Egg (Great Neck, Long Island) mansion in the much-hyped second adaptation of the F. Scott Fitzgerald novel. See What's There.

***Mr. North* (Newport, 1988):** John Huston's son,

Danny, directs Thornton Wilder's story of Newport society in the twenties. Dad cowrote, but Robert Mitchum had to sub for him onscreen when he took fatally ill.

RHODE ISLAND'S GIFTS TO HOLLYWOOD

★ ★ ★ ★ ★ ★ ★ ★ ★ ★ ★ ★ ★ ★ ★ ★

Nelson Eddy (Providence): Eddy and Jeanette McDonald teamed in the 1930s to become America's Singing Sweethearts in a series of popular films that seem absolutely nutty today. See What's There.

Van Johnson (Newport): Breezy leading man, a handsomer and more charming Ronald Reagan. He ruled the depleted MGM roost during World War II. Films include: *A Guy Named Joe, Thirty Seconds Over Tokyo, The Human Comedy.*

James Woods (Warwick): Intense character actor who is establishing a leading-man career. Films include: *Salvador, Against All Odds, True Believer.*

WHAT'S THERE

Newport: *High Society* (1956), the musical version of *The Philadelphia Story* that starred Bing Crosby, Frank Sinatra, and Grace Kelly (it was her last film), was shot at the Clarendon Court mansion, on Millionaire's Row. More recently the mansion belonged to Claus and Sunny Von Bulow, but it was unloaded when Sunny went into a coma; a presumably sane jury decided Claus had nothing to do with Sunny's condition. (The story's told in *Reversal of Fortune* [1990].) It's not open to the public.

However, the *Gatsby* locations, Rosecliff mansion and Hammersmith Farm, are tourable. Rosecliff, on Bellevue Avenue, also hosted shooting for *The Betsy.* For info, call: 401/847-1000. Hammersmith Farm, on Ocean Drive adjacent to Fort Adams State Park, includes the dock where Gatsby gazed longingly at Daisy's green light. Info: 401/846-0420.

Providence: The Rhode Island Heritage Hall of Fame honors great Rhode Islanders like Nelson Eddy, David Hartman, and early baseball great Nap Lajoie. Providence Civic Center, 1 La Salle Square.

VERMONT

MADE IN VERMONT

CHARMING AS HECK

***Way Down East* (White River Junction, 1920):** The famous Lillian Gish ice floe scene was shot at the junction of the White and Connecticut rivers for this D. W. Griffith epic.

***The Trouble with Harry* (Craftsbury Common, 1954):** A pesky corpse causes problems in a picturesque New England town. With future stars Shirley MacLaine, John Forsythe, and Jerry Mathers.

***Baby Boom* (Peru, Manchester, Weston, 1986):** Stood in for "Hadleyville," the town where Diane Keaton moves.

***Beetlejuice* (East Corinth, 1987):** The location was not central to the visual theme; it was simply somewhere a snooty New Yorker might buy a weekend house.

***Funny Farm* (Grafton, Townshend, Windsor, 1987):** Chevy Chase and Madolyn Smith try to get away from the nasty city, but instead encounter nasty Vermonters.

***Sweethearts Dance* (Hyde Park, 1987):** After filming, the state threatened to tax Don Johnson $50,000 on his earnings. Johnson threatened back, according to an Associated Press report, that he would spread the word to his Hollywood pals that Vermont was "a bad place to make movies."

VERMONT'S GIFT TO HOLLYWOOD

★ ★ ★ ★ ★ ★ ★ ★ ★ ★ ★ ★ ★ ★ ★ ★

Orson Bean (Burlington): "The Beanster" never quite realized his full potential, nor did we.

Cynthia Gibb (Bennington): Multitalented, cute-as-a-button Cindy romped with Rob Lowe in *Youngblood* and has graced many other films too numerous and dumb to mention.

WHAT'S THERE

Arlington: West Mountain Inn, where Michael J. Fox wed Tracy Pollan. Route 313 and River Road. Reservations: 802/375-6516.

East Middlebury: Or, you can stay at the Waybury Inn, of "Newhart" fame. It's on Route 125. Reservations: 802/388-4015.

Films Index

People Index

Places Index